CLINICAL BEHAVIOR THERAPY

Clinical Behavior Therapy

Edited by

ARNOLD A. LAZARUS, Ph.D.

Professor of Psychology, University College, Rutgers University
1970-72 Visiting Professor and Director of Clinical Training
Department of Psychology, Yale University

BRUNNER/MAZEL • NEW YORK

Third Printing

Copyright © 1972 by Brunner/Mazel, Inc.

published by
BRUNNER/MAZEL, INC.
64 University Place
New York, N. Y. 10003

Library of Congress Catalogue Card No. 70-184151
SBN 87630-051-4

MANUFACTURED IN THE UNITED STATES OF AMERICA

Preface

IT IS EVIDENT that the publication explosion has not yielded a parallel increase in useful information. Those interested in psychological treatment often deplore the fact that very few books can actually enhance their therapeutic skills. It is hoped that readers of this book will emerge with several new and different notions and techniques, thus enriching their own clinical repertoires. The book is addressed to service-oriented individuals who are especially interested in efficient psychotherapy.

In the field of behavior therapy (as may be the case in most other areas of scientific endeavor) researchers and academicians have both the time and incentive to publish their findings, whereas practitioners less often have the opportunity or inclination to share their ideas in writing. Of course, there are those who claim that only controlled laboratory studies are worthy of note and that the biased nature of most clinical impressions and observations renders them quite worthless. For a rebuttal of this viewpoint see Lazarus and Davison (1971) who underscore the fact that practitioners "may discover important individual nuances that remain hidden from the laboratory scientist simply because the tight environment of the experimental testing ground makes it impossible for certain behaviors to occur or for certain observations to be made" (p. 196).

The efforts of experimental psychologists and their burgeoning literature on behavioral procedures have resulted in a persistent view of behavior therapy as superficial and mechanistic. As a practitioner of behavior therapy, I have found that my treatment strategies and understanding of the field have consistently differed from those who espouse a "pure" experimental outlook (e.g., Eysenck, 1971). In the practical details of my day to day work with clients, I have found it necessary to broaden the base of conventional behavior therapy (Lazarus, 1971). Is this an idiosyncratic reaction, or in their daily work, do most (if not all) practicing behavior therapists find it essential to transcend laboratory derived principles and techniques which constitute the core of behavior therapy? This book grew out of the foregoing question.

The doctrine of *technical eclecticism* (Lazarus, 1967) has enabled me to learn from and work productively with therapists whose theoretical orientations differ widely from my own. The chapter by Akhter Ahsen and myself bears further testimony to this point of view. But what of other people who consider themselves "behavior therapists" and who work with patients rather than subjects? Do they employ assessment and/or treatment methods that do not easily fall within the conventional boundaries of behavior therapy? Do they find it necessary to modify, extend and revise existing procedures within their practices?

Accordingly, the following invitation was sent to ten of my colleagues:

"It has occurred to me to edit a book entitled CLINICAL BEHAVIOR THERAPY. The idea is to provide practitioners (rather than researchers or academicians) with an opportunity to air their own views and experiences concerning the active ingredients of effective therapy. The behavior therapy literature is flooded by the writings of individuals who seem to work with ideas rather than with people. The same names in the field (usually theoreticians rather than true clinicians) appear with monotonous regularity in journals and books. Hopefully, the proposed volume will allow some much-desired "new blood" to enter the field.

The aim of the intended book is to examine whether practitioners often transcend techniques derived from "modern learning theory" when called upon to make clinical decisions, and whether innovations in method and technique usually ensue. The scope of the book is bound up with the procedures, theories, methods, techniques, etc., which each contributor finds especially useful in aiding diagnostic and/or therapeutic processes.

The main thrust of the book is intended to be practical rather than speculative. I am inviting you to contribute a chapter outlining those methods and ideas which "turn you on" because of their productivity and effectiveness.

I truly hope that you will be able to contribute to what I hope will be a really exciting and much-needed publication."

My major editorial prerogatives were wielded in excising gross stylistic incongruities from initial drafts. The chapters contain several points of emphasis and various biases with which I do not agree, but in my view, an edited book of this kind should disseminate divergent "behavioral" opinions, rather than be forced to fit the constraints of one particular outlook. Personally, I found that the chapters refreshed my perspective and enriched my clinical repertoire. If most readers derive similar stimulation from this volume, its aims will most admirably be met.

ARNOLD A. LAZARUS

REFERENCES

EYSENCK, H. J. A mish-mash of theories. *International Journal of Psychiatry*, 1971, 9, 140-146.

LAZARUS, A. A. In support of technical eclecticism. *Psychological Reports*, 1967, 21, 415-416.

LAZARUS, A. A. *Behavior Therapy and Beyond.* New York: McGraw-Hill, 1971.

LAZARUS, A. A. & DAVISON, G. C. Clinical innovation in research and practice. In A. E. Bergin & S. L. Garfield (Eds.), *Handbook of Psychotherapy and Behavior Change: An Empirical Analysis.* New York: Wiley, 1971.

Contents

Contributors

AKHTER AHSEN, PH.D.: Private Practice, Yonkers, New York; former president, Institute of Eidetic Psychotherapy, Philadelphia, Pa.

BARRY M. BROWN, M.D.: Private Practice, Houston, Texas.

EDWARD DENGROVE, M.D.: Diplomate of the American Board of Psychiatry and Neurology. Private Practice, West Allenhurst, New Jersey.

HERBERT FENSTERHEIM, PH.D.: Clinical Associate Professor of Psychiatry, New York Medical College, New York. Private Practice.

PHILIP H. FRIEDMAN, PH.D.: Family Psychiatry Division, Eastern Pennsylvania Psychiatric Institute, Philadelphia, Pa.

MAX JACOBS, M.A., LL.B.: Private Practice, Johannesburg, South Africa.

THOMAS KRAFT, M.B., CH.B., D.P.M.: Private Practice, London, England.

ARNOLD A. LAZARUS, PH.D.: Professor of Psychology, University College, Rutgers University.

JOHN MARQUIS, PH.D.: Chief Psychologist, Mental Hygiene Clinic, V.A. Hospital, Palo Alto, California.

GERALD W. PIAGET, PH.D.: Behavior Therapy Associates, Los Altos, California; Staff Psychologist, Santa Clara County Mental Health Services, Palo Alto, California.

1

The Use of Behavior Therapy in a
Psychotherapeutic Context

THOMAS KRAFT, M.B., D.P.M.

WHEN READING ARTICLES on patients who have been successfully treated
by behavior therapy, one usually finds that the author has divided the
material into several sections: after an introduction, in which he draws
attention to previous work in this field, he then goes on to give a short
résumé of the case history, followed by the treatment, results, discussion
and a summary. While this makes for a neat article which is acceptable
for publication, it does not give the reader a clear idea of what happened
during the treatment. The case history of the patient cannot be divorced
from the remainder of the treatment as it forms an integral part of the
whole treatment process. History-taking is not a mere collecting of facts
but is an important interaction between patient and therapist. During
the first interview, the patient will discover some of the qualities of the
therapist, and also to what extent he will be allowed to discuss his problems or whether the treatment will be restricted to symptoms only.

3

The literature in behavior therapy gives the reader the impression that most psychiatric patients come to the therapist requesting treatment for their phobia or sexual disturbance, but while this does apply to a few, most psychiatric patients have no idea, except that they are in a muddle and need "sorting out." The therapist may have to spend several sessions with the patient in order to determine the precise nature of his problem. In the first interview, the patient may wish to talk about marital problems, difficulties at work, or inferiority feelings, and he may not know which areas require therapeutic intervention. These points are rarely discussed in articles on behavior therapy, possibly because behavior therapists are often given a selected group of patients, or because it is thought to be irrelevant. The object of writing this chapter is to highlight the interaction between patient and therapist during a course of treatment which is behavior-oriented, and to show that a great deal happens during the treatment other than that reported in the behavior therapy literature.

THE ART OF HISTORY-TAKING

While it is important to obtain factual data about the patient's background, emphasis should be placed on the patient's feelings about events in his life rather than their precise nature. He should feel free to elaborate where he feels a need to do so, and should not be pressurized into giving certain replies. It is important that the therapist have no preconceived ideas of what he expects to hear from the patient and that history-taking be a flexible process moulded by the patient's replies.

After giving the age of his father, the patient may wish to talk about certain aspects of their relationship, either at the present time or in the past, and he should be allowed to do so, as this may give valuable information about his problem. It is not sufficient to know that his father is a solicitor, but more important to find out whether this had a bearing on the choice of his own career. When inquiring about the physical health of the father, it is more important to find out the effect this had on the patient than the exact nature of the illness. The patient might volunteer certain information about his father—for example, that he was keen for him to play football even though he was not keen on the game. This may lead to a discussion about the significance of the game in relation to his other symptoms and why this should be a source of conflict between father and son. He may wish to talk about his father's drinking behavior, how this affected him or his mother, or the relationship between his parents, and all this information should be recorded at the time of the interview.

After obtaining information about the father, the therapist asks the patient about his mother, brothers and sisters, in much the same way, and any other members of the family who seem important to the patient. He may have been brought up by his grandparents, or he may wish to talk about a favorite uncle or some more distant relative.

After obtaining details of the family history, the therapist asks the patient for date and place of birth. While this may not lead to any further discussion, this may be very relevant to immigrants or patients whose parents were born in other countries.

The therapist then asks the patient about his childhood and often the patient will be able to remember important events and may inquire whether these are relevant to his present state. For example, a patient who had difficulty in swallowing remembered that during his childhood he had "choked" while learning to swim, and feared that he might not reach the side of the swimming pool. Later, this symptom was reactivated after the death of his father, who also had difficulty in swallowing. Immediately the therapist can show the patient how these are interrelated.

When asking about academic achievements, it is more important to know what significance these had for the patient than the actual level of achievement, though this should be recorded too. Academic ability may have been a large factor in the production of symptoms in the patient who failed intentionally because he did not wish to compete with a brilliant older sister. Neurotic symptoms can often be traced back to early childhood and early neurotic traits should be recorded.

When discussing his occupation since leaving school, the patient is asked whether he likes his present job, whether there have been frequent changes of employment, and if so, the reasons for this, also his relationship with fellow employees and staff. If there have been frequent clashes with members of staff, this will lead on to a discussion about problems with authority figures in general. The type of occupation selected is important in relation to his other symptoms, so that if a ladies' hairdresser seeks treatment for his homosexuality, it is pointed out to him at this stage that altering his sexual adjustment may well lead to a change in his employment too. The author feels that it is only fair to make this point early in treatment so that the patient is not disappointed at a later stage.

The next stage in history-taking is to make an assessment of the patient's sexual adjustment, taking note of overt sexual behavior as well as masturbation fantasies, whether the patient is married or single, and whether he has extra-marital ties, and their nature. In the case of the phobic patient, attention should be focused on her sexual adjustment before marriage and changes which occurred subsequent to the marriage, and the exact time of onset of phobic symptoms. It is frequently found that before marriage the patient made important relationships with two or more men and that phobic symptoms emerged when she attempted to make a relationship with one man only. The nature of the relationship between the agoraphobic wife and her husband needs to be thoroughly investigated, especially if she can go out only when accompanied by him, since it is usually found that the patient at the same time is dependent upon and wants to get away from him, and this is a central feature of the phobic situation.

The male homosexual patient is asked whether he usually takes the active or passive role, and whether he identifies with the male sex. It is also worth inquiring about intimate physical contact with important female figures early in life. It is pointed out that it is easier to treat those patients who have had some heterosexual contact than those who are exclusively homosexual, and that failure to identify with the male sex is a more complicated problem.

When asking about past physical illnesses, attention should be paid to the psychosomatic group, such as psoriasis, eczema, asthma, colitis, and whether these preceded the psychiatric symptoms. The patient is now asked about psychiatric treatment which he has received in the past, the type of treatment involved and the improvement obtained. This may lead on to a discussion about behavior therapy and its aims.

Having obtained information about the patient's background, the next stage in treatment is to obtain a history of the illness. A good way of starting here is to ask the patient when he last felt perfectly well and to continue from there. If the patient has already seen several doctors he may be able to give a coherent account, but if he has not had any previous treatment, he may be quite vague and say that he feels unwell, that he has a headache, lacks energy and feels tired for no reason. In this case one can help the patient by asking questions such as: "Do you have difficulty in social situations?" "Do you have difficulty traveling?" "When did you last go to the theatre?" In this way it is possible to work out with the patient the areas of difficulty and throughout the treatment emphasis should be placed on working things out together rather than the usual practice of the doctor administering treatment to his patient.

If the patient has difficulty in traveling, an attempt should be made to trace the early origins of this symptom and, if possible, to localize a particular traumatic incident. A patient may well recall a particular journey during which the train stopped for twenty minutes between stations and he became panic-stricken, developing symptoms from that time. Further inquiry may lead to important information about personal problems at that time. One patient recalled that this occurred after the death of her first husband, and recognized that this was related to the onset of her symptoms. During history-taking, the patient is asked whether she has difficulty with all forms of transport or only on public transport. Many patients find that while they cannot travel by bus, train or Underground, they can still travel in their own car, possibly because they feel that the car is an extension of the home. Some patients can travel only when accompanied by a husband or a relative, and here it is important to investigate the nature of the relationship between the patient and the person who accompanies her. During the discussion, the patient may wish to talk about other aspects of the phobic situation, and it is important to let the patient talk about these. It will soon become apparent that there are many factors in the patient's life situation which support the phobia and it is important to establish these maintaining factors. The patient is asked to describe the sequence of events in particular situations and the husband's reactions. It is usually found that the husband colludes with his wife in her phobic illness despite his outcries to the contrary. For this reason many therapists feel that it is important to see the husband of phobic patients.

If the patient has a drinking problem, he is asked when he began drinking, the type of drink involved, the quantity drunk, and whether he needs to carry a hip flask. Also whether he enjoys drinking or whether he just wants to rapidly increase his alcohol level. A guide to this will be found by asking the patient about the rate of his drinking and whether he gulps it down. Some patients are aware of the reasons why they need to drink to excess, while others just say: "I enjoy drinking!" In either case, it is important to determine the degree of social anxiety present. One patient may admit that he finds talking to other people extremely difficult unless he has had some alcohol first, while other patients flatly deny this. At this point in the discussion the author points out that the need for alcohol is related to social anxiety and that once patients have become socially competent they no longer need to drink to excess. Many patients accept this argument, but others remain unconvinced at this stage. After establishing the patient's need for alcohol, it is necessary to ask about drug-taking in general. Some may admit to smoking marijuana, but one must always ask specifically about the use of amphetamines, barbiturates and other drugs. For those patients who rely on alcohol or drugs for their support, one should always inquire about anti-social conduct.

After detailed history-taking of this kind, the therapist will have a good idea of the patient's problems and is in a good position to start developing a treatment program best suited for his patient. A sample of a history-taking interview will now be given as an illustration.

Therapist: How old is your father?
Patient: 72.
Therapist: I suppose he has retired.
Patient: No, he is still working two days a week. He works in a Delicatessen. He used to have a shop of his own, which he sold, and he now works for a friend of his.
Therapist: Has he had any illnesses?
Patient: In 1953 he had a serious illness and there was the question of amputation of both legs. They did some sort of by-pass operation. I think it was one of the main arteries. I was 16 at the time.
Therapist: What was your relationship with your father?
Patient: We never had much of a relationship all my life. When mother could not handle me, she threatened me with father. He never represented too much of a father figure to me. We never did anything together, as father and son. I wanted desperately to be part of "Smith and Son,"* but whenever representatives called, father sent me out. I felt rejected by my father.
Therapist: And your mother? How old is she?
Patient: She is a lot younger than father. She is 63. The business revolved around her rather than him (referring to father). She was the dominant figure—always has been and always will be. All she would have to do is to turn on the tears. . . .
Therapist: In order to get her own way with father?
Patient: Yes, that's right. She's extremely emotional and insecure.
Therapist: What do you mean by "insecure"?
Patient: Well, she is continually seeking praise for things which she has done in the past. (Pause). Little things. (He did not elaborate further on this point).
Therapist: Has she had any illnesses?
Patient: Yes, she had a spot on the lung. She was on anticoagulants in the past year, but she is off them now.
Therapist: Anything else?

---

* The name has been changed.

Patient: Yes, she has varicose veins in the legs. Otherwise she is quite healthy.

Therapist: How many brothers and sisters have you got?

Patient: I have one sister. She is older than I am. She is 37, married with one child. A son.

Therapist: Does she go out to work?

Patient: No, she is a housewife.

Therapist: Has she had any physical illnesses?

Patient: Yes, she had "colitis," but it ended up as appendectomy!

Therapist: What is your relationship with your sister?

Patient: Childhood relationship pretty bad. She took great delight in getting me into trouble. I took a more protective role towards her when I was 16 or 17. She is a tremendously educated person. When she came to visit me in America, my friends asked me not to bring her again. She had 7 Honors in Matriculation, including French and Latin. She was Head Wages Clerk for a company in television and films. She was pretty bright. She would get 100's or 98 at school and I would get much lower. Mother used to say: "You can't let your sister beat you," but I had no desire to compete with my sister.

Therapist: When were you born?

Patient: In 1937 in Tottenham. At my grandmother's place.

Therapist: Any bed wetting as a child?

Patient: No.

Therapist: Nail biting?

Patient: No.

Therapist: Thumb sucking?

Patient: No.

Therapist: Afraid of the dark?

Patient: No, it was always dark during the War.

Therapist: Tell me about your childhood.

Patient: I was sensitive about being Jewish. I had many fights with other children about this. There was a lot of antisemitic feeling at school. I was leader of one half of the class with my lieutenant and there was another boy who was leader of the other side with his lieutenant.

Therapist: What age were you when you went to school?

Patient: Five.

Therapist: And you left at 15. (The therapist remembered that he had already told him this at a previous interview.)

Patient: Yes, I was fighting against it. If I had tried to make it work . . . I regret now that I did not make much of school. I did not take School Certificate. To size it all up, I regret my education. I intentionally tried not to succeed.

(End of Interview.)

During an interview of this type, one obtains a lot of information about the patient, the nature of his relationship with his parents, his feelings of inferiority towards his sister and his intentionally failing at school. The patient also gives some indication that his choice of friends has been dictated by his educational level and that his friends rejected his sister because they did not reach her level. The patient felt rejected by his father and felt that his mother, though the dominant figure in the household, threatened him with father if she could not handle him.

CONSTRUCTING THE HIERARCHY FOR SYSTEMATIC DESENSITIZATION

It is unwise to use a standardized hierarchy for all patients even though they may be suffering from a similar type of disorder, and it is recommended that a hierarchy should be specially constructed to meet the needs of each individual patient.

Some patients find it quite easy to construct a hierarchy of their own and know which situations cause little distress and which are extremely anxiety-provoking, but this is certainly not true of all. The author has found that many patients are prepared to begin treatment using an easy item at a time when a hierarchy has not yet been developed, and then to progress towards more difficult situations, offering helpful suggestions to the therapist as treatment proceeds. This allows the patient to participate in the treatment program rather than being a passive agent to whom treatment is administered. This is extremely important because eventually the patient must learn to conduct his own affairs without the assistance of a therapist.

A patient who has a fear of heights may be able to construct a suitable hierarchy of increasing height quite easily. He has a ladder at home and feels that he can climb a little higher each day. On the other hand, many patients find it very difficult or even impossible to construct any sort of hierarchy, and need a lot of assistance from the therapist. One patient who had a severe dog phobia could not think of any situation involving dogs which would not provoke maximum anxiety, so it was suggested that she look at a picture of a dog in a children's picture book, which was quite acceptable to her. Soon she was able to hug a toy dog, and gradually she learned to cope with dogs in the street. A neighbor who owned a dog was very helpful in her treatment in that she gave her a graded series of situations, first when the dog sat still, then walking away from her, towards her, cuddling and feeding the dog. Another patient who had a fear of water learned to swim and later dive with the assistance of a life guard who happened to be an in-patient in the same ward at that time.

It may be necessary to construct two hierarchies and these can often be offered to the patient concurrently. For example, a male homosexual patient who had difficulty passing urine in public toilets was given one hierarchy involving heterosexual situations leading to sexual intercourse, and a second hierarchy for using urinals in public toilets.

It might be helpful at this stage to give some examples of hierarchies used in particular patients. The first patient was absolutely terrified of dogs, a fear which developed at the age of five when she was running down an alley and an Alsatian dog grabbed her by the hair and dragged her along the alley, though finally she managed to get away. Her friends called her mother, but she was reluctant to come and fetch her as she too was frightened of dogs. The hierarchy was very carefully constructed and the patient has made a very good recovery.

Dog Phobia    Table 1

1. Looking at a picture of a dog in a children's picture book.
2. Cuddling the children's toy dog.
3. Seeing a poodle on a lead a) 10 yards away.
   b) 5 yards away.
   c) A woman passing by her.
4. Touching a puppy behind a wire mesh in the market.
5. Looking at the neighbor's spaniel, Kim, held in the arms of its mistress.
6. Touching Kim when the dog is quiet, held in the arms of its mistress.
7. Touching Kim when the dog is quiet.
8. Stroking Kim.
9. Kim putting up her paws.
10. Looking at an Alsatian dog.
11. Watching Kim jumping on the road when she is indoors and the windows are closed.
12. Watching Kim walk round the room.
13. Feeding Kim with a biscuit.
14. Kim held by its mistress, and then jumping on the ground.
15. Kim running.
16. Kim jumping from a chair onto the floor.
17. Kim jumping on the floor and then putting up her paw.

18. Kim wagging her tail.
19. Kim wagging her tail and then putting her paw up.
20. Kim running down the corridor.
21. Kim running away from her.
22. Kim running towards her.
23. Kim roaming round the house without a lead.
24. Knocking on the door of the neighbor, and Kim running towards her, barking.
25. Dogs fighting.

This hierarchy was completed in 21 sessions.

The second patient was a 38-year-old docker who became phobic to water and heights after a serious accident at his work. He often stepped on and off ships without the safety precaution of a gangplank, but on this occasion, he missed the quay, fell onto a wooden fender and then dropped into the water below. Once in the water, he knew that the tide here was strong and that he could drown or be crushed to death between the ship and the quay. He was given two hierarchies and the first of these will be given in full.

Fear of Water and Heights

1. Taking a bath at home.
2. Taking a shower at home.
3. Going into the shallow end of the swimming pool.
4. Starting to swim at the shallow end of the swimming pool, breast stroke only.
5. Swimming at the shallow end, doing the crawl.
6. Jumping into the swimming pool at the shallow end.
7. Jumping into the pool and then doing the crawl.
8. Swimming at the shallow end, first breast stroke, then the crawl.
9. Pushing himself away from the bars and causing a splash.
10. Swimming in the middle of the pool at a depth of 5 ft. 3 ins.
11. Swimming at the shallow end and then at the deep end (10 ft. 3 ins.).
12. Going into the deep end of the swimming pool.
13. Watching people jump from the diving boards.
14. Standing on a step at the deep end of the pool and making a "little jump" into the water.
15. Backstroke at the shallow end of the pool.

16. Jumping into the water at the shallow end of the pool ("belly flop dive").
17. "Belly flop dive" at the deep end of the pool.
18. Racing dive at shallow end of the pool.
19. Racing dive at the deep end of the pool.
20. Swimming three times across the deep end of the pool without stopping   a) breast stroke
      b) crawl
      c) backstroke
21. Jumping into the pool at a depth of:
      a) 5 ft. 3 ins.
      b) 6 ft.
      c) 7 ft.
22. Several jumps at 6 ft., 7 ft., alternating these, and then remaining at the 7 feet depth.
23. Going onto the 1st diving board and jumping into the water.
24. Jumping off the 1st diving board, then diving from the 1st board.
25. Diving off the 1st diving board.
26. Jumping from the 1st diving board, jumping from the 2nd diving board, then diving from the 1st diving board.
27. Jumping off the 1st, 2nd, and 3rd diving boards, then diving from the 1st diving board.
28. Jumping off the 1st, 2nd, and 3rd diving boards, then diving from the 1st, and then the 2nd diving board.
29. Jumping off the 4th diving board, then diving off the 2nd diving board.
30. Jumping off the 5th diving board, then diving off the 3rd diving board.
31. Jumping off the 5th diving board, then diving off the 4th diving board.
32. Jumping off the top board, then diving off the 4th diving board.
33. Jumping off the top board, then diving off the 5th diving board.
34. Diving off the top diving board.
35. Random stimuli.
36. Looking round before jumping off the 3rd diving board.
37. Looking round before jumping off the 4th board.
38. Looking round before jumping off the 5th diving board.
39. Diving from the 5th diving board and looking round before diving.
40. Diving from the top board and looking round before diving.

This hierarchy was completed in 40 sessions, each lasting half an hour. He then started the second part of the desensitization program which involved standing near a lake, rowing on a lake, and crossing viaducts, bridges, canals, rivers, and finally going down the vertical ladder to the water's edge at the original site of the accident. This patient received 107 treatment sessions in all, and he has made a complete recovery, which has been maintained for over three years.

SYSTEMATIC DESENSITIZATION UNDER CONDITIONS OF RELAXATION

Most patients who are given systematic desensitization are given some form of relaxation, but little is said about this aspect of the treatment situation in the articles which are published. The author offers two forms of relaxation, either hypnosis or intravenous injections of Methohexital sodium, but in the case of drug addicts they are only offered hypnosis, since it is felt that injections should not be encouraged by the treatment. Other patients are given the choice, and some prefer hypnosis, particularly if they are afraid of injections, while others prefer injections which they regard as more "medical."

The patient is asked to lie on a bed, but if he feels very threatened by this, he can be hypnotized sitting in a comfortable chair. Intravenous injections of Methohexital sodium must not be given to a patient in the sitting position as this may prove dangerous.

For those patients who receive hypnosis, the author tends to use the hand levitation technique, which will be described in detail at the end of this section. Some patients, particularly adolescents, respond to a very quiet voice, while others respond better to loud instructions, and this varies from one patient to another. When the patient is hypnotized, he is given the first item on the hierarchy. A patient who is being treated for her frigidity might be asked to imagine being in the kitchen at home, talking to her husband. At first, she may find it difficult to imagine this scene and here the therapist helps to produce visual images. He can assist her in this by additional cues such as seeing the kettle boil, making a cup of tea, asking the patient to describe the clothes worn by her husband, and sooner or later the patient will say that she can see her husband quite clearly. The patient may say that she feels perfectly alright provided that her husband is two feet away from her. The scene is then withdrawn and the patient is told to stop thinking about it and relax. The second scene to be presented might be sitting with her husband watching television, and the third, saying goodnight to him, without any physical contact. The therapist suggests that she will reach a deeper level of relaxation next time, and that with practice, she will obtain stronger visual images as the treatment proceeds. Unfortunately, not all patients have the capacity to form visual images, but desensitization can occur in the absence of either visual or auditory imagery, providing there is the appropriate emotional component. Some patients find it helpful to be given a relief response between items, and this aids anxiety-relief. One patient might like to think of roses, another of strawberries, and young people often like to think of a favorite pop record.

If the patient is presented with a scene which she finds very disturbing, it may be necessary to withdraw it, because if the patient comes out of the hypnotic state at this point, she may refuse to be hypnotized again, either on this or on a subsequent occasion.

As each scene is presented, it is quite easy to see from the facial expression whether the patient feels comfortable in this situation. On the first presentation, the patient may bite his lip, or furrow his brow or show a pained expression, and the therapist may have to present the scene several times before he remains perfectly calm and relaxed when visualizing it. Although it is quite satisfactory to present the next scene when the patient shows no evidence of anxiety, the author continues to present it until the patient is so happy with it that he can smile and dismiss it as though it had never been a problem at all. This is based on the principle of over-learning. At the beginning of each session, patients find it very helpful to start with a scene which has been well rehearsed, as this increases their confidence, but this is not essential.

Before bringing the patient out of the hypnotic state, it is important to give a strong counter-suggestion that he will be able to open his eyes, be wide awake, and perfectly fresh, because otherwise he may remain in a semi-hypnotized state for the rest of the day. One patient could not understand why he was not fully awake and said that he felt confused and as if walking through clouds, and further counter-suggestions were given later. It has been the author's experience that drug-addicted adolescents are particularly resistant to the counter-suggestion, and this may be due to a reluctance to come out of the hypnotic state, which they say is somewhat similar to the drug-induced state.

When patients are hypnotized frequently, it will be found that the induction will become quicker on each occasion, so that eventually a deep trance state can be induced by a signal such as a click of the fingers.

Here it is important to emphasize that it will only happen in the treatment situation when the therapist clicks his fingers and in no other situation, as this might prove embarrassing elsewhere, for example, in a crowded department store.

For those patients who have Methohexital sodium-induced relaxation, the author usually uses a 2½% solution by adding 4 mls. of distilled water to 100 mg. of the powder. The 4 mls. (100 mg.) are drawn up into the syringe, and a fine needle is used, so that the drug can be injected slowly. The drug is given intravenously, and after an initial loading dose of up to 1 ml. (25 mg.), the patient becomes very relaxed. This level of relaxation can be maintained throughout the treatment session by keeping the needle in the vein and injecting a little more of the drug at regular intervals. The quantity of Methohexital sodium used varies considerably from one patient to another, and in the first treatment session, it is wise to start with a very small quantity, in case the patient is very sensitive to the drug. One patient was nearly asleep (this is not the aim of treatment) after injecting less than 0.5 mls. of the 2½% solution, and in this case it is wiser to use a weaker solution. Very tense patients often require quite large doses to obtain adequate relaxation, but this may vary from one treatment session to another.

Although Methohexital sodium is a relatively safe drug, especially in the dosage employed, one must not forget that this is an anesthetic agent and may only be given by medical practitioners.

During the treatment session using Methohexital sodium, scenes are presented to the patient in much the same way as under hypnosis. Towards the end of the session, the needle is withdrawn from the vein, and a few minutes later, the patient is ready to get up from the bed. No counter-suggestions are necessary in drug-induced relaxation.

Although the author likes to use hypnosis or intravenous injections of Methohexital sodium to induce relaxation, neither of these is essential for the desensitization process to take place, and many behavior therapists use simple muscle relaxation techniques. Recent work would suggest that it is quite sufficient to present a graded series of images, even in the absence of specific relaxation procedures.

After each treatment session, the patient is told to practice the situations which were rehearsed during the session, preferably on the same day as the treatment, or as soon after this as possible. Sometimes a patient finds that although he felt perfectly happy *imagining* the situation in treatment, he feels much less happy when putting it into practice. In this case, the patient should be reassured that this is frequently seen in clinical practice and all that is necessary is to repeat the situation in the next treatment session.

INDUCTION OF HYPNOSIS

In the first session, the patient might be given the following instructions: "Would you like to lie on the bed? You can cover yourself with a blanket if you wish. Make yourself perfectly comfortable. Now, hypnosis is just a method of relaxation. All I want you to do is to concentrate your thoughts on your right hand. As you begin to relax, you will find that the right hand becomes light, and later, the hand will begin to rise. This is perfectly natural, so there is nothing to worry about, just concentrate your thoughts on the right hand, and soon you will find that it starts to rise. You may close your eyes if you wish." As soon as the therapist sees a movement occurring in the right hand, this is immediately reinforced: "The hand has started to rise, soon it will rise more and more; as you relax more deeply, the hand will get lighter and lighter, and it will rise more and more." The patient may now feel his hand rising and may start to laugh. The therapist now reassures the patient: "That's perfectly alright. Patients often find this rather funny on the first occasion. Yes, you can laugh if you like, it doesn't matter at all. And breathe slowly and deeply and relax." (The author has found this comment particularly helpful to patients.)

As the hand starts to rise from the bed, the therapist gives further suggestions that the hand is rising: "The hand is rising quite quickly now. It has already left the bed, and soon it will rise more and more." Suggestions are also given that the hand feels light. "The hand is beginning to feel really light now, it is getting lighter and lighter, it is floating upwards, it is rising, moving upwards, it is as light as a feather, like a cloud drifting upwards, it is rising up and up and up." Here the therapist's voice gets quieter to create the impression of floating. When the hand has risen several inches from the bed (this varies from one patient to another), the therapist may now say: "Now that you are nice and deeply relaxed, you can put your hand down. I will now give you a "count-down" for ten. I shall count slowly from one to ten, and with each number you will find that you become more and more relaxed. One . . . two. . . ." The therapist counts from one to ten, each number coinciding with a breath out. It will be observed that the patient's breathing becomes slower during the hypnotic procedure. When the therapist has reached ten, he may now say: "Now that you are perfectly calm, relaxed and peaceful, we can begin." The first scene to be introduced is usually a "neutral scene" which does not cause any anxiety to the patient. After this, the therapist can introduce the first scene from the hierarchy.

THE COUNTER-SUGGESTION

Towards the end of the hypnosis session, the therapist must give a strong counter-suggestion. He might say to the patient: "I am now going to count from one to ten. With each number you will find that your relaxed state will become lighter and lighter, so that by the time I reach ten, you will be able to open your eyes, you will be wide awake and perfectly fresh. Your hand will be perfectly normal in all respects." It is probably a good idea to repeat this and say to the patient: "I repeat, by the time. . . ." Usually the patient opens his eyes when he hears the word "ten," but if not, it may be necessary to count again from one to ten, and give further counter-suggestions. It is important that the therapist is in perfect command of the situation and knows exactly what to do, as this transmits to the patient.*

COMBINED BEHAVIOR THERAPY AND PSYCHOTHERAPY

In the majority of patients treated so far, the author has found that after a few treatment sessions of the type described in the previous section, patients find that a lot of unexpected things are happening, which they would like to discuss with the therapist. For this reason it was decided to divide each treatment session into two parts, the first for psychotherapy and the second for behavior therapy. The content of the first part of each session depends entirely on the material which the patient chooses to bring into the treatment situation. Usually there are many problems arising out of the treatment which he is keen to discuss, and the patient should be given the opportunity to do so.

1. Responses of Family and Friends

It has been the author's experience that, as the patient improves, he meets strong opposition from his family and friends, who object most

---

* Editor's note: It is usually useful to count *backwards* from 10 to 1 when dehypnotizing patients whose hypnotic state had been increased by counting from 1 to 10.

strongly to any change, however small, in his behavior. The environment would appear to be extremely sensitive to these changes, and as soon as they are detected, (often before the patient has become aware of them), counter pressures are exerted onto the patient, to try and force him back into his former behavior. This may be formulated in the following way: *"There is a state of dynamic equilibrium between the patient and his environment and any attempt to change this will lead to opposing forces being set into motion to try and recreate the former state."* The patient in behavior therapy usually manages to survive these counter forces and makes a recovery, but if he fails to do so, he will return to his former state. The second point is that once the patient's behavior has changed, if the environment fails to exert sufficient counter pressure to reverse the treatment, then there is a change in the nature of the relationship between the patient and the people in his environment. This may be formulated as follows: *"If the state of dynamic equilibrium between the patient and his environment is upset, and the opposing forces cannot survive the alterations in the patient's behavior, then this leads to an alteration in the environment."*

These two formulations may be illustrated by the case of a 22-year-old male homosexual patient who was receiving treatment from the author. As he was being desensitized to heterosexual situations, he soon learned that his male companions did not approve of any alteration in his sexual adjustment. When he started dating girls, his friends did not encourage him in this; on the contrary, they told him that he had no right to do this, especially on a Saturday night, and that his first responsibility was with them. This caused considerable conflict in the patient and he began to wonder whether he was doing the right thing after all. He was being given one set of instructions from the therapist and another from his friends. Up to now he was experiencing the opposing forces which were set in motion in an attempt to force him back into the homosexual position. This is in keeping with the first formulation. Later in treatment, when his friends realized that they could not achieve their aims, they began to show changes themselves in the direction of heterosexuality, and found that they were dating girls too, and dancing more. This is in line with the second formulation. The patient met similar problems in relation to members of his family.

The successfully treated alcoholic patient who can drink socially without the need to drink to excess finds that his friends do not appreciate his altered attitude towards drinking. They expect him to drink as much as before, and when he does not do so, they cannot understand it. At first, they think this is of a temporary nature and "cannot last," but later, they realize that this is a new pattern of behavior which will be maintained. One patient who had just completed a course of treatment reported that his mother had warned him that she had detected his finger prints on the wardrobe where she had hidden a large supply of whiskey. Presumably she had hoped to sabotage the treatment and encourage further drinking in her son, but she failed to achieve this, for he no longer wished to drink to excess.

The successfully treated drug addict meets fierce opposition from his friends. If he tells them that he no longer needs to take the addictive drug, they become so angry that they may use physical violence and injure the patient. The sister of one successfully treated addict became extremely hostile and accused the therapist of brainwashing him.

A frigid patient who was treated by behavior therapy thought that her husband would be delighted if she could show more interest, but when this happened, he felt less inclined to make love to her, and became impotent. Her husband said that he did not like his wife to show sexual interest (this is the reverse of his original attitude) and that frigid women were "more sexy." He resented her more feminine approach, found it strange when she started preparing elaborate meals for him, and was alarmed when she dismissed her maid because she was not satisfied with her standard of cleaning. Later, the husband readjusted to his wife's improvement, though this took a long time, and several joint sessions were needed where husband and wife were interviewed together.

2. Relationship with the Therapist

When the patient has received intensive treatment of any kind over a prolonged period, whether this is behavior-oriented or not, he develops an attachment to the therapist who is treating him. Behavior therapists tend to deny the importance of this, though some recognize that it may be a useful adjunct to treatment.

After a few sessions of behavior therapy using hypnosis, the author has found that the patient develops feeling for the therapist. This may be quite strong and the patient finds himself thinking about the therapist when he is working or at other times, and he may wonder why he is thinking about the therapist at all. Sooner or later, the patient may develop complex thoughts relating to the therapist. On the one hand, he may look forward to the next treatment session when he can see the therapist again; on the other hand, he may consider the possibility that the therapist has come to some harm which will prevent him from seeing him. One patient feared that the therapist might be killed on the road and wanted to ensure his safety by escorting him across the road. The author interprets these comments and tells the patient that his ambivalent feelings towards the therapist are a reflection of emotions which were felt by him at an earlier stage in relation to important figures in his life and that these are not in fact intended for the therapist. The fear of death of the therapist is interpreted in terms of death wishes, and the patient may remember harboring death wishes for his father.

Though the exact nature of the relationship which the patient makes with the therapist during a course of treatment varies from one patient to another, all patients who recover in treatment make a strong attachment to their therapist. One female patient who was treated for frigidity and housebound syndrome wanted the therapist to make love to her, and when this was refused, she was very angry and cried bitterly, saying that if she had known that treatment would produce such an emotional turmoil she would rather not have had the treatment at all. Later, she was pleased that the therapist had not been influenced by her demands and that these had been interpreted to her in the light of earlier emotional experiences.

CONCLUSION

It is hoped that the author has been able to convey that, during a course of treatment which is essentially behavior-oriented, there are many important changes other than the target symptom being treated. Treatment of a frigid woman brings about an alteration in the relationship with her husband, and altering the sexual adjustment of a homosexual leads to severe repercussions in his immediate environment. A few examples are given in the text to illustrate the magnitude of the reaction in the environment to changes occurring in the patient. An attempt has also been made to show the importance of the relationship with the therapist during a course of intensive treatment. It is felt that psychotherapy is necessary for all patients receiving behavior therapy, and a broad spectrum approach to treatment would seem to offer the best help to our patients.

2

The Initial Interview

HERBERT FENSTERHEIM, Ph.D.

BEHAVIOR THERAPY TENDS to focus upon specific target symptoms and has a wide array of treatment techniques at its disposal. It differs from the more traditional psychotherapies in a number of ways that bring diagnostic considerations closer to the "blueprint for action" (Cameron, 1953) ideal than is true of the more traditional settings. Behavior therapy requires a series of meaningful decisions on the part of the therapist from the very first contact with the patient. Hence, the initial interview in behavior therapy takes on a special importance.

The problems presented from the very first contact with the patient are accentuated in the private practice of behavior therapy. In an institutional setting, at the very least, the patient has been filtered through a screening process which minimizes the chance of a completely inappropriate referral. The patient may be preceded by a chart containing the results of an intake interview which will include a description of the problem, a brief history and a mental status examination. There may also be an extensive social work case history, an intensive psychological examination, a medication chart, and, perhaps, voluminous notes of previous treatment.

In a private practice all one usually knows is that there is a voice on the telephone asking for an appointment. At this point two major decisions have to be made: should any appointment be given at all and, if so, how quickly should the patient be seen.

Because it is novel and holds the promise of more effective results, many patients while undergoing more traditional forms of treatment decide to change to behavior therapy. Many times such a change is appropriate and beneficial to the patient. There are times, however, when the change of treatment may be inappropriate (as when the patient is misinformed about the nature of behavior therapy or expects a magical solution to rather complex problems). There are other times when such a change may actually be harmful to the patient as when a change of therapies is an avoidance of making necessary changes in behavior during the course of an otherwise successful ongoing treatment. Hence, every new patient should be asked whether he is currently in treatment and whether he has discussed the change with his therapist. The therapist should always be contacted prior to giving the first appointment.

CASE 1: The case of Mr. A. illustrates some of the ethical problems involved with patients under treatment. He had been in psychoanalytic treatment for about three years with the presenting problem of sexual impotency. At the time of his first contact he was still in treatment and there had been no improvement in the symptom. He had discussed behavior therapy with his therapist who was very much opposed to it. No appointment was given until his therapist had been contacted.

The therapist involved had a good professional reputation and, in my discussions with him, appeared to be competent, sensitive and mature. He was not against the use of behavior therapy for the treatment of sexual impotence either in principle or for the specific patient. His concern was with the timing of such intervention. The patient, he stated, was a general underachiever in all areas of his life, vocational, social, and personal. He was given to periodic temper outbursts and was unable to form close emotional relationships with anyone. Motivated mainly by his desire to overcome his sexual symptom, he had been working well analytically. Recently he had made some major behavioral changes and had achieved some important insights. He appeared to be at the point of a major analytic breakthrough. This possibility carried a good deal of anxiety in its wake and, to avoid this anxiety and still relieve the symptom, he had sought out behavior therapy. To treat the symptom behaviorally *at this point* could very well distract him from a potential growth experience of major importance to all areas of his life and, in that sense, would be destructive. This formulation, supported by many details, seemed quite credible.

Under these conditions should I see the patient? I described his therapist's formulation to him over the telephone to make certain that he understood it. I also told him that so far as I could determine this formulation was most reasonable. When he still insisted on the behavioral approach, I followed the principle that he had a right to choose the form of treatment he was to receive and I accepted him for treatment. As he could not afford the cost of both treatments simultaneously, he stopped the analytically oriented therapy.

A combination of systematic desensitization through imagery and graded sexual tasks in life yielded complete symptom relief in fourteen sessions. His other problems (difficulty in achieving emotional closeness and irrational temper outbursts) appeared to remain unchanged nor did he desire to work on these problems. The fourteenth session was therefore the terminal session with me. He did not return to his previous therapist nor did he continue any treatment at all. He remained quite satisfied with his "symptomatic gains."

It may be noted in this case that it was not only the fact that the patient was currently in treatment that posed the problem. Part of the problem stemmed from the fact that behavioral techniques can be used to modify specific symptoms while leaving others unchanged. This, too, can bring about certain ethical problems.

CASE 2: During his first telephone contact with me, Mr. B. stated that he had a problem of sexual potency. He was a homosexual, his difficulty occurred in his homosexual relationships and he did not want treatment for homosexuality. In fact, he would enter treatment only if I agreed to confine my treatment attempts to the specific problem of sexual potency and to avoid completely any attempt to influence the homosexuality. He did recognize that there could be no guarantee that the homosexuality would be unchanged but he insisted that there be no deliberate attempts to change it.

Consultation with colleagues yielded three distinct sets of opinions concerning the propriety of accepting these limited treatment goals. One group claimed that it would be like treating a diabetic ulcer without treating the underlying diabetes and so would be unethical. The people holding this point of view also held the basic belief that the homosexuality and the impotency were merely expressions of the same underlying pathology and their conclusions stemmed logically from this conceptual position. Several of them also held the belief that it would be impossible to treat the impotency without also treating the homosexuality. (This is untrue for I have now treated six such patients with a simple systematic desensitization and all have responded successfully in from two to seven sessions.)

A second group of colleagues was more practical. They held that I should agree to the conditions imposed since the patient himself may come to change the goals. They argued that the only reason the patient did not want the homosexuality treated was because he felt hopeless about it, he did not believe treatment would work. If, through the treatment of the impotency, it could be demonstrated that the behavioral techniques were effective, he would gain hope and decide on further treatment. This position was not supported by any evidence. In fact, of the six such patients I have treated only one showed any desire to give up an exclusively homosexual mode and that one patient wanted "the best of both worlds."

A third group of colleagues, mainly people involved in the behavioral, hypnotic or psychopharmacologic approaches (i.e., those approaches directed towards target symptoms), held a different view. There was no reason to believe, they argued, that the two conditions were directly related. It might be assumed that the patient had two separate and distinct sexual problems. They felt that he had the undeniable right to seek treatment for one condition and to reject it for the second. The important point was that the patient should be aware that available techniques do exist which may modify the homosexual pattern should he so desire.

This last approach is the one I adopted for Mr. B. and for all such patients. I do agree to confine the treatment to the specific target symptoms as best as I can. However I also state that I will present for their consideration a plan for the treatment of homosexuality. All I ask is that

I be permitted a brief time to present a possible treatment plan and that the patient listen to it. When I do present such a treatment plan I do so as objectively as possible with no attempt to "sell" it to the patient. During the terminal session I once again refer to the possibility of modifying the homosexual behavior. In this way I accept the patient's right to seek treatment for one condition and to reject treatment for the other while knowing what treatment is available.

Beyond the problem of ethics, there is the problem of the urgency of the appointment. As with any form of therapy, the content and the affect must be assessed during the initial contact to determine the acuteness of the condition. If there is intense distress the patient should be seen within forty-eight hours or even sooner. If this cannot be done, he should be referred to a colleague who may be able to see him at once. There are patients who, having taken the important step of calling for an appointment, are impatient or manipulative and demand to be seen immediately. Such patients usually can wait for a convenient appointment time and should not be confused with the more acutely disturbed people who do need to be seen immediately. As mentioned, the clinical decision to be made here is essentially the same no matter what type of psychotherapy is practiced.

There is a difference between behavior therapists and other therapists concerning patients who do have to wait a week or longer for a first appointment. Behavior therapists, probably more as a matter of style than of conceptual differences, tend to rely more on questionnaires than do other practitioners. Hence, while a patient is waiting for an appointment I often mail him a life history form, a fear inventory, an assertion questionnaire and an MMPI. The patient completes these and brings them to the first interview or mails them back prior to that interview. This procedure helps to make the initial interview more efficient and also provides a supportive function while the patient awaits the appointment date.

The last point about initial contact, unique to a private practice, concerns fees. Fees should be clearly stated before making the first appointment. Unlike most other forms of treatment, because behavior therapy is so new, few low cost treatment facilities exist at present and the problem of the patient with limited financial resources is a major one. I have attempted to meet this problem to a small extent through the use of a therapeutic assistant to perform certain of the routine treatment procedures, through the use of small groups for desensitization and through the use of "mini-groups" for assertive training. In this way there is some lowering of fees but the major problem remains and will be overcome only when many more trained behavior therapists are available.

FORMAL DIAGNOSTIC CONSIDERATIONS

The initial interview for behavioral treatment is closely allied to therapeutic action. In actuality there are two major types of initial interview, each with a different goal. For patients not in acute distress the major purposes of this interview are to obtain a clear statement of the most important problems, to form some working hypothesis concerning these problems, and to develop a beginning approach to treatment. For the person in acute distress, the goal of the first interview is to furnish some measure of relief even if it means a delay in the systematic gathering of information.

Formal diagnostic considerations do play some role. Although it has been well established that the major diagnostic categories tend to be unreliable and often unrelated to treatment, certain diagnoses are indeed related to behavioral treatment. This area has not been well researched and what follows are clinical impressions.

A differential diagnosis between a character disorder and a neurosis is often important. Neurotics tend to have anxiety and guilt connected with crucial problem areas and the treatment of choice usually centers around some form of desensitization and tension reduction. Character disorders, when they do show anxiety, usually experience it as a consequence of the symptom rather than as a cause of the symptom. Desensitization may be difficult because of the inability to experience anxiety when picturing scenes or even in the actual situation. At best, the desensitization procedures lead only to peripheral changes in that the patient becomes more comfortable with an inadequate mode of life. The treatments of choice for character disorder usually center around a combination of operant methods, aversive techniques, assertive training, education and guidance.

Another important differential diagnosis is between hysterical neuroses and obsessive-compulsive neuroses. The obsessive tends to be intellectualized, rigid and to have a shallow affect. The hysteric tends to be impulsive, given to strong feelings and is often described as childish and immature. Witkin and his colleagues (1954, 1962) have found that obsessives tend to be field independent whereas hysterics tend to be field dependent; that the perceptual fields of obsessives tend to be highly differentiated while those of hysterics tend to be global and undifferentiated.

In general, my clinical impression is that there usually are fewer problems in relaxation among hysterics. Also hysterics seem to require simple hierarchies, with relatively few steps, and in all, fewer hierarchies are required for a given behavioral change. Obsessives, probably because of their highly differentiated thought and perceptual processes, usually require more steps in the hierarchies than do the hysterics and may require a number of hierarchies to be applied to a given problem.

A comparison of two young men, one generally hysteric and the other decidedly obsessive, with anxieties in social situations may illustrate this difference. With both patients systematic desensitization to images of being at a party were used. The scenes used for the hysterical young man included speaking to a friend, to a stranger, to a girl he had dated, to a strange girl, asking for a telephone number, etc. In all, a fourteen step hierarchy was used with successful symptom relief. The obsessive young man required four different hierarchies of twelve to twenty-one steps each. These hierarchies concerned rejection, disapproval, doing something "gauche" and expressing anger. The symptom was not completely alleviated until the desensitization was supplemented by some assertive training in a group situation.

Perhaps the most important differential diagnosis to be made concerns the distinction between "neurotic" and "psychotic" conditions. With the overt psychotic, the significance of this diagnosis is obvious and will not be considered here. It is the borderline or the pseudoneurotic schizophrenic where the differential diagnosis may become difficult yet crucial.

The relation of such a differential diagnosis to behavior treatment may be illustrated by considering pervasive anxiety and pananxiety. Although both types of anxiety are generally chronic and at a high level, there is a qualitative difference between them. As used here, pervasive anxiety is a neurotic reaction to a large number of different stimuli. Pananxiety is an expression of a psychotic process and may even be due primarily to an organic dysfunction within the central nervous system. The differential diagnosis between a neurotic and a psychotic condition is crucial in making the distinction. Neurotic patients with pervasive anxiety often respond to a treatment plan of intensive relaxation training and nonsystematic desensitization (to be described later) followed by systematic desensitization and assertive training as the general level of anxiety decreases. Such patients should be seen initially two to three times a week and definite changes may be expected to occur during the first month of treatment. Initial treatment of psychotic patients with pananxiety involves the use of proper medication supplemented by relaxation training, and, eventually, by guidance concerning life situations. The relaxation exercises I use take about twenty minutes to perform and are tape-recorded for the patient. He is instructed to play them once a day. Extremely tense patients also receive half-hour relaxation sessions in my office. Generally, though, I see such patients on a once-a-week basis, progress is slow, beset by unpredictable panic outbursts, and goals are limited. I have found that after long periods of relaxation training, which consists of playing the relaxation tape every day for a period of well over a year, marked changes in pananxiety may occur, panic reactions may become less frequent, but the basic inadequate life style may show only minimal improvement.

One final caution must be made about the formal diagnosis. A problem oriented approach may sometimes underestimate pathology; problems which initially appear to be rather simple may turn out to be most complicated. To guard against this underestimation I always try to make a formal diagnosis and to supplement it with the scores from an MMPI. The information needed for the making of such a diagnosis often alerts me to pathology I may otherwise have missed.

PROBLEM FORMULATION

It has already been noted that with patients who are not in acute distress the initial interview should attempt to gain a clear definition of the problem. Very often (but far from always) the patient is able to state exactly what is wrong: he has a sexual problem or he is frightened of flying or he cannot sleep at night. Sometimes, however, the complaint is more general and vague: he cannot form close emotional ties, or he is in trouble with his work, or he is generally depressed. Both of these sets of problems can be handled in the same manner although the more general set of questions may take somewhat longer to explore and to formulate into working terms.

To investigate the problems in a systematic manner I attempt to answer the following questions:

1. What is the basic problem? How intense is it? To what extent is it disruptive?
2. When did it start? What was going on in the patient's life at that time? What were the exact circumstances under which it first occurred?
3. When is the problem greatest? When is it least disturbing?
4. Is there a specific fear, or some other feeling or thought connected with the problem? What is the worst that can happen?

The answers to these questions, combined with other information about the patient, may provide the basis for a behavioral therapy diagnosis and a tentative treatment plan. However, it would be premature to formulate such a plan until one further evaluation is made.

At this point we are attempting to deal with a problem of greater or lesser specificity presented by the patient and refined by the interview procedure described. However, all problems, all disrupted behavior, all disturbed emotions, do not stem from incorrect learning, psychopathology, or the characteristics of the person. If only for the sake of parsimony certain other variables must be investigated. Among these variables are:

Environment: A nonoptimal environment may often lead to psychological disruption. While this may be a particularly common variable among poor people (cf. Normand, Fensterheim and Schrenzel, 1967), it may influence people at all socio-economic levels. The approach to these problems usually does not involve psychotherapy but rather social casework to help solve the reality problems.

Stress: Life itself holds many stressful situations. People under such stress may become quite upset but their reactions may be completely appropriate to the situation. When people seek help under such circumstances, all that is usually required is reassurance that they are not going crazy, plus emotional support. The latter is often best provided by close friends and family rather than by a professional therapist.

Misconceptions: Some people become concerned with behaviors that are not really problems simply because they have incorrect concepts of the nature of "normality." The following illustration is an unusually clear example of this:

CASE 3: A 22-year-old man stated that he had a "sexual problem." Whenever he went to bed with a girl whom he did not like or whom he found unattractive, he had difficulty in obtaining an erection. When he did like the girl or when he did find her sexually attractive, he had no such problems. In all other areas of his life he appeared to be functioning normally.

His misconceptions were twofold: he believed that he should jump into bed at every possible opportunity whether he wanted to or not and he believed that a "real man" obtains and maintains an erection at any time or place or under any circumstance. These misconceptions were discussed with him and he left much relieved. A three-month and a six-month follow-up (I myself found it hard to believe it was quite that simple) showed a more discriminating pattern of sexual behavior and no further doubts of his manliness.

Style: People sometimes find the wrong approach for themselves in work or in social life. They try to fit into a pattern that runs counter to their own intellectual or temperamental style. Thus introverts try to become salesmen and extroverts try to become bookkeepers. This may be particularly common among students who, for a variety of reasons, attempt to major in subjects not really suited to their mode of function. These people would be most helped by the techniques of counseling and guidance rather than by psychotherapy.

While still other variables could be noted, the major point has been made. All problems presented by patients do not require psychotherapy and a careful evaluation may actually contraindicate a formal behavioral approach.

However, most problems presented to the therapist will require psychotherapy. The major behavioral approaches would tend to formulate the problems in terms of (a) phobias, (b) assertion problems, (c) absence of desirable habits, and (d) presence of undesirable habits. Although these are stated in simple form, let it be noted that "habit" may refer to a rather complicated series of behaviors, overt or covert. Because I have little that is new to offer about the last two sets of problems, this discussion will center around the diagnosis of phobias and assertive difficulties.

DIAGNOSTIC CLASSIFICATION OF PHOBIAS

In the behavior therapy lexicon, a phobia is any disturbed feeling elicited by a given class of stimuli. Although the published literature yields the impression that all phobias are basically the same, any good behavioral clinician is aware that there are different kinds of phobias requiring different kinds of treatment approaches.

1. *Direct Phobias:* These phobias tend to be the most simple and straightforward, with the much studied snake phobia as the paradigm. Cooper and his colleagues (1969) notwithstanding, the clinician does see many of these problems in an office practice. The usual, but not exclusive, form of treatment is systematic desensitization using relaxation and imagery. Even when the fear is intense and long hierarchies are needed, signs of progress are often evident from the very beginning.

A variant of this direct phobic condition concerns those fears that are present simply because the person does not know how to behave in certain situations. Fear of dating among adolescents and young adults is one example. Although systematic desensitization may be used here, the main approach involves education, fact giving and behavior rehearsal. Again, signs of progress are usually evident from the beginning of treatment.

2. *Direct Generalizations*: This is probably the most common type of phobia. Some fears do not stand alone but are generalizations of other fears. Thus, a fear of riding in subways may be a generalization of the fear of being trapped. The importance of this distinction is that without using the correct variables the results of desensitization may be most limited or may fail altogether. All behavior therapists are aware of the importance of this type of phobia, although it sometimes is difficult to determine the correct core fear.

3. *Indirect Generalizations:* This type of phobia is less well recognized by behavior therapists. Direct generalizations appear to make sense, to bear directly on the problem situation. It is easy to understand how the fear of being trapped may lead to a fear of riding in subways. However, some generalizations are not quite so obvious. As this type of indirect generalization has not been extensively considered, I will cite two examples.

CASE 4: Miss C. was a woman in her late twenties who was being treated for her difficulties in relating to men. A crucial point appeared to be her tension concerning a rejecting father and a desensitization to this was attempted. At the beginning of the desensitization session the patient casually mentioned that at some time we ought do something about her fear of heights; prior to the session she had become upset while looking out of a sixth floor window. There was no discussion of this and the desensitization concerning her rejecting father proceeded. The very next day (she reported) she was at a cocktail party and suddenly was made aware that she had been looking down from a twenty-first floor terrace with no anxiety at all. The fear of heights was completely gone and stayed gone. Upon questioning, no evidence was obtained to suggest that during the desensitization there had been intrusions of scenes concerning heights. Although there are a number of possible interpretations of this event, one reasonable interpretation is that in some way the fear of heights was a generalization of the fear of a rejecting father. When the latter was removed (as it was during that one session), the former also disappeared.

CASE 5: The patient was a former airline stewardess who had become terrified of flying. The treatment was a straightforward desensitization to flying and to airplane crashes. Towards the end of treatment she brought up the fact that her fear of tough-looking men in the street, a fear not previously elicited, had completely disappeared. No evidence of intrusion of tough-looking men into the flying images could be elicited.

The connection between a rejecting father and the fear of heights, or between airplane crashes and the fear of tough-looking men, is not quite as evident as those in the direct generalization category. These indirect generalizations become important when such a fear as agoraphobia is considered. Several colleagues and myself, based upon clinical experience, have come to consider many cases of agoraphobia as an indirect generalization of the fear of the loss of a significant person by an otherwise dependent person. With a married person it most often is the fear of losing the spouse. With such people I tend to get best results not through a desensitization to outdoor excursions, but through working on the marriage relationship.

4. *Excessive Inhibition:* People who lack assertive or excitatory behavior (Salter, 1949) tend to develop many different symptoms. Specific fears or phobias may be one such set of symptoms. My own clinical experience suggests that most hypochondriacal fears, as well as certain sexual fears, stem from an excess of inhibition. The desensitization procedures do not work with fears of this type and assertive and excitatory training is the treatment of choice.

Thus, I diagnose four different kinds of phobias, each requiring a different treatment. However, it must be noted that there is no diagnostic method presently available that will predict with certainty which treatment approach should be used. I have unsuccessfully attempted to treat hypochondriasis with assertive training only to find that it responded to a simple desensitization. I have improved the marital relationship of an agoraphobic woman with no change in the major symptom only to find that it did respond to an *in vivo* desensitization to going outside. I have unsuccessfully attempted to treat an airplane phobia as both a direct phobia and as a direct generalization only to find that it disappeared with assertive training.

At present, unless there are strong indications to the contrary, I always use the most simple therapeutic approach first. If I diagnose a phobic condition, I first treat it as a direct phobia or a direct generalization. Unless technical problems such as difficulty in relaxation or difficulty in visualizing scenes intervene, changes should be noted rather quickly. If changes in the symptom are not forthcoming, I then investigate one of the other approaches.

DIAGNOSTIC CLASSIFICATION OF ASSERTIVE PROBLEMS

Disturbed psychological functioning is usually intimately bound up with disturbed interpersonal relations. These disturbed interpersonal relations are often due to problems in assertion. These types of psychological disturbances almost invariably include a low self-esteem and an inadequate mastery of life situations, and often include depression, rages, apathy or withdrawal. Since phobias, psychosomatic disorders and other symptoms may also be included, a differential diagnosis must decide which aspects of the psychological disturbance and the disturbed interpersonal functioning are primary. If the primary focus is upon person-to-person interactions the area of assertion must be carefully investigated.

A working definition of assertion is "an open and direct, honest, and appropriate expression of what a person feels and thinks." Before a treatment plan can be prepared to remedy dysfunctions in this area, several different aspects of these behaviors must be formulated.

1. *Area of involvement*. The Casper Milquetoast who is unassertive in all areas is easily identified. However, in most cases the lack of assertion seldom generalizes into all areas of life. A man may be assertive at work, in his social life, and with his children, and yet be unassertive in his relations with his wife. A man may be direct and open about his tender feelings and uncommunicative about his angry feelings, and vice versa. Whenever the presenting problem is one of a mood disturbance, even though the patient may indicate a generally assertive life style, particular care should be given to the search for meaningful areas where unassertive

behavior may dominate. In those areas where assertive difficulties are encountered, discussion and behavior rehearsal usually bring about marked and rapid change. The more general the lack of assertion, the more complex the treatment usually must be.

2. *Type of difficulty.* Some people do not act assertively because they have never learned how to do so; others know what to do but cannot bring themselves to do it. These latter are usually phobic patients. They fear scrutiny, or rejection, or aggression or any number of other consequences of assertion. Once the fears are identified and mitigated or removed, assertive behavior usually emerges quite spontaneously. The former type, the people who had never learned to be assertive, may be typified by the young adult who has never dated. With these persons education, modeling, and structured experiences (often preceded by tension reduction as with a direct phobia) are usually the treatment of choice.

3. *Type of Behavior:* As assertion has been defined it has three behavioral characteristics: (1) openness and directness, (2) honesty, and (3) appropriateness. People with assertive difficulties may be deficient in any or all three areas. However, it is not uncommon to see people who are deficient in only one area. It is possible for people to appear to be open and direct and yet to be dishonest in what they express. To be inappropriately honest and so to create a distance between themselves and others is not an uncommon technique used by those who fear closeness.

3a. OPEN AND DIRECT. People whose assertive problems are limited to this area tend to be wordy. This often is accompanied by shallowness of feeling, difficulty with close relationships and lack of clear-cut desires. I have often found them to be related to circumscribed work difficulties such as report writing. Practice and exercises in the use of the pronoun "I" and in making simple direct statements often change this entire pattern. Group therapy may be particularly helpful because other group members can model the desired behaviors and can provide immediate feedback when necessary.

3b. HONESTY. These are the people who appear to be open and direct, generally appropriate, often extraverted, but who are dishonest in what they express. They appear to be assertive but, because of the lack of honesty, are not genuinely so; hence the label of "pseudo-assertive." They are the hail-well-met salesmen or politicians. Many alcoholics and drug addicts would fall into this category. Those who are not alcoholics or addicts usually come with a presenting problem concerning closeness ("I can't make up my mind to marry her."), lack of satisfaction in life ("Nothing turns me on."), or mood difficulties. I have been generally unsuccessful in treating these conditions and therefore I shall make no recommendations for treatment.

3c. APPROPRIATENESS. This is the most rare of the specific behavioral deficiencies. These are the people who are open and honest in their behavior but, because they are often inappropriate in these expressions, they usually encounter numerous interpersonal difficulties.' Such people are often naive and immature and are often at the extremes of an exploitation continuum, being highly exploiting or highly exploited. They tend to have rapid and fairly great (but not extreme) mood changes. They have not learned the realities of social relations within our complex society nor have they learned the appropriate expression of feelings. Education and behavior rehearsal, particularly in a group setting, often work well. Those who do not respond to role-playing techniques may respond well when desensitized to a fear of closeness, followed by some training in assertive behavior.

One last caution must be presented when dealing with problems of assertion. The patient's subculture is of great importance and the therapist must have a genuine understanding of the social patterns and modes of function within these subcultures before diagnosing and planning treatment for an assertive difficulty. That subcultural atmosphere, ideology and values tend to select and to reinforce certain patterns of social behavior is well known and has been illustrated many years ago by Fensterheim and Birch (1950) in their analysis of the behavior of Displaced Persons in an UNRRA camp following World War II. The subcultural group sets the type of social pattern a person may encounter, influences the patterns of confrontation with and relations to other people and, above all, defines what is considered to be appropriate interpersonal behavior. The role of physical combat in different social groups is but one obvious example of this. The therapist must take all these into account in planning his treatment for an assertive problem.

THE ACUTELY DISTRESSED PATIENT

The foregoing emphasis has centered around the usual initial interview where the patient comes in with a problem, where a first formulation of the nature of the problem can be made, where a tentative treatment plan can be drawn up, and where the patient leaves with homework to do, (i.e. questionnaires, tests to complete or assignments to perform). With most patients all this can usually be accomplished in one session although, at times, two or three interviews may be necessary. The formulations are of course subject to modification as more data concerning the patient becomes available.

Some patients, however, come for the initial interview in a state of acute distress. They may be in a panic, have a severe depression, be suicidal, or suffer from a mild psychotic break (the more violent or florid psychotic episodes will not be discussed here). Under these conditions the goal of the initial interview must shift from one of a systematic problem formulation to one of bringing immediate relief to the patient.

The interview with the severely disturbed patient begins with a discussion of the symptom, its content and its origin. At some point, based upon the clinical judgment of the therapist, this inquiry is abandoned and energies are directed towards bringing relief to the patient.

There are a series of traditional tension reduction methods available to the therapist. These include reassurance and support, making a human contact with the patient and so breaking through the isolation, and allowing opportunity for catharsis. There are also several behavioral techniques which are helpful for this purpose:

1. *Relaxation.* This is usually used where tension and anxiety are general and where a secondary reaction to the tension has been set off. These secondary reactions are usually a fear of loss of control, a fear of the anxiety itself or an overwhelming feeling of helplessness in face of the tension. Almost invariably relaxation procedures bring about at least a slight and temporary reduction of the tension level and this I draw to the patient's attention. I point out that *we* reduced the anxiety by about 12% or 20% or 30%, as the case may be. Often the anxiety quickly spikes to its former level and it is necessary for the therapist to reflect this too with some statement that as the patient practices it may last for longer periods of time. Sometimes the relaxation exercises reduce the tension level quite considerably and the patient leaves feeling much better. At other times the patient leaves just as tense as when he came but with a knowledge that he is not completely helpless in the face of the disturbance. At all times I tape record the relaxation exercises and the patient leaves with the tape and with the homework assignment of using the relaxation tape at least once daily. This provides both structure and

support to the patient as well as the potential anxiety reduction of the exercises themselves.

Some patients are too agitated to perform the lengthy relaxation exercises or even some shortened version of them. Yet it may be necessary to bring about some tension reduction. I use a very brief relaxing exercise with these patients. While they are talking I can see the tension build up. At some point I stop them and tell them to take a deep breath, to hold it, to slowly let it out, to picture the word or image of "calm" and to relax their muscles. The entire exercise takes about ten seconds. It often results in a very temporary and slight, yet a definitely noticeable, reduction in tension. After doing this several times, the patient often appreciates the fact that there is some simple way of controlling tension and may even begin to do it himself. This can be an extremely supportive procedure.

2. Non-systematic Desensitization (NSD). This method has not been published although I have reported on it at a meeting of the New York Chapter of the Association for Advancement of Behavior Therapy. Basically, it fits within a counterconditioning paradigm where the anti-anxiety aspects are a task orientation and the attempts to relax, rather than relaxation itself. The patient is instructed to think about or to picture whatever is disturbing him, the very worst aspects of it. He is to signal at the very first sign of tension. Upon signalling, the patient receives instructions and help in picturing a pleasant scene and in attempting to relax. It is hard work for the patient, boring for the therapist (the disturbed scene should be repeated fifteen to twenty-five times) but fairly successful in cases of extreme anxiety or depression in well over 50% of the time.

This method is indicated during an initial interview when the disturbance is fairly extreme and centers around a relatively specific content area. It is contraindicated in psychotic conditions where at best it is usually ineffective and where it may actually increase the disturbance. A decision to use this method during an initial interview must be made early in the session, for close to a half hour must be allowed. When it does work, the major relief often comes about several hours after the session or even during the next day.

Other behavioral methods may also be used to bring relief to the acutely disturbed patient during the very first interview. Thought stopping (on occasion even covert sensitization) may be used to stop these and other obsessive thoughts and the shocker may be given the patient to take home.

Any other behavioral technique, when used with sound clinical judgment combined with a good understanding of the basis of the technique itself, may be used to ameliorate the acute distress during the first interview.

At the close of an initial interview, three important questions must be answered. Unfortunately, the professional literature provides few guidelines that will be of help and the therapist must rely on his own clinical judgment.

1. *Is behavior therapy the treatment of choice?* Perhaps some other form of treatment would be best for the patient. The guideline I usually use is that if I can formulate a reasonably precise therapeutic program with which to approach the major problems, a behavioral approach is worth trying.

There are patients, however, where it becomes obvious that the major therapeutic thrust must be non-behavioral. One such type is the patient who requires closely supervised medication as the core of treatment. Another type of patient is the one who is so isolated, so in need for "working through" some kind of relationship with another human being, that the usual symptom relief and behavior modification, while necessary, is not sufficient. Finally there is the person who is so immersed in the psychoanalytic mode of thinking that he really cannot understand the behavioral perspective, does not really want it and could not tolerate it for more than a few sessions.

2. *Can I work with this patient?* All therapists find certain problems or certain people difficult to treat. I have already noted in this paper that I get poor results with the pseudo-assertive patient. There are other patients with whom I have difficulty. The identification of such patients is as important in behavior therapy as it is in any other form of psychotherapy. It is important for both patient and therapist that this judgment be made during the initial interview so that it can be tactfully explained to the patient, and so that he be referred to a colleague for treatment.

3. *How fast should treatment proceed?* There have been no studies of drop-outs from behavior therapy. Recently I have surveyed my own patients who have dropped out early in treatment. The largest group of these patients appeared to have dropped out because I moved too fast in treatment. These are people to whom I had explained the treatment plan but who did not truly accept it. They are people who needed the feeling

of being understood, of being able to trust the therapist and his judgment, before specific behavioral techniques could be used.

With such patients it is necessary to spend several sessions establishing rapport and a feeling relationship as a context for treatment. A smaller group of patients appeared to drop-out because of their magical expectations; when they were not "cured" in two or three or four sessions, they became angry or bitter and left treatment. To attempt to work too fast is to reinforce these magical expectations. The initial part of the treatment should temper the patient's unrealistic demands and help him gain a more realistic expectation. Again, a proper context for treatment must be established.

SUMMARY

The behavior therapist must be primarily a clinician. The application of an effective behavior therapy program calls for a meaningful relation between diagnosis and treatment. Hence, the initial interview takes on a special significance. During this interview the therapist must take into consideration certain aspects of formal diagnosis, make a behavioral formulation and confront several ethical and clinical judgments, all of which are directly influential in determining the most productive course of treatment. However, because he has behavioral techniques at his disposal, he may attempt to bring relief to the patient even before making his basic formulations.

REFERENCES

CAMERON, E., A theory of diagnosis. In H. Hoch and J. Zubin (Eds.), *Current problems in psychiatric diagnosis.* New York: Grune & Stratton, 1953.

COOPER, A., FURST, J. B., & BRIDGER, W. H., A brief commentary on the usefulness of studying fears of snakes. *Journal of Abnormal Psychology,* 1969, 74, 413-414.

FENSTERHEIM, H. & BIRCH, H. G., A case study of group ideology and individual adjustment, *Journal of Abnormal and Social Psychology,* 1950, 45, 710-720.

NORMAND, W. C., FENSTERHEIM, H., SCHRENZEL, S., A systematic approach to brief therapy for patients from a low socioeconomic community, *Community Mental Health Journal,* 1967, 3, 349-354.

SALTER, A., *Conditioned reflex therapy,* New York: Creative Age, 1949.

WITKIN, H. A., *et al., Personality through perception,* New York: Harper & Brothers, 1954.

WITKIN, H. A., *et al., Psychological differentiation,* New York: John Wiley & Sons, 1962.

3

An Expedient Model for Behavior
Therapy

JOHN N. MARQUIS, Ph.D.

WHEN I WAS IN HIGH SCHOOL I had a friend who was interesting to talk to because he spent a lot of time in the library reading strange and wonderful things about philosophy and psychology. The ideas that he talked about were heady and quite alien to the things discussed in high school in a small midwestern town in those days. Such ideas were almost categorically relegated to the college curriculum. I was overwhelmed with the multiplicity of ideas that he expressed, and asked him where would be a good place to start reading in order to gain an understanding of psychology. He suggested that I read William James' *Principles of Psychology*, (1890), Watson's *Behaviorism*, (1924), and Freud's *General Introduction to Psychoanalysis*, (1917).

The following year as a freshman in college I was taking too many courses to be able to do my homework anyway, so I found time to follow his advice. I returned home from Christmas vacation full of enthusiasm about the new world that I had discovered and told him about my decision to seek a career in psychology. His answer set a very good goal for me: "That's nice. Maybe you can help get psychology out of the witch doctor stage."

The three books he recommended still strike me as being very well chosen. The perspective of seeing the three giants exemplifying, first, the finest of general academic psychology struggling to free itself from philosophy, a position which James represented so well; second, the vigor and rigor of Watson's scepticism and his strong emphasis upon an objective scientific approach; and third, the subjective, individual approach of Freud with his willingness to pursue counter-intuitive hypotheses, enabled me to see in perspective the works of men who followed them. In particular, their criticisms of one another were enlightening. James was a little too preachy for my taste, but I was fascinated by his approach of specifying concrete things to be done in order to modify habits. Freud's hypotheses were untestable and untested, and Watson's almost complete rejection of mental content seemed too limiting and austere. Watson's accusation that James made rhetorical geese that laid golden eggs has left me with an unremitting suspicion of any pat analysis as being arbitrary, especially if it forms an acronym or has three basic points. Each approach held considerable appeal but left me with a high level of uneasiness.

In the late Forties I met with a seminar led by Arthur Broadbeck at the University of Illinois which tried to cast psychoanalytic hypotheses in empirically testable forms. By 1955 I was very much the behaviorist and was attempting to get group members to talk in eclectic psychotherapy groups by passing them the M&M's. (This, of course, backfired, since the alcoholic patient saw the procedure as "Kid stuff" and negatively reinforced members for speaking and for accepting candy (see Buehler, Patterson and Furniss, 1966). Nevertheless, I was always impressed with the early, isolated instances of behavior treatment. That movement, as I see it now, was considerably thrown off the track by the work of Dollard and Miller (1950) who translated psychoanalysis into learning theory terms. (See Marquis, 1970.)

Thus paradoxes persisted throughout my graduate studies until one day in the spring of 1960, at about the time that I finished my dissertation, Joseph Wolpe gave a colloquium at the University of Michigan. I was more intrigued by what he said than by anything I had ever heard, and spent the evening eagerly questioning him about his new psychotherapy. I was intrigued by the realization that one can use behavioral treatment methods and at the same time see a human being as being able to imagine, and thereby provide himself with his own stimulus material for deconditioning. Furthermore, I immediately appreciated the value of using a person's complex past conditioning and learning history, and then rehearsing behaviors in order to learn new modes of action rather than in order to gain insight into repressed complexes.

I read everything about behavior therapy I could get my hands on and, as I moved to Palo Alto, began trying to apply what I had learned. For some time I had been instructing patients in a behavioral view of life combined with the use of some psychoanalytic techniques and some confrontational techniques which I construed as extinguishing maladaptive behavior patterns by withdrawing from them the reinforcement of success in deceit and manipulation. Intellectually I felt that a very broad learning model was sufficiently complex to account for all human behavior with certain physiological and structural characteristics taken into consideration. However, I had difficulty in construing old diagnostic concepts in behavioral terms. How to account for feelings of inferiority and inadequacy, of depression, withdrawal, schizoid characteristics, and manipulative behavior? No one seemed to have the specific phobias that would lend themselves to desensitization. The severity of this problem is exemplified by my long search for an initial patient who would be suitable for behavioral treatment, and, conversely, the large number of people who fell between the cracks in my new-found theory. I have since found this to be the most serious problem of students learning how to do behavior therapy. A great step forward came when Arnold A. Lazarus came to Stanford for a year and later when he returned to the Behavior Therapy Institute in Sausalito for a year, giving many of us in the San Francisco Bay Area a chance to place behavior therapy in a broader theoretical and practical perspective. With experience, behavioral methods resulted in improvement of patients and other methods dropped out as they were not reinforced. At the same time more and more problems were easily construed in behavioral terms.

Traditional methods of psychotherapy are not only inefficient, they are also hostile. A classical psychoanalyst may go for six months without doing anything but instructing the analysand in the techniques of free association, and interpreting his resistances. Almost everything that the patient says is considered as being wrong. At best it represents some sort of derivative of his unmentionable impulses filtered through ego-mechanisms whose primary function is to deceive the patient and others about him. At worst it is a deliberate attempt to evade and subvert efforts to help him. The analyst is the expert on everything, including how the patient feels. Non-directive therapy is perhaps more respectful and certainly there is much to be learned from Carl Rogers (1951) about respecting our fellow human beings, no matter how troubled they may be. Nevertheless, it is an extremely hostile act to refuse to answer a direct and reasonable request or to withhold information from patients instead of providing the data that they need in the form of expert help in solving life's problems.

Perhaps the benign approach of the behavior therapist is made most clear in Patterson and Reid's (1967) *Reciprocity vs. Coercion.* The essence of their position is that people can control one another's behavior either by coercive demands or threats, or by reciprocal positive reinforcement. Surely a better understanding of these principles would do much to bring peace and love to the world.

Wesley G. Morgan of the University of Tennessee deserves credit for a model which is useful in construing all kinds of behavior change, but the writer takes full responsibility for discussing it in its present form. In my opinion, when the approach of a behavior modifier approximates this model, his methods become more effective and are perceived as being more benign. To the extent that the approach deviates from this model it tends to become more ineffective, or more judgmental and hostile. The model is really very simple and there is nothing really new about it. It divides therapeutic transactions into three parts. First the client and the behavior modifier must come to a clear understanding of the service that is to be performed. Behavior change has a starting point and a goal, and it is important at the outset to come to as clear an understanding of both of these as possible. A careful diagnosis is made of the patient's present state of affairs in relation to the behaviors he wishes to change. Then a careful analysis is made of the terminal behavior desired. This may involve the patient's doing something that he was not able to do formerly. It may involve his learning how to do comfortably something that he currently can do, but with considerable suffering and loss of effectiveness. He may need to learn how to be comfortable without doing something that he currently does and would rather not do.

After a careful diagnosis and analysis of the client's present condition and the desired terminal behavior have been made, the second step is to analyze the paths that can be taken to get from one to the other. Often several courses of action must be taken in order to produce the desired results. Also there are frequently several alternative courses of action which would lead the client from his present state to the terminal behavior. The third step is to construct a program, usually based on small incremental steps leading from the starting point to the goal.

Figure one gives an example of how the model might be applied to a hypothetical case. Treatment planning would also include orchestration of the several programs with proper timing. David Fisher *(Personal Commun.)* reports the results in treating a homosexual of getting an *in vivo* program ahead of a desensitization to women, which resulted in the following midnight phone call: Client, *"Hey Doc, I kissed her."* Dr. Fisher, *"Gee, Charlie that's great!"* Client, *"and then I went out in the alley and heaved."*

Although difficulty in changing behavior can result from the client's providing inaccurate information, a usual problem is a faulty analysis by the therapist, or even more likely, a programmatic mistake which usually consists of making the steps too big. If one has one hundred thousand dollars to develop a programmed text in mathematics, he can do a pretty good job of avoiding this difficulty. In working with an individual client on personal problems, precise programming is almost impossible. Therefore, the important thing is to be patient, constructive, and goal-oriented when the difficulty occurs.

It is easy at such times to become frustrated and blame the client for being unable to accomplish the task which we have set for him. Probably all of us have had a good deal of this kind of behavior modeled for us as children, and I doubt if there exists a human being so saintly that he does not at times feel angry when his attempts to influence the behavior of another person are not going ahead according to schedule. But we should keep in mind that anytime we blame another person for anything that he does, and when we claim that he ought to have done something else, we take leave of the reality of psychological determinism. Realistically we all know, as Andrew Salter (1949) says, that people do not do what they ought to do, they do what they have learned to do. They can do no other. When the client fails to do something that we think he should be able to do, we have made a wrong prediction. There is much to be said for George Kelly's (1955) formulation of hostility which points out that when a person makes a wrong prediction about another's behavior, he often attempts to coerce him into behaving in such a way as to validate

FIGURE 1

Diagnosis	Problem	Treatment	Incremental Step	Terminal Behavior
Homosexuality	Afraid of criticism from women	Desensitization[1]	Increasing stimulus intensity with no anxiety	Comfortable with critical women
	Afraid of control by women	Behavior rehearsal[2]	Increasing assertiveness, less anxiety with assertiveness	Able to handle dominant women
	Not attracted to women	Orgasmic[3] reconditioning	Picturing women earlier in masturbation	Attracted to women
	Ignorant about how to give pleasure to women	Instruction	Increasing information about female sexual responses and elicitation of useful feedback	Confident of being a good lover
	Afraid of "nice girls" who are seen as like mother	Implosion[4]	Decreasing anxiety on picturing sex with mother	Able to be intimate with "nice girls"
	Attracted to men	Covert[5] sensitization	Increasing anxiety to men as sex objects	Not attracted to men
	Unable to relate intimately with women	In-vivo program	Increasing intimacy with women with little anxiety	Good heterosexual relationships

[1] Marquis, Morgan and Piaget (1971)
[2] Lazarus (1966)
[3] Marquis (1970)
[4] Stampfl & Levis (1967)
[5] Anant (1969)

the theory instead of accepting the validational evidence that the other person's behavior presents him with.

I do not mean to imply that all attempts to change behavior need to be done in tiny steps or even that social censure is not effective in changing people's behavior. Mowrer (1950) discusses the problem of reconciling determinism and responsibility very cogently. When a person is punished for being irresponsible, the point is not that he can logically be held responsible for his behavior in a moral sense. Rather it is that, having acted irresponsibly, if he is held responsible, he will hopefully act more responsibly in the future. The question then becomes the empirical one of whether punishment will be effective in changing his behavior.

Of course one of the nice things about a behavioral model is that the hypotheses used as a basis of treatment are tested in every case. Not only are we made aware of the places where we have erred in the microstructure of programming, but we also get feedback that makes it possible to see areas of anxiety which have been neglected and faulty hypotheses which may have been used in setting up treatment. To the extent that behavioral methods are effective in eliminating anxieties we are enabled to see what remains to be eliminated. As the client becomes more and more relaxed and fewer things bother him, the remaining hang-ups stand out dramatically against the background of relaxation and disinhibition.

This process of utilizing feedback to correct the treatment program and to eliminate remaining problem areas is of particular importance in helping the client to the highest possible level of functioning. Most practicing clinicians, in contrast to the academic experimenter, are eager to ferret out and eliminate all unadaptive responses. Experimental psychologists are usually interested in demonstrating a reliable result from a treatment method. The results of seeking a statistically significant difference on one variable are quite different from those obtained when seeking an optimal level of functioning for the human being who happens to be one's client.

I have had the experience a number of times of referring patients to colleagues whom I know to be skilled in behavioral methods only to have them treated by somewhat less effective methods based on somewhat less parsimonious theories, primarily therapeutic approaches around the periphery of behavior therapy such as Gestalt therapy or other existential approaches, neo-Reichian techniques, or family therapy based on communications theory. Although there are certainly times when these therapies are useful, patients usually learn to be aware of their feelings and to communicate more clearly with very little time and trouble when their basic anxieties and behavioral deficits are removed. Relaxation training, hierarchy construction, desensitization, and, in particular, shock aversion and anxiety relief conditioning can be meticulous, exacting tasks which can become very dull and boring. Nevertheless, I feel that it is the responsibility of the therapist to use the most effective techniques in dealing with patients, rather than the most enjoyable. It is natural enough when faced with immediately non-reinforcing consequences to drop down the habit family hierarchy to the next most salient response, but I think we should try to avoid it when it is not in the patient's best interest. When I first started doing behavior therapy, I would drop back to an analytic approach to the problem and search for some secret key to the patient's behavior. Such efforts almost universally met with failure.

This points to an interesting phenomenon which tends toward conservatism. Some clients are eager, able, and ripe for improvement. Others have difficulties which are rigidly ingrained and are highly resistant to change. Therapists try their favorite techniques first and reserve innovations for those clients where the favorite techniques have failed. These are usually the people who are less likely to respond well to any technique. Thus the usual techniques are tested under much more favorable conditions.

What kind of relationship develops from a learning model of human behavior? If, indeed, the client's behavior is the result of the experiences he has had, it is irrational to blame him for being what he is. If the therapist had had the same experiences as the client and vice versa, each would be sitting on the other side of the desk. Therefore, there is no justification whatsoever for the therapist to look down his nose at the client. The relationship is as direct and straightforward as that of the therapist consulting his attorney about a legal matter, or his accountant about his income tax. The expert is supplied with data, and a request for help with a specific problem, although the expert may also be called upon to formulate the problem more precisely. Perhaps a better example would be the more personal and complex relationship of the architect using his technical skills to design and build for the client a house which matches his needs and his lifestyle.

Armed with effective means of building self-reliance and independence in the client, the therapist need not worry about the client becoming dependent upon him for answers, or even for sympathy. The resulting relationship is one in which I have felt quite comfortable having good friends as clients and good clients as friends. If the therapist can succeed in teaching the client to construe the world of his own behavior and that of other people in terms of learning and psychological determinism, a number of benefits can accrue. Most of our clients—indeed most of us—have been reared by moralistic Christians and Jews. Even those of us whose parents have not been too moralistic and judgmental have grown up in a society whose institutions march to the beat of a moralistic drum. Until recently, teachers meted out rewards and punishments on the basis of the child's guilt or virtue, rather than in a specific attempt to increase or decrease the frequencies of certain behaviors. Most still do. Crime and punishment, guilt, innocence, and the categorical imperative run through the warp and woof of all our mass media. Even the basic ritual of the institution of divorce is an adversarial process in which one of the unfortunate parties must be blamed, found guilty, and treated punitively in terms of the settlement of the practical problems involved in dissolving the marriage.

Many patients find it a great relief to lay down the burden of obsessively adjudicating every action which they or those about them perform in terms of guilt or innocence. For many it is a real revelation to realize that it is not necessary to find someone to convict and hang every time things go wrong.

Therapists from other schools often see behavior therapy as a useful way of dealing with very specific symptomatic problems, but find it hard to understand how it can be used to deal with problems of existential despair, alienation, feelings of inferiority and inadequacy, etc. I feel that such highly generalized problems are usually the result of an inadequate diagnosis of the specific areas of anxiety and lack of skill. Usually a few minutes of careful questioning of a person who claims no specific areas of anxiety, but generalized depression or philosophical ennui, will suffice to reveal a number of very discrete and specific problems, often of considerable severity. Certainly a careful analysis of a fear survey schedule will provide reason enough for the feelings of generalized despair or inadequacy. A careful behavior analysis often reveals dozens of specific subjective fears. Indeed, such a person can often be found to have an area in his body which is in a chronic state of such intense tension as to cause excruciating pain. Conversely when those persons who are seeking philosophical solutions to difficulties construed in over-generalized terms have found basic solutions to their specific problems such as fear of .criticism, rejection, disapproval; fear of being the center of attention; inability to reinforce others, or to accept affection or kindness without anxiety; and when they have become relaxed and effective in dealing with other people through shedding the burdens of anxiety and acquiring necessary interpersonal skills, then one can look in vain for the existential problems which brought them to the consulting room.

I do not mean by this to deny the reality of existential problems. All of us live in a world where there is gross injustice and where innocent people suffer, starve and die. Indeed, if you believe in determinism, only innocent people can suffer. We all must grow old and someday die. Alone among the species of the earth our breed of ape knows it. And each man in his own way must deal with these unpleasant facts. It is a bearable burden for people who are relatively free from morbid anxieties and have the skills necessary to cope with the daily problems of life with relative equanimity. It is probably also of considerable help to see the world in terms as realistic as possible in order to avoid the confrontations with false attitudes and discrepant data which plague the lives of people whose views of the world involve too much self-deception and romanticism. It is also of help to be involved in working to solve the problems of the world and increase the quality of human life. I am not prevented by any scientific snobbishness from discussing these problems with my clients on a philosophical level.

There are some situations which the incremental programming model as previously described does not seem to handle very well. One example is those situations in which the client or clients come to an agreement with the therapist and promise to do certain things or refrain from doing certain things, usually until the following interview. For example, a set of parents may agree with each other and with the therapist to ignore some noxious behavior on the part of the child. In other situations a contract is negotiated in which a husband and wife agree that each will behave in certain ways or refrain from doing certain things in return for reciprocal concessions on the part of the other spouse. Also a client may resolve and promise not to engage in some behavior which has been very gratifying for him. For example, a transvestite may promise not to dress up or an alcoholic will resolve not to drink during the week. Such agreements are sometimes effective in changing behavior for the short run or even permanently, which gives the appearance of a discontinuous behavior change involving no incremental steps.

In such cases, advantage is taken of the fact that many clients are made quite anxious by the prospect of violating a promise because of their past conditionings. By tying the promise to specific behaviors, one changes the reinforcing consequences of alternative behaviors. Such agreements are effective only when the client has more anxiety about breaking his promise than he has about following the course of action to which he has committed himself. Meanwhile, two forces are operating in the direction of a permanent change in the client's habits. First of all, if the course of action is a realistic one, the natural reinforcers in the environment will take over and permanently support the new behavior. (The parents are rewarded by a decrease in frequency in the child's whining; the alcoholic is rewarded with a clear head which does not ache in return for refraining from drinking. The assertiveness which the client shows in acting on his promise to ask for a raise is often rewarded with a raise.) The increase in strength of the new response is thus incremental, if not programmed specifically by the therapist. The other process can be variously construed in terms of extinction or implosion. Initially, following the agreed upon pattern of behavior, the client's anxiety level may rise, but as the feared consequences do not occur—again if the therapist has been realistic in his assignment—the anxiety response diminishes incrementally, and relatively permanent, stable change is achieved.

Another situation takes a metaposition to any therapeutic model. It is difficult to help a client who is not being honest with the therapist. The most common examples include the client's motive for therapy consisting of the desire for a pleasant hour of conversation and understanding. The therapist is trying to bring about more permanent change. The client may be interested in making a good impression on the therapist and therefore may simulate improvement rather than achieve real improvement. The danger of this is lessened by the therapist convincing the client that he is not being judged or condemned. The situation is less likely to develop when the therapist has independent information as to the client's behavior between sessions, as in a hospital setting, or when the spouse is included in therapy sessions.

CASE HISTORIES

The first two following cases have been chosen to illustrate the strategy and tactics of broad-spectrum behavior therapy (Lazarus, 1966 A) applying the model proposed above. It is often the custom to report dramatic and exceptional cases. Instead of selecting unusual cases, I have chosen two who represent the most common types of problems dealt with in a usual suburban private practice. Thereafter two other cases will be described broadly and one aspect will be discussed in detail. Some identifying data have been changed in each case in order to protect the identity of the clients.

CASE #1. Jane was an attractive 22-year-old graduate student whose chief complaint was frequent tension headaches and severe neck pain due to muscular tension. She had been treated with tranquilizers and physical therapy with slight relief. Her father was a retired Air Force sergeant and she had lived in many places around the United States and in Europe, largely growing up on air bases. She had difficulty in asserting herself and in expressing either displeasure or positive feelings. This led to a number of difficulties.

Jane had recently effected a reconciliation with her parents after an open break of some two years' duration occasioned by telling her mother about an affair she had had. Her mother was quite upset about this and Jane had become too upset to go to school and had dropped out for a semester. At that time her headaches started. She disagreed with her parents on a number of things and had been unable to come to terms with them.

She had felt comfortable with her original boy friend and only one of the six men she had gone with since then. In the year previous to beginning treatment, she had been living with a boy friend. A friend of his moved in for the summer in order to share the rent. She went to bed with the roommate (said she didn't know why), and her boy friend was furious with her. At his insistence she told off the roommate, although she was not really angry with him. After that, she and the boy friend went on a back-packing trip which turned out to be a terrible ordeal for her because of the cold and the dust. They argued and he broke up with her, but they completed the month living together because the rent was paid on the apartment. She cried most of the time.

Careful questioning revealed that Jane was extremely submissive, although capable of bitter arguments involving considerable self recrimination. She had great difficulty in saying no, whether to a boy's sexual advances or her mother's request for information. She was quite sensitive to criticism and rejection, anxious about being the center of attention, and worried about papers and examinations.

Because Jane was bright and well motivated, because she had considerable sophistication and social skills, because her anxieties were moderate, and because she had limited financial resources, it was decided to use *in vivo* relaxation and behavior rehearsal as the primary therapeutic tools rather than desensitization treatment. Plans are outlined in Figure 2.

After the second diagnostic session she was given a tape of relaxation instructions. The procedure was adapted from that used by Wolpe and Lazarus (1966, pp. 177-180), but with special emphasis on relaxing the eyes and the vocal apparatus. At the third session she reported that she had listened to the tape twice. It had not gone very well the first time, but by the end of the second time she had been completely relaxed. She was in a psychodrama group at school. One of the other members of the group was a boy who had told the group of some of his sexual exploits. She was afraid to go out with him for fear of being seduced when she did not want to. He had asked her out and she was very proud of refusing him. Meanwhile, she was going with another boy a year younger than she who had had no sexual experience. She was very fond of him and wanted to have intercourse with him, but he said that he did not believe in sex before marriage.

She was told that both of these situations presented her with an opportunity to learn that she did not have to be a passive victim of circumstances. She was given the homework assignment of calling the boy from her group, going out with him, and not allowing herself to be seduced. We then rehearsed several ways of saying no and she was given the information that he would not likely be insulted by her refusal. In the second case she was told that she should see the situation as one in which her boy friend had anxieties about sex which she could desensitize by engaging in sexual behavior that he felt comfortable with for longer periods of time and moving very gradually toward the goal of intercourse. It was predicted that after intercourse his rationalizations would disappear and he would be proud of having made it.

Jane came into the fourth session very happy and excited. She had called the boy in her group, gone out with him, had no trouble in not being seduced, and had decided she was not interested in him anyway. He had called her several times since, in spite of her refusing to go out with him again. She succeeded rather easily in seducing the boy she liked. His response was to tell her that he had been considering it seriously for the past couple of weeks and had decided that his ideas on the sub-

FIGURE 2—JANE

Diagnosis	Problem	Treatment	Incremental Step	Terminal Behavior	
Psychophysio-logical reaction	Tension (Headaches and stiff trapezius muscles)	Relaxation	More deeply relaxed. Relax in wider range of stimulus conditions	Relaxed in most circumstances. No headaches or stiff shoulders.	2.
	Can't assert self with others. Difficulty speaking in class. Difficulty expressing feelings. Sensitive to criticism and center of attention	Behavior rehearsal followed with home-work assignments	Assertive in wider range of circumstances, more comfortable being asser-tive, more able to express feelings	Able to avoid being dominated. Able to speak in groups. Able to express positive feelings.	2.
	Infrequent orgasms	Instruction. Homework assign-ments	More knowledge of female sexual response. Reinforcement for applying knowledge	Usual orgasms	1.
	Worry	Relaxing vocal apparatus. Discussion	More able to control. See worry as unnecessary	Infrequent worry. Constructive planning	2.
				1. Apparently cured 2. Much improved	

ject were in error. The episode had led to a great improvement in their relationship and she now felt comfortable in being silly with him.

She had listened to the tape twice and realized that she was not succeeding in relaxing her eyes. Her headaches were unchanged. She was asked to bring in a list of her various daily activities arranged in hierarchical order according to how tense they made her. In addition, she was offered a reduction in fee if she spent a half hour relaxing on six of the seven days before her next appointment.

The following week she reported having relaxed six times as specified and also at a folk music concert on Saturday night. Things were going well with her younger boy friend and she had broken relations with a former boy friend whom she had been seeing once a week. We rehearsed class speeches on dress codes and women's rights.

A program of *in vivo* relaxation was set up which consisted of three parts. My notes do not reflect the first part in detail, but the general procedure is as follows. The inital skill in the program consists of being able to relax completely with the help of relaxation instructions from the therapist, either in person or by means of a recording. The depth of relaxation is tested carefully by observing the client visually and by manipulating the extremities.[1] The arms are checked by putting one hand around the wrist and grasping the elbow with the other. The arm is then shaken and rotated and will move with complete ease if the muscles of the arm and shoulder girdle are completely relaxed. Similarly the leg is supported with one hand at the knee and one just above the ankle. Again, if the foot flops, the knee swings easily and the hip joint rotates freely, we know that the pelvic girdle and leg are completely relaxed. The head is rotated to determine if the neck muscles are relaxed. In this procedure it is advisable to introduce rapid and unexpected changes of direction to make sure that the client is not moving in response to pressure, a response which is often learned in helping the dentist or barber.

Relaxation is practiced initially in conditions of reduced stimulation, on an easy chair or bed, and in a quiet place with little chance of interruption. These conditions are kept constant while the client first practices relaxing without verbal instructions, usually before going to sleep at night. This practice is begun only after several successful attempts to relax deeply with instructions and is usually continued for a week before

---

[1] Psychologists and social workers are often reluctant to touch a client, but even most clients with phobias about being touched accept the procedure easily.

moving on to the following program, although athletes and dancers can often move very rapidly because of their familiarity with muscular control.

The client is encouraged at all times to program his relaxation by kinesthetic cues rather than by using a verbal or visual program. This makes possible deep relaxation of the eyes and vocal apparatus and also makes it possible to use these structures for some other activity while relaxing. Kinesthetic cues also allow for more efficient increase in the speed of relaxing and facilitate development of an automatic and unconscious motor skill. Witness the dancer who is forever tied to the verbal program learned in dancing class and therefore cannot converse with his partner because his head is full of "one-two-three."

When the client can relax without verbal instructions with some efficiency, he is asked to time how long it takes to get from an average level of tension to a state of moderately deep relaxation. This is recorded and he then performs some everyday activity for a few minutes and then returns to relax again. The time is recorded and the process is continued until he can relax in a few seconds.

The rest of the first phase consists of moving from the conditions of low stimulation to more usual situations. First the task is to stay relaxed during the new situation, usually in the consulting room, and he is given homework of relaxing in the new situation. Whenever difficulty is encountered, the process is broken into smaller steps.

The client is relaxed deeply and asked to open his eyes while trying to stay relaxed. If difficulty is experienced it may be necessary to start by opening the eyes for a few seconds and gradually increasing the amount of time. Others cannot stay relaxed with their eyes shut and the process is reversed. The client is asked to sit up and stay relaxed. At this point differential relaxation is introduced since some tension is needed to hold oneself loosely erect. Then he stands, leaning over with head and arms hanging and gradually rises to an erect position, using only the minimum amount of tension necessary to maintain his posture. Then he flops around the office, imitating a drunk, and subsequently adds enough tension to walk without flopping, but with no unnecessary tension.

At this point he may practice some simple task, such as passing a pencil from one hand to another. Most people have trouble staying relaxed while working fast and the next step involves starting with some simple task, such as sanding or polishing something, or doing writing exercises such as making cursive ovals or push-pulls. This is done very slowly at first and the speed is gradually increased until the movement is at maximum speed. Most of my clients end up with a shiny automobile at this point.

At this stage the basic components of most activities have been practiced while staying relaxed. The second part of the program consists of working on staying relaxed during increasingly difficult, naturally occurring activities. Here the procedure followed is the one developed by Haugen, Dixon and Dickel (1958). Basically it consists of setting up one's entire life as an anxiety hierarchy and desensitizing the hierarchy by staying relaxed during the easiest activities or times and gradually adding more difficult ones.

The third phase consists of finding recurrent stimuli to nag the client to check his muscles. This control is particularly effective if the stimulus occurs as the client begins to tighten up. The list is endless, but things I have found most useful are reaching for a cigarette, looking at one's watch, recognizing a worried thought, biting one's fingernails, or any nervous habit, the telephone ringing, the dog barking, and commercials on radio or television. I often send a client out with a parking meter timer set to go off every fifteen minutes. When he begins to find himself relaxed when the alarm sounds, he increases the interval.

Let us return to the sessions with Jane. We discussed her hierarchy of activities and decided that she would attempt to stay relaxed while showering, reading and listening to the radio. We also rehearsed sending back an order of food in a restaurant.

In the next interview, Jane reported that she was relaxing much better and proved it by relaxing in the office in thirty seconds. Her boy friend had challenged her ideas about "The Feminine Mystique," and she had given in too easily. She had made progress in interrupting herself when she started to worry, and managed to relax her vocal apparatus. We reheased a couple of scenes from the previous list. For homework she was to ask questions she would like to ask in class while observing herself in the mirror in order to eliminate a phony smile which she displayed when self conscious. She was instructed in the physiology of sexual responses and agreed to tell her boy friend precisely what she found most stimulating and to continue foreplay into the high plateau phase (Masters and Johnson, 1966), in order to insure her orgasmic response. Staying relaxed during meals was added to the existing list of activities.

In the ninth interview she reported that she had not been relaxing as she should and her headaches were still not improved. She had seen herself making funny faces in the mirror but had finally been able to relax her mouth and yet be comfortable while talking aloud. She had some concerns about what kind of job to look for and this was discussed. She was quite concerned about meeting her boy friend's mother whose social status was considerably higher than that of her own parents. She was encouraged to consider her own status in the future as the holder of an advanced degree and as an attractive and articulate person. Talking to other people and walking were added to the list of times she was to stay relaxed and she was once again offered an incentive for remaining relaxed at least one-half hour a day and asking a question in one class. She was to keep a schedule of her activities and record how relaxed she had been. She reported difficulty in concentrating on her studies and was assigned a program described by Ljndberg Fox (1966). She was to break her work into pieces that should take approximately five minutes to complete. She was then to study until she began to feel restless and then do one more piece. The n-1 pieces would be done quickly and easily because she was within the limits of her concentration and the nth piece because she would follow it with some pleasant activity. She was to put the onset of study under the control of some appropriate stimulus by beginning immediately upon entering her apartment or putting her dishes in the sink in order to avoid procrastination.

In her tenth and last interview she reported that the study technique was working and she was now studying effectively for thirty minutes with a five minute break. Stimulus control for initiation of studying was working well. She was remembering to relax better and more frequently. Her headaches were somewhat improved and she was becoming quite effective in relaxing her neck. She had been comfortable with her boy friend's mother. During sexual intercourse, orgasms were usual and often multiple. She was speaking freely in class.

At this point it was decided to terminate therapy in spite of her continuing headaches and arrangements were made for Jane to send me a schedule indicating how much of the time she was relaxed for the following eight weeks. She reported increasing success and by the end of the time reported that she had headaches rarely and only when she forgot to relax. She was on vacation from school and was working as a receptionist, which required considerable social contact. A year later she sent me a check for her treatment. She reported that she had continued to improve and that the same boy friend she had seduced was paying all of her bills as a wedding present.

One day after writing up this case and a year and a half after terminating therapy, a letter from Jane arrived. In the last few months she had been increasingly tense and her headaches were again increasing in frequency. Therefore she requested referral to a behavior therapist near her new home.*

CASE #2. Bob, a 32-year-old unemployed truck driver was seen for thirty hours over a period of two years. He had eight children ranging from four to seventeen but had had a vasectomy four years before starting treatment. He was of stocky build and was warm, direct and confident in his social relations. Three years previously he had been well established, owning a tavern and two trucks in a town in northern California. He had found the temptations of a tavern-keeper's life too great and had gotten into a pattern of drinking too much, gambling and chasing women. He sold his tavern and trucks, moved to a town on the coast south of San Francisco and took a job as a long-line truck driver.

He traced his anxieties to his father's death at age twenty-nine of a coronary occlusion. At the time Bob, who was seven years old, became afraid of death. When Bob was nine years old, while on a picnic he was playing with the other children and fell on his head. He heard his neck pop and thought that he had broken his neck and was dying. He experienced an extreme panic and was taken to the doctor who reassured him that he was only suffering from a sprain. Since that time he had been afraid of dying and saw anxiety attacks as threatening imminent death. He had been somewhat afraid of being trapped away from help but his anxiety attacks had been infrequent until one day about a year before treatment, when he had been crawling up a hill in his semi-trailer truck and it occurred to him that he could have an attack and die before he could get to town to seek medical attention. He took one more trip in his truck in a constant state of severe anxiety.

He had then retreated to his house, spent the last of his savings and had gone on welfare. He could venture out on short trips with his wife, a practical nurse, but was severely agoraphobic and claustrophobic. It was only because of his great faith in the psychiatrist who referred him that he was able to make the fifty-mile trip over the mountains to see

* *Editor's note*: In my experience, relapses of this kind usually respond well to a second course of behavior therapy. During "booster therapy," hitherto unsuspected factors responsible for the deviant behavior emerge and lend themselves to direct treatment.

me. He worried constantly about how to get to the nearest doctor and about his car breaking down. He was afraid of any physical exertion leading to rapid breathing which he saw as a symptom of a heart attack. He was afraid of having anyone know about his neurosis but was otherwise confident socially.

His anxieties were often greater in anticipation than in actuality. If he had only one car in running condition (he liked to have two or three), he would change one spark plug at a time. However he sometimes changed a tire on the highway with less anxiety than he experienced in contemplating the possibility of such an event. He usually dreaded his trip over the mountains to see me early in treatment but often experienced little anxiety on the road.

At the end of the first interview the client was given a brief talk about the nature of behavior therapy and was encouraged to think of his problems as solvable in a reasonable amount of time. At the second interview Bob reported that he had felt elated at the prospect of solving his problems and had enjoyed the ride home and felt better all week. A tentative plan of treatment was set forth which included most of the features of the final plan described in Figure 3. Relaxation training was begun and anxieties about death were explored in preparation for the construction of a hierarchy. Interestingly, Bob was not afraid of accidents or injuries in the least. He was bothered by doctors, hospitals, funerals, sickness, sirens, obituaries and high blood pressure.

Because of vacations, inclement weather, occasional anxiety too severe to make the trip and crises of various kinds with the eight children, the first thirteen hours spanned a period of six months. Bob learned to relax well and began to use it erratically *in vivo*. Hierarchies of his two major anxiety areas were constructed and desensitization commenced. When feasible Bob was to follow desensitization of an item by going through it *in vivo* before the following session. He did so about half the time. At the sixth session he reported that he was eating with the family for the first time in five years, much to their delight. He was relaxing each night and sleeping better. By the eighth hour he was able to remove three spark plugs at a time from his car and take a son to the hospital without anxiety.

At one point Bob was worried about his mother being killed while driving back to Oregon after a visit. I showed him how to estimate the probability roughly. We guessed one fatal accident in a thousand years of driving, one chance in three that it would be his mother who was

FIGURE 3

Diagnosis	Problem	Treatment	Incremental Step	Terminal Behavior	
Agoraphobia	Fear of being trapped away from help	Desensitization in vivo program	Increasing distance from home or car with little or no anxiety	Able to travel freely or repair car without anxiety.	2.
	Fear of death (shortness of breath, doctors, hospitals, funerals, illness, sirens, obituaries)	Desensitization	Increasing stimulus intensity with no anxiety.	Able to tolerate stimuli listed under 1 without anxiety.	1.
		Hyperventilation training	Increasing realization that dizziness does not portend death, ability to control dizziness.	Able to catch himself starting to hyperventilate. Anxiety therefore less regenerative.	1.
	General anxiety	Relaxation in vivo	Stay relaxed in increasingly difficult situations	Relaxed most of the time.	2.
		Stop smoking	Decreasing anxiety without smoking	Stopped	
		Exercise program	Increasing ability to tolerate vigorous exercise	Perception of decreased probability of coronary.	1.
		Weight reduction diet	Decreasing weight	Slim and keep weight off	
	Mediocre relationship with wife, wife anorgasmic, client chasing women. Premature ejaculation	In vivo desensitization of wife's sexual anxieties. Facilitation of communication, Seman's method.[1]	Wife's increasing sexual arousal without anxiety. Increasing awareness of wife's needs, increasing freedom of communication. Increased time to ejaculation	Wife orgasmic, client faithful, greatly improved relationship, client reasonable time to ejaculate.	1.
	Fear of having an anxiety attack	Anxiety relief conditioning[2]	Increased anxiety relief conditioned to word calm	Able to reduce anxiety by saying "calm."	2.
		Pocket shocker	Less likely to obsess about possibility of an attack	Less worried	

[1] Semans, 1960
[2] Wolpe and Lazarus, 1966

1. Apparently cured
2. Much improved

killed, one chance in 365 that an accident this year would fall on a particular day. 1,000 $\times$ 365 $\times$ 3 is one chance in more than 1,000,000. He was thereafter able to assess probabilities of feared events more accurately and found it comforting.

After a month's hiatus between the eighth and ninth hours, Bob reported that he had not been going much of any place, but that he was relaxing well at home. He had seen a surfer wiped out and was right there with the rest of the nosy people. He had ridden in a friend's car to the next city down the coast, which was an accomplishment since it was a situation in which he was not in control. In the tenth session he was given a pocket shocker with instructions to shock himself when he started to obsess about getting stranded. The correlation of smoking, obesity and lack of exercise with coronary disease was discussed and Bob agreed to start a diet which ultimately took him from 214 pounds down to 185.

The following week he reported that he had only had to use the shocker twice, but had found it a great comfort. He keeps the battery fresh and carries it in his glove compartment to this day, although he never uses it now. He forgot it while riding down the coast to the next city with a friend, but comforted himself with the thought that he could pretend to hear a miss in his friend's car, get under the hood, ostensibly to check the spark plugs, and shock himself with the plug wires. In this hour (number 11) the death hierarchy was completed and he pictured walking 490 yards away from his car down the beach (item 5.5 on the Loss of Mobility hierarchy, a parametric item, Marquis, Morgan and Piaget, 1971).

In the twelfth session Bob reported that he had suffered three flat tires and run out of gas, with considerable anxiety (up to 60 suds) but no panic. He was feeling better about riding in other people's cars and had been as far as forty miles. At this point an *in vivo* relaxation program beyond relaxing in his bed or easy chair was begun. He was given homework of relaxing with eyes open, relaxing in the shower, and walking down the beach.

In the thirteenth hour he reported walking a block and a half from his car and feeling comfortable in heavy traffic. He reported that things were not going well sexually and agreed to have his wife join us during the next session to discuss it.

This was not done because shortly after the thirteenth hour Bob slipped on his wet front porch and fell through the window, cutting his arm to the bone. He remained calm through emergency surgery but panicked when settled in his room at the hospital. He got his wife to bring him his clothes and some money and had her park his car outside the window where he could see it, giving him the keys. Then he was able to relax somewhat for his three weeks stay in the hospital.

LOSS OF MOBILITY

1. You and your wife have won a trip to Tahiti and you are on deck looking off the fantail while the coast disappears.
2. You are one-half way up El Capitan pounding in a peton and rigging a rope to it.
3. On a flight to Hawaii the pilot says, "Ladies and Gentlemen, we have now reached the point of no return."
3.5 Landing at airport, Honolulu.
4. You are pulling out of Salinas on a train non-stop to Los Angeles.
5. You are on a bus going up Highway 1 to San Francisco.
5.5 Gradually walk one mile from car.
6. You are driving a Porsche across the Bay Bridge.
7. Take a bus from your house down to the beach.
8. Drive down by the beach, pick up density of traffic by degrees.
9. You are riding downtown with Bill for coffee.
10. Drive from summit to here.
11. You are in the car, ready to go to the store and the car doesn't start.
12. Your wife takes the car down to the store.
13. You come out to find a flat on your car in the driveway. Change it.
14. You're putting in a new spark plug.

Pleasant scene: Relax in a boat fishing on the reservoir.

FEAR OF DEATH

1. You are seven years old looking at father lying in the coffin.
2. You are nine years old, at a picnic, and fall on your head. Your neck pops and feels kind of stretched and you wonder whether it is broken.
2.5 The doctor says your blood pressure is dangerously high and that you need to lose weight.
3. You are at Bill Clausens' funeral, A) thinking about how they were killed, B) looking into the coffin.

4. You visit your wife at Star Lodge and she says, "just a minute, honey, this woman just died and I have to wait until the coroner comes."
5. You are driving down the street and come upon an accident. A woman has broken her arm, a compound fracture, and you put on a tourniquet.
6. The doctor says your wife has a strep throat and a temperature of 104°.
7. You're having a beer with Stan and he's explaining how they embalm a body.
8. You are at the hospital to visit someone with a broken leg and look in and see a man, pale, tube down his nose, tube in his arm, bottles, etc.
9. You hear on the radio that Lloyd Gandy has been shot.
10. The doctor says, "Bill, this is a little skin cancer. I'm going to send you to a dermatologist—99 times out of 100 no more trouble."
11. You are at home reading funnies and a siren sounds outside.
12. You read an obit in the paper that Bill Finley of Finley's store died at 45 of an apparent heart attack.
13. You read in the paper that Grandma Moses died at 102.

A week after being discharged from the hospital, Bob reported that he had gone four hundred yards from his car in a wrecking yard, panicked for a moment, and then relaxed. Otherwise he was close to normal and much more relaxed around town. His wife joined us and I outlined a sexual program of doing only what she could do comfortably with her directing him at every step. Foreplay was to continue until she felt that she was just short of having an orgasm before starting intercourse.

The following week they reported having intercourse three times during which she experienced prolonged orgasms. Bob reported doing better at relaxing in the car and increased his mobility. He was given twenty-five trials of anxiety relief conditioning (Wolpe and Lazarus, 1966) and then deeply relaxed and instructed to say the talisman word, "calm control," each time he exhaled for ten minutes, a technique for which Gordon Paul deserves credit.

The following (eighteenth) session, Bob reported feeling great. The "calm control" was working well, he had filed for bankruptcy, and was off to a good start with an automotive specialty business. In the nineteenth session we set up an exercise program which he followed for a while and then dropped, but his work required considerable exercise and kept him in fairly good condition. We bypassed item 5.5 on the loss of mobility hierarchy and proceeded without completing it. The last I heard Bob had still not made it a mile from his car. On the sixteenth session things were still slowly improving.

Bob did not come in for two months. At that time we finished the Loss of Mobility hierarchy and pictured taking a trip to Oregon where Bob's aunt was dying of cancer. The following week he returned on the eve of his trip to Oregon, the aunt having died. He was anxious at the prospect and his wife and I reassured him and we discussed ways of handling his anxiety.

In the next session (twenty-four) we discussed his trip to Oregon. He had been scared when he left—a little shaky, concerned and worried—but relaxed as the trip progressed and did not panic once. He took one town at a time by reassuring himself that there was a doctor in each one. He handled three flat tires with minimal anxiety. At the funeral he was sad but not anxious. He drank only one beer on the trip and enjoyed the drive and the scenery. He had since gone six blocks from his car with slight discomfort.

In the twenty-ninth session Bob reported that he had been in a very good mood. "Nothing bothers me." His wife sat in and they said that their sexual problem had returned. More careful questioning revealed that he suffered from premature ejaculation. They were instructed in the Semans method (see Masters and Johnson, 1970, although it had not been published at the time). In addition they were to practice scratching each others backs. He was to reward her for any expression of bodily sensations in order to facilitate feedback. He was to concentrate on his sensations when thoughts of inadequacy arose. If either masturbated they were to picture having intercourse with each other (both had been picturing other people). Then they were to re-introduce the program of *in vivo* desensitization (see Wolpe and Lazarus, 1966).

Four months later I visited them at home. Bob's business was thriving and he was working very hard. He and his wife had completely solved their sexual problem and were communicating freely with each other and were enjoying each other as never before. The weather had been bad and he had been too busy to go anywhere. Although his fear of death was completely gone, his fear of being stranded away from help had returned—not so much within fifty miles of home, but at the prospect of a trip. He had taken on the responsibility of a business trip down the coast and was quite upset at the prospect.

Bob came over two months later. His trip had gone badly and he was almost back where we started as far as his fear of loss of mobility was concerned. We started desensitization over at the beginning of the hierarchy and he was once more encouraged to exercise and to relax. He also reported that he had quit smoking after nineteen years. He had been smoking three packs a day. He has not smoked since.

He returned for two more sessions the following month. He had been exercising and his wind was better. He was feeling more comfortable with not smoking and by the second interview was able to drink without a strong desire to smoke.

In the second interview he said that he was still afraid of going crazy and I started out to contrast his classically neurotic problems with some psychotic symptoms in order to reassure him. In the process I mentioned the delusion that people were going to poison him and he had a panic attack because when he was a boy his mother had been so mean and irritable that he had developed a fear that she would put poison in his food. This was my first opportunity to see one of his anxiety attacks and I expressed surprise at how mild his anxiety seemed to me. I told him that I knew a famous behavior therapist who went around more anxious than that all the time. I had him tip the recliner back and in fifteen minutes he was deeply relaxed and cheerful again.

I saw him again a month later and we progressed to item 5 on the loss of mobility hierarchy. His business was prospering and he was once more able to move about comfortably within fifty miles of home as long as he didn't get too far from his car. Several months later he did some work on my car and at that time his gains had persisted. He was enjoying life and his wife reported that he was a pleasure to live with. He still was reluctant to travel to San Francisco.

CASE #3. Rutherford. This case is chosen to illustrate what can happen to an intellectualizer who learns to relax and stop obsessing. Many people have the conviction that if they can only find the right philosophy of life it will hold the key to all of their problems. It is certainly possible for people to be inspired by a philosophy to fulfilling patterns of behavior or led by a philosophy into self defeating patterns, especially if the philosophy is taught by a powerful model. Nevertheless, most human problems result from the individual having learned to feel anxious in harmless circumstances or from not having learned the necessary skills to deal with the situations in which he finds himself.

Skills Rutherford had in ample supply. He was a twenty-five-year-old space scientist who had risen from a deprived childhood to excel in almost everything. He was keenly intelligent, handsome, and very well coordinated. Having fought his way up from the bottom, at first by his fists and later by his intelligence, he was fiercely competitive and preferred being hated to being ignored. He was afraid of being second in anything and of being laughed at, but his response to either threat was aggressive.

He came to me in a state of frenzied anxiety occasioned by the impending breakup of a very mediocre marriage. He was seriously contemplating suicide. Probably the greatest threat occasioned by the breakup of his marriage was that it meant losing to a professor of his wife's with whom she was probably having an affair eight hundred miles away. He had read countless books in the areas of philosophy and psychology and was glib but frantic in his pursuit of new ways of construing his life. In spite of his unusually good intellectual grasp of the content of these theories all it amounted to was constant worry.

The first hour was taken up by giving an account of his life and his present predicament which was surprisingly lucid considering his extremely high level of anxiety. He was extremely cynical and saw everything as being absurd. During the second hour he volunteered the information that he had noticed that he had been "squeezing his toes up." I took this as the occasion to ask him to consider a new view of himself and a possible road to salvation.

I suggested to him that he was not likely to find philosophical solutions to his problems since the source of his discomfort was physiological, i.e., the fact that he kept his muscles tight all the time. "Worry is an activity that consists of saying anxious things to yourself and tightening up your muscles." Although he saw this activity as an attempt to solve his problems, in fact it *was* his problem. Many people go through life worrying about improbable eventualities and are reinforced by the belief that the worry has prevented their occurrences. They feel that they would be unable to survive if they stopped worrying.

This is simply not true. Man alone among the species on the earth is capable of worry. The elephant lives for a hundred and twenty years, rears his young through a long helpless period in a land full of lions, and provides himself daily with huge quantities of food and water—all without worrying.

Perhaps some external stimulus starts the process. Either it is conditioned to elicit tension or reminds the person of something that does. Being in a state of tension the person reaches into his hippocampus for a tape that is appropriate to that level of tension. Soon an idea comes that arouses a higher level of tension and the process escalates.

As Jacobson (1938) long ago pointed out, there is a simple way to break this vicious circle. The tape of worried thoughts is played by the vocal apparatus. If these muscles are relaxed, the tape stops. So all that needs to be done is to watch for the first sign of a worry. The process is usually quite distinct from constructive planning or creative thought, and is usually inimical to such thinking, so nothing is lost by interrupting the worry without even finishing the phrase. The only value of worry is to indicate that you have some tight muscles somewhere. Then you relax your vocal apparatus and proceed to check the rest of your muscles and relax any you find to be tense.

Rutherford eagerly took up the idea. Here was a new philosophy and a new obsession. He listened to the relaxation tape I gave him two and a half times before his next session four days later and found that "When everything is relaxed, everything is OK." He had been working on staying relaxed on his own initiative. The next few weeks were very stormy with the marriage off-again-on-again, the wife coming and going, threatening suicide, Rutherford being unable to reach her by phone for days at a time. At such times he was unable to relax but between crises he made it his full time occupation to relax and between discussing crises we worked in the hour on perfecting his skills at relaxing.

At the eighth hour, which followed the first by three weeks, Rutherford reported that he was reconciled to the fact that his marriage was through. At the end of the hour we decided that during the following meeting we would set up hierarchies for desensitization. The next day he was in an automobile accident and suffered a concussion and a broken arm.

He returned a month later with his arm in a cast saying that he had lost the ability to relax and was being driven wild by the itching. He had trouble relaxing in the hour and found that he was trying to support his broken arm and was picturing the broken ends of the bone which he had seen in the X-ray. We discussed the fact that the cast and sling would support the arm without effort on his part and worked on differentiating between tension and the strain and fatigue in the arm. I had him picture being injected with novocaine by the dentist and when he could make his jaw numb quickly and easily, we transferred it to the arm with considerable relief in the itching.

The next week he had mastered relaxing again. Things were so much better that he decided he could handle his remaining anxieties just by relaxing and we terminated without ever getting around to desensitization. His parting statement was to the effect that as his efficiency at relaxing goes up his need for omnipotence goes down. He now sees nothing to panic about. If someone says something threatening he considers his motives and finds that it becomes the other person's problem and not his.

I invited Rutherford to my house for a drink a month or two later and he had almost completely eliminated his remaining hangups. His gains persisted when I stopped by his apartment a few months later.

Two years after treatment he came to my office once more. He had been happy and relaxed in the meantime. He had married a much more satisfactory wife and was doing outstanding work in a very difficult doctoral program at Stanford University. He was planning to take a preliminary exam ahead of schedule just for practice. He became afraid of failing the exam even though he could do so without prejudice.

I told him that I had failed my major prelim once and survived* and reminded him of some of the things we had discussed. He relaxed well in the office and went out resolved to work on staying relaxed. He called in a couple of days to say that he had been successful in staying relaxed and was no longer worried about the exam.

CASE #4. Carl was a twenty-two-year-old man whose phobias were extremely difficult to treat. The main reason for this was that the keystone of his anxiety response was severe stomach tension of rapid onset. Each time this response occurred it took five or six minutes for his stomach to relax, which made desensitization very slow. I have generally had poor luck with such persons and Carl was no exception. He was seen for 144 hours before a successful conclusion. Discussion will be limited to one interesting sequence in this very complex case.

By the 106th interview, Carl had become quite proficient at relaxing *in vivo*. His most severe phobia had to do with his parents leaving town. During the few periods when they were not planning a trip Carl was by now able to spend much of the time relaxed. However, he noted two things which were not related to any of his anxieties. He would be

* There were some psychoanalytic people on the committee.

driving to work, checking his muscles faithfully and feeling fine when suddenly for no reason he would be up to 50 suds. Also, he had noticed that he would become extremely tense when doing bench work. Coincidentally I had noticed that his eyes were often the first part of his body to become tense and the last to relax. I determined to work intensively on teaching him to relax his eyes.

To this end I asked him to look hard to the left as the first step in studying the eye muscles. He rose up in the chair as though he had been stuck with a pin and reported that his stomach had tightened up. I asked him to fixate upon the eraser of a pencil and moved it back and forth before his eyes while he reported anxiety responses. By this means it was determined that he began to tense if he moved his eyes beyond approximately 30 degrees from the straight ahead position in any direction. This included anxiety when the pencil was moved closer to his eyes than would permit remaining within the 60 degree cones.

He was instructed to try turning his head instead of his eyes when he had to look in the rear view mirror when driving and to drop his head instead of his eyes when working with something below his line of vision on the bench.

He returned the next session to say that the tactic had been successful. He no longer suddenly found himself tense for no apparent reason when driving and was able to stay relaxed while doing bench work. He was asked to relax deeply and then to fixate the pencil once more. I moved it back and forth, up and down and closer and closer to his eyes, going slowly enough not to arouse tension. Gradually the response-produced stimuli were desensitized and in twenty minutes he was able to look as far as his anatomy permitted, including the closest convergence, without anxiety. I have since encountered two other similar cases and many others in which response-produced stimuli from tension in certain muscles caused tension in other muscles.

I believe in a behavioral approach to life as an effective and comprehensive philosophy. I try to organize my life and see the behavior of my fellow human beings in behavioral terms and certainly encourage my clients to do the same. On a more philosophical level I believe in working to better the lot of mankind and feel that it contributes to the mental health of my clients if I can convince them to join me in the endeavor. I believe that a man should be himself and do what he feels like and say what he thinks as long as it doesn't harm anyone. Then you know who you are and who your friends are. They like you as you are instead of for some custom-made act you put on for their benefit. Again I encourage my clients to try this philosophy.

There is nothing unscientific about this and there are indeed good behavior principles which predict that a more uninhibited and genuine person will be more free of anxiety. Honesty can be the best principle as well as the best policy.

REFERENCES

ANANT, S. S., (Ed.) *Readings in Behavior Therapies.* New York: MSS Educational Publishing Co., 1969.

BUEHLER, R. E., PATTERSON, G. R., & FURNESS, J. M. The reinforcement of behavior. In Institutional Settings *Beh. Res. and Therapy*, 1966, 4, 157-167.

DOLLARD, J., & MILLER, N. F. *Personality and psychotherapy.* New York: McGraw Hill, 1950.

FOX, L. Effecting the use of efficient study habits. In Ulrich, R., Stachnik, T., and Maybry, J. (Eds.) *Control of Human Behavior.* Glenview, Illinois: Scott, Foresman and Co., 1966. Pp. 85-90.

FREUD, S. *A General Introduction to Psychoanalysis.* Garden City, N. Y.: Garden City Publishing Co., 1917.

HAUGEN, G. B., DIXON, H. H., & DICKEL, H. A. *A therapy for anxiety tension reactions.* New York: Macmillan, 1958.

JACOBSON, E. *Progressive Relaxation.* Chicago: U. of Chicago Press, 1938.

JAMES, WILLIAM. *Principles of psychology.* New York: Henry Holt, 1890.

KELLY, G. A. *The psychology of personal constructs.* New York: Norton, 1955.

LAZARUS, A. A. Broad-spectrum behavior therapy and the treatment of agoraphobia. *Behavior Research and Therapy*, 1966, 4, 95-97. A.

LAZARUS, A. A. Behavior rehearsal vs. non-directive therapy vs. advice in effecting behavior change. *Behavior Research and Therapy*, 1966, 4:3, 209-212.

MARQUIS, J. N. Orgasmic reconditioning: changing sexual object choice through controlling masturbation fantasies. *Journal of Behavior Therapy and Experimental Psychiatry*, 1970, Vol. 1. Pp. 277-285.

MARQUIS, J. N., MORGAN, W. G., & PIAGET, G. W. *A guidebook for systematic desensitization.* Palo Alto: Veteran's workshop, Veterans Administration, 1971 (2nd Edition).

MASTERS, W. H., & JOHNSON, V. E. *Human sexual response.* Boston: Little, Brown, 1966.

MASTERS, W. H., & JOHNSON, V. E. *Human sexual inadequacy.* Boston: Little, Brown, 1970.

MOWRER, O. H. In Jon, M. R. (Ed.) *Nebraska symposium on motivation.* Lincoln: University of Nebraska Press, 1950.

PATTERSON, G. R., & REID, J. Reciprocity and coercion: two facets of social systems. Paper prepared for the Ninth Annual Institute for Research in Clinical Psychology, sponsored by the University of Kansas, Dept. of Psychology, *Behavior modification for clinical psychologists.* Lawrence, Kansas, April, 1967.

ROGERS, C. R. *Client centered therapy.* Boston: Houghton Mifflin, 1951.

SALTER, A. *Conditioned reflex therapy.* New York: Creative Age Press, 1949.

SEMANS, J. H. Premature ejaculation: a new approach. *Southern Medical Journal,* 1956, 4a, 353-357.

STAMPFL, T. G.. & LEVIS, D. J. Essentials of implosive therapy: a learning-theory-based psychodynamic behavior therapy. *Journal of Abnormal Psychology,* 1967, 72, 6, Pp. 496-502.

WATSON, J. B. *Behaviorism.* New York: Peoples Institute, 1924.

WOLPE, J., & LAZARUS, A. A. *Behavior therapy techniques.* Oxford: Pergamon Press, 1966.

4

Practical Behavioral Diagnosis

EDWARD DENGROVE, M.D.

ALL BEHAVIORAL THERAPIES must be preceded by a proper behavioral diagnosis. The application of behavioral principles is so precise that without a proper delineation of the "target" symptoms one can go astray. It is worth emphasizing that target behaviors involve the identification of "emotional habits" and faulty cognitions. "Symptoms" merely denote the patient's awareness of the reactions that go on within him.

I recently treated a young, married woman who worked as a waitress. Her presenting complaints were the usual phobic ones: fear of shopping, fear in church, fear of crowds, and other interpersonal tensions. In addition, she presented three rather unusual features: difficulty with vision in that things seemed small (micropsia), a tendency for her voice to sound far off, and a feeling that she was fading away, all indicative of a need to avoid facing her problems directly. Asked what she could not face, she described her fears again. I proceeded with systematic desensitization. At first she made excellent progress and returned to her job. Then she struck a plateau and I discovered that she was not fully relaxed, though she had so indicated. Simultaneously she was having problems with her mother, daughter, and husband. It took a longer period to relax her sufficiently for further progress to ensue. She then left her job because she did not want to get involved in her boss's personal problems.

She had resolved her external problems with her husband, daughter and mother, but in other areas of her life progress was lacking and she complained bitterly of not feeling well. By this time she had lost the specific fears which had brought her into treatment initially and now addressed herself to the fact that she could not find another job and feared she could not keep it if she had one. I faced her with her fear of work and she replied that people at work—and at no other place—made her nervous. I was not happy with this answer, so I injected Methedrine intravenously to lighten her mood and increase her ability to talk. She then confessed that it was not concern for the people at her job that made her nervous but the fact that if she went to work her family would suffer. If she worked the morning shift, her daughter would have no way of getting to school two miles away; her mother, whom she visited daily, would not have her comfort and help in shopping. If she went on the evening shift, her daughter would not have a hot meal, nor would her husband. She felt that she had to do the right, good, and expected thing. On the other hand she complained that she was not doing what she wanted to do: go to work, and have time to go out with her girl friend. She feared her husband would beat her as her first husband had done. Though they were not getting along well, this was not true. The therapeutic focus was now far removed from her original fears. A different approach involving marital counselling and assertive techniques seemed strongly indicated.

If this conflict had been disclosed earlier in treatment, much time would have been saved and treatment results would have been more certain. How can a therapist determine these events sooner? A simple listing of fears is insufficient for diagnostic purposes. As Wolpe (personal communication) remarked, "Without correct identification of the relevant stimulus elements, one may expend a great deal of time and effort without result." One can form conclusions about important hierarchical items through skillful interrogation, the use of fear surveys or other questionnaires, autobiographical notes, the letter association technique (Dengrove 1962), and various psychophysiological measurements. Unfortunately patience and luck still play an important role. More of this later.

Stevenson and Hain (1967) decry the failure to identify with sufficient precision the exact stimuli of the patient's neurotic responses, declaring that the therapist can waste valuable time by tackling the wrong elements in the patient's neurotic reactions. They illustrate their point by analyzing the barber shop phobia, and insisting that one does not merely settle for the general environment in which it occurs, e.g. the barber shop as a whole. There may be a fear of scrutiny by others, a rebelliousness against social customs, impatience with delays, fear of confinement, fear of mutilation, anxiety-arousing experiences with chairs resembling barber chairs, sexual arousal, issues of seniority, and other explanations for the phobia; a multiplicity of stimuli which touch off the phobic response.

A stutterer I had been treating stuttered more while dictating to his stenographers. He changed stenographers without effect, and desensitization to these girls produced no reduction in his affliction. Further diagnostic probing indicated that he was not bothered by individual stenographers but by the fact that what he was dictating was being made a matter of public record and he would be held accountable for it. A change to assertive techniques helped overcome this complication. Similarly an agoraphobic who feared walking away from her home was really afraid of encountering dogs, and desensitization to these animals enabled her to walk freely again.

According to Meyer and Crisp (1966) the presence of historically earlier sources of anxiety may complicate recovery. Thus, the presenting symptom may be the result of higher order conditioning or secondary generalization, yet the basic source of the symptoms may still be present, acting upon the individual and influencing the course of the presenting complaints. Consequently, it too must be ferreted out and dealt with in addition to the secondary complaints. I have not found this to be much of an obstacle, particularly if I utilize the letter association technique. (Details of this technique are outlined in the section dealing with diagnostic procedures.)

Davis (1958) points out that memory images are perceptions, just as those caused by current people or objects, and we respond to the stimuli in memories just as we do to those in other perceptions. The recall of a scene once painful can then evoke anxiety *not* as an old de-repressed emotion, but in response to the stimulus for anxiety occurring in the *immediate* perception. Thus *memory* of the cruel mother may stimulate *present* anxiety rather than release old anxiety.

Clarke (1968) concluded that the permanence of early learning will depend not only upon the age of the child and the duration and intensity of the experience, but more particularly upon its later reinforcement. Early learning will fade if not reinforced. Similarly, Montenegro (1968) suggests that rather than concern ourselves with the past history, we should become more involved in the present conditions that are maintaining and reinforcing the patient's symptomatology. Behavior therapy is directed primarily to removing or counteracting the circumstances that are perpetuating the given behavior problem. Yet it is important to stress the fact that when treating higher order learning and bypassing the original learning situation, relapse is likely to be the net result.

Lazarus (1966) emphasizes the part played by others in the continuance of a symptom. In one instance he had to call in the patient's husband and mother and inform them how they were reinforcing the patient's dependency by displaying concern and expressing reassurance whenever she complained of minor somatic discomforts. They were requested not to pay attention to these negative statements, but to reward by attention, encouragement and approval all positive self-references and independent responses. He states that it is presumably impossible to become an agoraphobic without the aid of others who will submit to the inevitable demands imposed upon them by the sufferer, who play a vital role in sustaining and maintaining the agoraphobic behavior and making lasting therapeutic changes unlikely without treating them concurrently.

One needs to desensitize not only to the act, but to anticipation of the act, as a separate hierarchy. Sometimes the anticipation takes on an obsessive quality, at which time we must revert to thought blocking procedures. Furthermore, it is not merely the anticipation of the act per se which must concern us, but also the general anticipation of the future. As one patient told me, "I can do the little things, like drive around the block, then I think ahead to what will be expected of me, and I fall apart and don't even want to do the little things." We must—in some way—convince the patient to look at the scene, one portion at a time. Particularization prevents or reduces feelings of overwhelming anticipatory anxiety.

Wolpe (1964) writes of pervasive aspects of anxiety which may be difficult to ferret out, such as space, time, one's own body, light verticality, light-shade contrasts. I recall treating a woman who developed a phobic state after a car had rammed into her home in the dark. She became sensitized to the dark and to outside car noises and was not aware of these specific irritants, complaining only of general nervousness with tension headaches.

Lang (1964) writes of the pressure of partially digested food against the wall of the intestine, or a phase of peristalsis itself as interoceptive conditioned stimuli for anxiety, such as might follow family arguments during or following a meal. Gantt (1964) notes that the Russians have successfully conducted conditioning experiments employing many subtle internal cues such as urinary secretions, thyroid endocrine secretions, metabolic changes, etc. He adds that it may be very difficult to extinguish these, and certainly that the individual himself would be unconscious of what is producing the changes in his visceral system.

The emphasis thus far is upon the need to distill basic and primary problem areas in endeavoring to diagnose the covert and overt factors responsible for the patient's presenting complaints.

Lazarus and Serber (1968) point out that in making a behavioral diagnosis one should carefully separate deficits from basic anxiety responses. For instance, it is important to keep in mind that a male patient's inability to approach eligible females may not be a function of anxiety toward women but rather a reflection of inadequate learning, simple naïvete, and poor verbal skills; that phobic complaints may be secondary to a psychotic process requiring antipsychotic medication; that with some phobic reactions, depression may be the predominant illness and need anti-depressive medication, environmental manipulation and assertive training; that other phobic cases may warrant re-education and direct instruction, modeling and practice, plus rational discussions of ethics and morality.

Lazarus (in Abramovitz 1970) further points out that one of the chief limitations of behavior therapy is the application of specific techniques which ignore the patient's values, attitudes and beliefs and do not define the particular goals of the patient and orient therapy toward their attainment. Individual therapy, he (Lazarus, 1970) states, obviously imposes limitations upon the person-to-person exploration of these specific behaviors, and adds, "Many facets of a problem which may elude the scrutiny of even the most perspicacious therapist often become clearly delineated during or after an intensive group discussion." All in all, the clinician should strive to obtain information about his patients from many sources—observation, measurement, inquiry, outside opinion and above all, a detailed exploration of stimulus antecedents and behavioral consequences.

PROCEDURES FOR DIAGNOSTIC EXPLORATION

A systematic approach to history taking (Table A) leads to a practical

TABLE A

HISTORY-TAKING

How do you feel? What are your complaints?
Headaches—Any other aches or pains?
>   Ascertain: Where do you feel the pain? Does it stay there or go to any other place? What is it like: aching, pressing, throbbing, etc.? How often do you get it? How long does it last? What brings it on? What relieves it? Do you suffer nausea or vomiting with it, visual difficulty, dizziness? Other accompaniments?

Nervousness: Are you tense, restless, irritable or impatient, jittery or jumpy, tire readily, shaky?
Appetite and weight loss.
Sleep difficulty: Trouble falling asleep, interrupted sleep, restless sleep, early waking? Do you have nightmares or bad dreams of any kind?
Memory—concentration.
Sweating—hot flushes—faint feelings or fainting spells—dizziness—weakness—noises in the ears.
Trouble with stomach: indigestion, nausea or vomiting, diarrhea or constipation, pains in abdomen, heartburn.
Trouble with heart: palpitations, double beats or skipped beats, pains in chest.
Trouble with lungs: tightness in chest, shortness of breath, coughing, choking feelings, things sticking in throat, hard to swallow.
Trouble with bladder: difficulty holding or passing water, go too often during day or night.
Any fears: delineate and detail, circumstances, onset, etc.
Depression, crying spells, suicidal thoughts.
Trouble with sexual life: detail.
Trouble with social life: detail.
Smoking habits—drinking habits—drug habits—taking medications at all.
Worries of any kind: health—future—ability to work—finances.

PAST and PERSONAL HISTORY: Any serious illnesses, operations or injuries in past: details. Any nervousness: detail, treatments previously.
>   Married or single. Children. How get along with spouse. Details of marriage relationship.
>   Family history: Mother and father, siblings. Details. How get along, etc.
>   Work history.
>   Any police record, juvenile or adult.
>   Military service: details, including type of discharge and hospitalizations.
>   Education.
>   Hobbies: other interests.

DRAW-A-PERSON PRODUCTION

THREE WISHES

WHAT KIND OF PERSON ARE YOU (Self-evaluation)

REQUEST: AUTOBIOGRAPHY
    LIST OF FEARS. LIST OF ANGERS.
    LIST OF WHAT HE/SHE WOULD LIKE TO SEE DIFFERENT
      ABOUT SELF

OPTIONAL: FEAR SURVEY (Wolpe and Lang)
    REINFORCEMENT SURVEY (Cautela and Kastenbaum)
    Specific questionnaires: re alcoholic habits, etc.
    Other psychological tests: Maudsley Personality Inventory
                             MMPI
                             Others.

LETTER ASSOCIATION technique for pinpointing etiology.

diagnostic evaluation within the first half-hour of the first session; the latter half of the initial interview can then be devoted toward initiating treatment. I like to see the patient leave, after the first visit, feeling considerably better and more hopeful for the future.

The questions asked in Table A cover fairly completely the complaints of most patients. Simultaneously the patient's mode of dress, speech and comportment are observed: whether anxious or depressed, restless or apathetic, intelligent, responsive, and the like. First impressions, though fleeting, are valuable. One can tell much of a patient's inner feelings by the facial expression, particularly about the eyes. Telling the patient one's impressions in a conversational and interested voice often puts him at ease.

The Draw-A-Person production is a favorite addition of mine because of the wealth of information it gives about the patient in a very short time. I offer the patient a pad and pencil and ask him to draw a picture of a person from head to toe, not just a head, and not a stick figure. Interpretation of these drawings is beyond the scope of this paper but there is much literature on the subject. There is nothing like experience, however, to give one the feel of the response, particularly when every patient seen and treated is given the test.

I also use the Three Wishes test as a matter of routine. For those unfamiliar with it, one simply asks the patient, "If you had three wishes, what would you wish for?" The information derived assists in helping the patient to establish goals of treatment.

The patient's self-evaluation is often helpful, and may tend to corrob-

orate or refute your own evaluation of him. Sometimes added data are
thereby obtained for hierarchy building.

The patient is requested to bring in a list of fears, as complete as
possible, in order to add to the facts and impressions already secured
during the first session. It is highly important to "target in" upon the
symptoms and to be certain that what the patient claims he fears is truly
the "target." Detailed interrogation will usually supply the items needed
for setting up of hierarchies, emphasizing the people, places, objects, and
situations that engender anxiety.

I ask the patient to prepare an autobiography (Annis 1967). The
length of the manuscript is left to the discretion of the patient but should
be at least several pages long. The purpose is to fill in possible gaps in
the history secured at the first session, in hopes that further material for
therapy will be supplied. It also has the effect of making the patient
participate more actively in therapy.

Requesting the patient to list, at his leisure, those traits he would like
to see different about himself adds to the determination of treatment
goals. It is also helpful to add all the things that irritate and make him
angry, and the times he may have wished to be more aggressive but
failed to assert himself.

Useful information may sometimes be obtained from the addition of a
Fear Survey Schedule (Wolpe and Lang, 1964, Lanyon and Manosevitz,
1966, Rubin, B. M., 1968, Scherer and Nakamura, 1968, Rubin, S. E.
1969, Bernstein and Allen, 1969), of a Reinforcement Survey Schedule
(Cautela and Kastenbaum, 1967), and other specific questionnaires, or
psychological tests.

The Letter Association technique (Dengrove, 1962) was devised some
years ago and has proven most useful to me in pinpointing targets. It
shortens the necessary time immeasurably and is used in each treatment
session for ongoing diagnosis. In essence, the mood of the patient is set
by asking him to close his eyes and to relax as much as possible. He
is to think of a particular symptom, to relate it to the last setting or event
in which it was felt, and to attempt to relive or reconstruct—to whatever
extent is possible—the feeling tone of the complaint. As a rule only a
few seconds are required for this phase.

Then he is asked to give the very first letter that comes to mind—
not the second or third, but the very first one. This is necessary since
there are times when the patient will toy around with the alphabet.

The letter is noted, and the patient is then asked to give the very next letter that comes to mind. In all, five letters of the alphabet are obtained. If any letter that follows is sequentially related to the one given before it, the patient may be instructed to scatter the next one, to pick it out from any other place in the alphabet. The initial letter, A, and difficult letters, such as Q, X, Z are most often used to resist the process and may be disregarded.

There will be occasions when the patient will insist that he cannot think of a letter. In this case, one urges the patient to make some attempt. After all, who does not know the alphabet? Remind the patient that there are only 26 letters. If there is still resistance, one need only point out the letters of the alphabet in written form and ask the patient to look at the list and to choose one. I prefer to ask him to think of all the letters as printed on bits of paper, placed in a hat, and then thrown into the air; he is to choose the one that he grasps as the pack comes down in a shower.

When five letters are taken—the number is arbitrary and could be only one—they are listed vertically in order. The patient is then allowed to open his eyes and requested to give the first word—again only the first one—that comes to mind and which begins with each of the letters previously chosen.

In this way we have five words listed. The patient is asked to make a sentence using each word, or to free associate with each word, i.e. saying what it brings to mind, how it connects up with the symptom. Almost always the words form a battery of information related to the original difficulty and no word is without meaning in relation to the person's difficulty, no matter how far-fetched it may seem at the time. The information so derived is often dramatically related to the patient's difficulties; often the patient himself sees the connection.

Timing is important. When the patient delays in giving a letter, he should be urged to do it as quickly as he can. It is essential to prevent the patient from mulling over the alphabet, particularly during second or subsequent experiences with this method. Thinking about the subject is not desired; the more quickly the letter is pulled out of the air, the more useful it is for our purpose. Tell him not to think about it, just to say it. Nor is one to be distracted by a patient's desire to give a full word, since the word may only be a "red herring." One wants only the letter. Associations may be given afterwards.

As an example of this approach, a 37-year-old housewife presented complaints of "ungodly thoughts going through my head. I sit and cry and cry and cry, and I don't know why." Asked to give five letters, she produced the following and their associations:

F-free-the boat won't let me be free financially.
G-good-it's good for my husband. He enjoys it.
P-poor-it's making us broke.
B-boat-the same thing.
B-Bob-my husband.

This led into the precipitating event of her depressed state, which was the purchase of a boat by her husband, with the consequent strain upon their finances. Further exploration led to her other conflicts and underscored the way she used the purchase of the boat as a means of expressing antagonism toward her husband.

As another example, a 16-year-old high school youth was found in a neighbor's house, dressed in feminine attire, doing his homework on a bed. He declared that he felt like a girl at times. There was no psychotic material. Asked to give five letters, he presented the following:

B-boy-body build, most usually masculine, and I'm not. I'm so weak. I can't do things like other kids can, like play sports.
F-failure-I'm afraid I'll be a failure in life. Be a bum.
N-Neal-myself.
O-open-open the box-any kind of box-you put something in or pull something out of it.
T-top-top of a mountain-above sea level-usually forests and woods around there.

I was able to follow the first three associations into his relationship with his father; the last two were not pursued, since they presented material he would not be ready to cope with.

I find the technique interesting, rich in profusion of material, and direct in approach. Its use is not limited to initial contacts with the patient but may be applied at any time in therapy. It is a time-saver. The patient cannot claim that nothing comes to mind, since all that he has to do is to give a letter of the alphabet.

Following the end of the interview, I ask the patient—now that I am aware of the information he has given me—what he wants me to do for him: a therapeutic goal is set. It is surprising how often the goals set by the patient will differ from those presupposed by the therapist.

PHOBIAS AND THE COMPULSIVE PERSONALITY TYPE

General personality attributes are important when arriving at a differential diagnosis. For example, if one separates those phobic conditions associated with post-traumatic states and schizoid disorders, one is left almost entirely with patients who display a basic compulsive personality pattern—perfectionism—in varying degrees. These people are, for the most part, neat, systematic, orderly, conscientious, and concerned that everything should be in its right place and that there is indeed a right place for everything. They want to do the good thing and be the good person, to please everyone (except their spouses). They range from the woman—and 15 to 1 it is a woman—who will pick up the ash tray to empty it the moment someone drops a cigarette into it, to the much less frequently seen artist whose studio may be messy but whose concept of her work must be perfection.

All of these people have one thing in common: a highly developed conscience which sits heavily upon them. The majority have a mother, or much less frequently a father, who is compulsive and perfectionistic also, and who has dominated them, often to the point of distress.

The phobic symptom is precipitated at a particular time in their lives when they are undergoing a stressful situation and feel particularly helpless. It is important not only to delineate the basic compulsive character structure but to pinpoint the original stressful situation, and, if necessary, to desensitize to it; it may have been continually reinforced to the present time.

The compulsivity and perfectionism call for a broad array of techniques in order to help the patient to cope with a stressful environment. These patients often need to be desensitized to feared authoritative figures, and have the burden of their compulsivity lessened. An important feature of therapy is to help them to a point of not caring so much about what others think of them.

ONGOING DIAGNOSIS

Diagnosis is not limited to the first session but is an ongoing process. Each time the patient comes for therapy, he is asked, "What has occurred since the previous session?" Any symptom, old or new, is immediately elaborated upon and its time and setting specifically described, often with the patient closing his eyes and attempting to relive the situation as in the present. Then, if the patient cannot state why the symptom occurred at a particular moment in a particular setting, in its special way, the letter association technique is often able to determine these details.

The source of the reinforcement of the symptom must be dealt with on each occasion. There may only be a repetition of material previously unearthed but it is important to make the patient aware of what it is that keeps him ill. As noted previously, there is extinction of the symptom unless something or someone is keeping it alive, much as a hoop will run down if not given a push from time to time.

Each patient is asked to relate both the good and bad things that have happened since the previous session. When a patient speaks of several anxiety attacks, each is traced back to its original time of onset, the setting in which it occurred, and if the patient cannot discuss the origin of the attack, the letter association technique is used, quickly pinpointing the source. As an example, a patient opened the session with, "Why do I get nervous whenever I think of coming here?" She was asked to sit back in the chair, close her eyes and become aware of the feeling of nervousness. When she indicated that this was present, she was told to give the first letter that came to mind. In this instance it was the letter, F. The first word she connected with it was "fear." She was then asked to give a letter after thinking, "Fear of what?" This turned out to be "Y-you." Asked to think of the word, "because," she said, "Because I don't know what you're going to do." Further discussion of this point allayed her anxieties.

Ongoing diagnosis is important where there is delay or inability to transfer improvement from office to real life, and directs attention to motivation in particular. For example, a 20-year-old woman was doing well—in the office—with systematic desensitization to her fears of walking and driving from her home, but actually had made no progress at all in the actual situations. Asked to attempt movement in real life situations, she produced only excuse after excuse during each session as to why it had been impossible throughout that week. She had an anticipatory fear response but she would not make the slightest attempt, even with proffered help. Further diagnostic exploration revealed the reason for her lack of progress to be her fear that if she would be free to come and go as she pleased, she would simply go and not return. She had no respect for her immature husband, yet feared giving up the kind of life that she was leading.

Similarly, a 34-year-old housewife had been doing quite well with her fear of driving away from her home when her infant child died suddenly under circumstances for which she blamed her pediatrician. Immediately she relapsed and no coaxing could get her to drive again, until diagnostic exploration revealed her fear that if she could drive on her own, she might drive to the doctor's office and commit mayhem there. She dreamed of it, and was protected against these effects of her hostility by her inability to drive at all.

Finally, it is worth noting that some patients may appear to suffer a relapse (i.e. the return of initial symptoms) when in fact new organic or different environmental forces are operative. For example, one of the first patients whom I treated with systematic desensitization was a woman in her early forties. She had suffered a phobic state for about 12 years. With systematic desensitization she progressed to a point where she could travel, not only from her home but for great distances. She was a most grateful patient because her husband always wanted to travel with her and she had held him back. One day she phoned for an appointment. She was frightened; her symptoms had returned. Diagnostic exploration, however, proved her alarm to be unfounded. She was suffering from some of the symptoms of her menopause, had mistaken them for the return of her previous illness and developed an anxiety over them. Reassurance and estrogens limited her visits to one, and thereafter she phoned to say that she was her renewed self again. Another woman who returned for further treatment had developed symptoms about a fear that had not shown itself before because she had had no occasion to encounter similar situations previously. Treatment of this item through desensitization quickly returned her to her previous symptom-free state.

Behavioral diagnosis requires versatility, together with a sharp, inquiring mind. Properly done, its end results enhance therapeutic progress.

REFERENCES

ABRAMOVITZ, C. M. Personalistic psychotherapy and the role of technical eclecticism. *Psychological Reports*, 1970, 26, 255-263.

ANNIS, A. P. The autobiography: its use and value in professional psychology. *Journal of Counseling Psychology*, 1967, 14, 9-17.

BERNSTEIN, D. A. & ALLEN, G. J. Fear survey schedule (II). *Behavior Research and Therapy*, 1969, 7, 403-407.

CAUTELA, J. R. & KASTENBAUM, R. A reinforcement survey schedule for use in therapy, training, and research. *Psychological Reports*, 1967, 20, 1115-1130.

CLARKE, A. D. B. Learning and human development. *British Journal of Psychiatry*, 1968, 114, 1061-1077.

DAVIS, R. D. *British Journal of Medical Psychology*, 1958, 31, 74.

DENGROVE, E. A new letter association technique. *Diseases of the Nervous System*, 1962, 23, 25-26.

GANTT, W. H. Autonomic conditioning. In J. Wolpe, et al (Eds.) *The Conditioning Therapies*. New York: Holt, Rinehart, and Winston, 1964, Pp. 117, 125.

LANG, P. J. Experimental studies of desensitization psychotherapy. In J. Wolpe, et al (Eds.) *The Conditioning Therapies*. New York: Holt, Rinehart, and Winston, 1964, Pp. 51-52.

LANYON, R. I. & MANOSEVITZ, M. Validity of self-reported fear. *Behavior Research and Therapy*, 1966, 4, 259-263.

LAZARUS, A. A. Broad spectrum behavior therapy and the treatment of agoraphobia. *Behavior Research and Therapy*, 1966, 4, 95-97.

LAZARUS, A. A. Behavior therapy in groups. In G. M. Gazda (Ed.) *Theories and Methods of Group Psychotherapy and Counseling*. Springfield: C. C. Thomas, 1970.

LAZARUS, A. A. & SERBER, M. Is systematic desensitization being misapplied? *Psychological Reports*, 1968, 23, 215-218.

MEYER, V. & CRISP, A. H. Some problems in behavior therapy. *British Journal of Psychiatry*, 1966, 112, 367-381.

RUBIN, B. M., et al. Factor analysis of a fear survey schedule. *Behavior Research and Therapy*, 1968, 6, 65-75.

RUBIN, S. E., et al. Factor analysis of the 122 item fear survey schedule. *Behavior Research and Therapy*, 1969, 7, 381-386.

SCHERER, M. W. & NAKAMURA, C. Y. A fear survey schedule for children (FSS-FC). *Behavior Research and Therapy*, 1968, 6, 173-182.

STEVENSON, I. & HAIN, J. H. On the different meanings of apparently similar symptoms; illustrated by varieties of barber shop phobia. *American Journal of Psychiatry*, 1967, 124, 399-403.

WOLPE, J. Behavior therapy in complex neurotic states. *British Journal of Psychiatry*, 1964, 110, 28-34.

WOLPE, J. & LANG, P. J. A fear survey schedule for use in behavior therapy. *Behavior Research and Therapy*, 1964, 2, 27-30.

5

Eidetics: An Internal Behavior Approach

AKHTER AHSEN, Ph.D.
and ARNOLD A. LAZARUS, Ph.D.

IT SEEMS WIDELY AGREED that most problem behaviors are learned in some manner and that psychotherapy is a relearning and unlearning process. Behavior Therapy has given explicit direction to the basic thrust of learning adaptive habits while unlearning maladaptive responses, but unfortunately the S-R formulation of learning adopted by some behavior therapists is too limited to account for the realities of life (Lazarus, 1971). This limitation inherent in the theory is also generally apparent in the techniques developed within the counter-conditioning framework.

"Learning" in its widest sense of acquiring a "pattern" is a meaningless term and it should properly include insights, images, symbolic materials, ideas and cognitive-affective interchanges that stretch between all these. A proper theory of behavior in our view will only emerge as a result of the interaction of clinical theories and experimental psychology in which clinical data will be obtained primarily from controlled studies

87

of patients rather than subjects. One can see that such a scientific approach in psychology would not be particularly restricted to "learning theory."

Our main objection to non-cognitive learning theory is that it does not aim at understanding what generally passes between the patient and the therapist and it has no means available which can help us in so doing.

In an endeavor to emphasize the need to extend therapy beyond the narrow boundaries of conventional behavior therapy, Lazarus (1971) described the case of Mrs. D, a housebound lady stricken with anxiety. If she ventured further than her front porch, she would become faint and panicky. When Mrs. D consulted Lazarus, his first therapeutic objective was to enable her to come on her own to the clinic, which was achieved by hypnotizing her and asking her to picture herself accomplishing this feat without undue disturbance. After this followed a period of extensive history-taking and more hypnosis in which she was repeatedly asked to picture herself travelling unaccompanied to and from the clinic. Then came the evidence that her husband was subtly attempting to undermine her progress by encouraging her extreme dependency. Her husband admitted a sense of security in knowing that his wife was always at home and was dependent on him and felt that if she were mobile and self-sufficient, she would leave him for another man. This fear on his part was traced to his own sexual ineptitude. After this revelation the husband and wife were seen together and discussions were devoted to ways and means of improving their relationship. She was encouraged to stand up for her rights through goal-directed role-playing which subsequently made it easier for her to contemplate standing up to her father. After enacting several role-playing sequences, Mrs. D improved further and now enjoyed taking long walks alone and was able to go shopping and visiting without distress. However, she continued to consider herself a worthless person and was not able to overcome her negative self-evaluation during therapy. Some time after she had terminated therapy, she became active and established an organization of a charitable nature and, as its president and founder, discovered self-worth and meaning. The last act of healing carried out by Mrs. D was totally self-initiated but what had been done prior to the final goal (self-worth) was considered a necessary turning point.

Follow-up studies of cases treated by behavior therapy indicate that durable outcomes usually require philosophical as well as behavioral changes (Lazarus, 1971). This leads to the open question of the possible advantages of combining external behavioral and internal behavioral treatment strategies. Of course, in the sense that our only access to clinical data is through some form of behavior (verbal and non-verbal), all therapy is behavioral. Nonetheless, it is useful to separate therapies that deal mainly with external observable behavior from those that concentrate on internal experiential phenomena. Basically, the question then is whether there are specific advantages in combining eidetic therapy (Ahsen, 1968) with behavioral techniques. What follows is an important case in which both methods (eidetic analysis and behavior therapy) were employed.

The circumstances which made the demonstration of this case possible were very interesting. Mrs. Jay, aged forty-one, had been treated at the Eastern Pennsylvania Psychiatric Institute by a group of behavior therapists for more than a year, during which time she had initially showed improvement and finally surprised everybody by relapsing and developing her symptoms all over again. Mrs. Jay was still visiting the Institute but had completely regressed to her pretreatment symptoms, namely, severe irrational anxiety which made her homebound, chest pains, palpitations, nausea, pins and needles, dizziness, extreme feelings of personal unworthiness, etc.

At this time, one of the therapists who had treated Mrs. Jay happened to meet Akhter Ahsen and a somewhat heated debate ensued regarding their respective theoretical and technical differences. The meeting culminated in a challenge to Ahsen to demonstrate his methods of eidetic analysis before a group of professionals. Ahsen had stressed that his theories of eidetic symbolism (Ahsen, 1965) would enable him to select appropriate therapeutic strategies at various stages of therapy and to predict the specific consequences of each intervention. Before the meeting ended, it was decided that Ahsen would treat a case at Eastern Pennsylvania Psychiatric Institute in the presence of the staff and that he would utilize short steps and demonstrate each step through a definite causal link and predict beforehand what results were expected and how they would be achieved.

The use of eidetics provides testable predictions and deductions and the methods of treatment they employ often eliminate surmise, hunch and intuition. They replace oversimplifications with realities about subjective phenomena, and the complexities of these realities are, in turn, testable and demonstrable.

These assertions will become more clear when we describe eidetic methods of treatment in respect to Mrs. Jay. The description of Ahsen's treatment will be discussed in detail to provide an idea of how eidetics actually appear to an outside observer and how they seem to work internally. Ahsen's demonstration suggested that where narrow behavior therapy failed to provide a valid change inside the patient, the eidetic approach succeeded in swiftly eliminating what appeared to be psychotic states, proving them to be memories of important events which formal behavior therapy had completely ignored.

CASE HISTORY OF MRS. JAY

Mrs. Jay, a forty-one-year-old white, married female of Jewish extraction, was suffering from symptoms of pain located in the upper left abdomen, chest and left breast, excessive irrational anxiety involving fear of death and numerous other manifestations of anxiety, such as palpitations, dizziness, nausea, pins and needles, fainting spells, as well as strong uncertainties and feelings of personal unworthiness, so much so that she was finding it impossible to perform daily chores and was unable to go places, especially crowded places. The treatment under behavior therapy was started in the regular way as a typical laboratory model involving principles of extinction, counter-conditioning, positive and negative reinforcement, including aversive conditioning and punishment with a small electrical gadget which she was expected to carry with her all the time and to shock herself if she entertained a negative idea involving a maladaptive approach to a life problem. Her symptoms were being treated in isolation from their origin and background because all the behavioral questionnaires and case history procedures had failed to bring out any causal link between the symptoms and her developmental past.

The previous formal behavioral approach had initially succeeded in reducing Mrs. Jay's anxiety for a short time but the symptoms returned in full blast one day when the patient came to the clinic and found nobody there. She reacted so badly to the incident that her condition deteriorated below pretreatment levels. The situation grew from bad to worse. After many more attempts, she was finally pronounced a borderline schizophrenic. It is obvious that formal behavior therapy had proved ineffective in ridding the patient of her maladaptive fears. All along she had shown a difficulty in absorbing behavioral treatment and in the end she threw all the training and conditioning overboard, making scores of hours just another negative experience in her life. Nothing much was known about her real emotional life. All said and done, the patient now stood at the threshold of no hope. Her original behavior therapist had described this case as the "acid test" for any other system of therapy.

At the commencement of eidetic analysis which took place early in 1967, Mrs. Jay was acutely disturbed. She was panting for breath and perspiring and complaining about dizziness and palpitations. She wanted the windows to be opened wide so that she could breathe cool, fresh air. Ahsen had already explained to the small group of observers that he would first assemble the character of her symptoms and then give her what he called the Age Projection Test* (Ahsen, 1968, Pp. 253-261) to see if the symptoms were "hysterical" and to determine whether any particular event in her past was connected with them. This, he said, would be possible to establish through an eidetic (self-image) which she would see during the Age Projection Test. Ahsen stated: "If the symptoms are in any way directly connected with specific past events, this self-image will provide us with the ability to exacerbate or to ameliorate her symptoms."

After Ahsen had noted down the main features of the symptoms, namely, how Mrs. Jay tended to describe them, how they tended to reflect in various parts of her body in the form of somatic feelings, and how they tended to get particularly localized in a certain area, a graphic picture of the symptoms emerged. These were noted down in the actual words which Mrs. Jay used to report them, including her elaborations. The chest pain and palpitations were thus localized around the region of the heart. Her other symptoms, like nausea, dizziness, needles, etc., emerged as secondary responses which described generally the feeling side of the main symptoms of chest pain. During this phase Mrs. Jay was lucid and described things very well. Ahsen passed the word among the main observers by writing on a piece of paper, "When I repeat the actual symptom descriptions to Mrs. Jay, she will react to my constant repetition by developing acute symptoms. When they reach an intolerable pitch, I will suddenly start talking about the opposite, of relief, of absence of pain, of, in fact, pleasant sensations and feelings in the same areas of the body. Then I will suddenly request her to see herself in the form of an image somewhere in the past. This image will shed light upon the etiology of her somatic symptoms."

After circulating this message, Ahsen started repeating the symptoms back to Mrs. Jay in her own words and, as he had predicted, her symptoms gradually became so acute that she begged him to stop repeating them to her. At this point, Ahsen reversed his procedure by repeating pleasant

---

* Editor's note: Ahsen now refers to this as the "Symptom Oscillation Test." For complete details, the reader is referred to Ahsen, 1972.

opposite descriptions (e.g., calmness, no pain, no discomfort, etc.). The patient showed clear signs of relaxation and relief. When asked to project herself into the past, she reported a self-image around age twenty-six while wearing a red blouse and black skirt. As to the memories around age twenty-five, *she recollected the death of her father during that year.*

The circumstances surrounding Mrs. Jay's father's death were found to be particularly traumatic upon inquiry. The father, who was a coronary patient, had suffered a heart attack and was brought back to life temporarily through cardiac massage by the attending doctors. The patient had been present throughout the procedure and for her to see the father returning to life and then dying again all within a few minutes was extremely distressing. She recalled begging the doctors not to massage the heart and to let the father die peacefully. The doctors, however, did not listen and performed what they considered their duty, not minding Mrs. Jay's reaction to it. She stated that she had felt extremely traumatized at this point and had an experience of choked hysteria inside.

At this point, Ahsen circulated another written message to the observers: "Her symptoms of pain in the upper left abdomen, left breast and part of the chest are probably related to this traumatic memory of cardiac massage. If the hypothesis is correct, we should be able to ameliorate her symptoms as well as make them acute if we repeat images of the two opposed ends of the event, namely, (i) massage of the heart and (ii) death of the father immediately after cardiac massage. Symptoms should react to (i) by becoming more acute and will decrease and even disappear when the image belonging to (ii) is concentrated upon by the patient. Images belonging to these two opposed areas are of the eidetic nature."

After circulating this note, Ahsen proceeded to develop (i) and (ii) eidetic images. By the end of this inquiry, it was found that the two lucid images had been clearly arrived at and Mrs. Jay showed a clear tendency to react to them: to (i) by developing the acute symptoms and to (ii) by becoming relaxed, though not without some symptoms. Ahsen then circulated another piece of paper saying, "My hypothesis is that just as the doctors wanted to actively revive the father, Mrs. Jay wanted to actively let the father die, amounting to images of aggressively rendering the father to death, a form of 'murder fantasy.' If the hypothesis is correct, the symptoms should disappear if Mrs. Jay is encouraged to discover her need to actively render the father to death in images."

Ahsen proceeded to arrive at further images pertaining to Mrs. Jay's hidden feelings toward the father. As questions and answers proceeded, we saw an unusual phenomenon, namely, that Mrs. Jay did, in fact, on her own see images in which she suffocated her father with a pillow and put him to death on the hospital bed. As she did so, she bitterly cried and then became completely peaceful, as if the storm had passed. After she "killed" the father with the help of the pillows, her somatic symptoms disappeared.

All the observers were examining the proceedings closely and saw that Ahsen was not feeding ideas or images to her and that eidetics were somehow emerging and expanding her awareness as she came to recognize that her symptoms were linked with the death of the father and that somehow or other she wanted her father to die. She was reproducing her needs and fantasies as far back as ten years. Her previous Behavior Therapy had never explored this area and there was no hint of any of this material in the history-taking when Mrs. Jay gave her extensive history in the initial stages. The eidetic procedures moved with a sure foot and showed no looseness in this direction and were able to lay open the probable causal link in the very first session. One could only say that the extensive stimulus analysis previously carried out was rudimentary, vague and indeterminate and clearly lacked the ability to unearth basic elements, at least in this area.

The eidetic approach disclosed that, to start with, Mrs. Jay's symptoms were of a hysterical nature and that her subjective states tended to split up into two distinct, significant image configurations—cardiac massage and death after the cardiac massage—and concentration on the image of the cardiac massage produced chest pain, profuse sweating, shortening of breath, feelings of giddiness and nausea, whereas concentration on the father's death released feelings of relaxation and comfort in the patient. Subsequent to repeated testing and oscillation of the symptoms through the two image states, Ahsen suggested that the patient now consciously repeat the images pertaining to the death of the father and concentrate only on this end of the image and drop the other side altogether. In reaction to these instructions, Mrs. Jay related further material involving how much her father loved her and how he used to take her out on long walks and sing songs for her on the way when she was a little girl. Now she seemed to be preoccupied with the father's two previous heart attacks.

After Mrs. Jay had overcome her main debilitating symptoms through a single session, she was able to cooperate more with psychotherapy. Now started further unfolding of her past as well as her fantasy life in relation to her symptoms. The theme of her father's cardiac attack seemed to be a continuous one and connected to two previous heart attacks, especially the first one when the father suddenly developed a heart attack when the mother was boiling water. The image pertaining to the boiling water appeared to be laden with powerful affect which threw the patient again into an experience of symptoms around the region of her heart. This image, however, proved "cathartic" instead and left the patient stronger in the end. The memory passed like a cloud, bringing to the surface other memories in which their house was robbed and a thief mugged her father inside the store which was directly below their living apartment. The memory pertaining to the mugging brought out other hidden fears concerning strangers and her own feelings of aggression. She experienced an image of herself attacking a thief in the store which helped her in mastering the memory. After this came memories of her stealing candy from the store and her concern about her weight and the father's insistence that she should try to hide herself behind the counter because she was too fat. As a result of this memory, she saw herself clobbering the father on the head and the image was similar to the thief attacking the father.

The patient showed keen understanding of the symbolism involved and also developed a clearer realization of why she wanted her father to die during the cardiac massage. However, the eidetics did not merely demonstrate the negative side of her wishes because there was also a jolly father in her mind and the images pertaining to the jolly father brought tears and sorrow to the patient. In the images, the two of them sang together on the footpath while going to school or just going for a walk. The profound experience of this jolly father restored a feeling of worth in her. She immensely enjoyed picturing these images.

The images then moved in the direction of her fears at the school when her classmates ridiculed her for being fat. She remembered some of these classmates and saw their images and repeated the visual experience and understood why she had grown to be so passive in respect to others. These children had cruelly persecuted her. After this came images pertaining to her growing up and her first menstruation. The eidetics in this area gradually led to her fears concerning conception and problems of miscarriage, a theme which had also appeared in the second part of the Age Projection Test.

She described her miscarriage experience and the fear that she could not have another baby. The doctor had told her that he could not hear the baby's heart and that "dead babies don't grow." This had been extremely traumatic for her. She remembered experiencing severe anxiety and uncertainty and horror at what she was facing. It appeared that her desire not to have a child was offset by an equally strong wish to have a child. She remembered thinking on those contradictory lines but was unable to resolve the conflict. A range of additional images (Ahsen, 1968, Pp. 258-261) enabled her to work through this conflict and led to various realizations that many problem areas were connected with her rejecting mother.*

Mrs. Jay's mother seemed to lack warmth, understanding and tolerance for the patient. She emerged as an impatient and critical person who did not hide how disappointed she was in her daughter. Her main concern seemed to be her daughter's being overweight. She was a martyr who had dominated her husband and had a loud voice without any comforting words in it. The father on the other hand had been an understanding person in her life. The mother was ashamed of her daughter and the daughter knew how she felt about her. She had infused her daughter with her feelings of worthlessness and guilt.

She began questioning whether her mother had normal attitudes toward life and whether her feelings of martyrdom were directly responsible for creating feelings of guilt in Mrs. Jay. By understanding the source of her guilt and by knowing in an experiential manner how it affected her, Mrs. Jay then drew a parallel between herself and her mother, suggesting that perhaps she was acting in the same manner toward her own family. The feelings of worthlessness and guilt had been engendered by the mother and were now being reinforced by her, and Mrs. Jay felt that she might even be punishing her mother in this manner. At this point she understood images of her mother as they appeared in the Eidetic Parents Test (Ahsen, 1968, Pp. 262-288) as the images of a martyred individual. She experienced feelings of tension and rage inside her and felt that she really wanted to punish her mother. At this point she

---

* Editor's note: While the psychoanalytic undertones reflect Ahsen's orientation, it should be understood that his *active* use of imagery departs radically from the passive and indirect stance of psychoanalytic therapy. Upon reading this chapter, one may not be aware that Ahsen is, in fact, very directive in selecting images, identifying their polarities, exploring them with the patient, and in assigning "homework" for the patient in the form of rehearsed images and fantasies.

expressed many images of anger against her mother. The Eidetic Parents Test brought a decisive awareness in Mrs. Jay and created an ability on her part to understand some important psychological interactions. Mrs. Jay made further progress through this test when she expressed concern as to whether she was doing the same thing to her own family. Her mother worked hard and was good, but was also a martyr. Mrs. Jay did not work hard, was "bad" and was a martyr.

As a next step in therapy, Mrs. Jay continued to experience a series of images in respect to the mother, covering situations of extreme frustration from the mother and her reactions to those situations involving the discharge of anger, etc. It was through these images that she gradually came to feel that she needed to separate herself from the mother. All along she had been bringing her mother to the clinic as an escort but now she decided to try and come alone. She understood that by being passive and afraid she was allowing herself to be destroyed by the mother. Her mother's support and her feeling of martyrdom were serving her own needs in making the patient feel worthless.

The realization that Mrs. Jay was also identifying with the mother and doing the same to her own family was naturally the next step in the therapy. These feelings of identification became more obvious when she reported that her son had recently complained of heart symptoms somewhat similar to her own and she had felt frightened on that account. She was consciously fantasizing that her son had suffered a heart attack, or an epileptic attack or had symptoms of high blood sugar because her own father had diabetes before he died. This is how she expressed her concern in respect to her son:

"Yesterday my son had mowed the lawn and he was fixing the lawnmower. After he was done he came in and said that for a few minutes his circulation went fast. I think he meant his pulse was rapid and his heart pounded. He did not seem frightened. He said he thought it may have happened once before, a few years ago.

"I get petrified inside when he is sick. He once had a staph infection that wouldn't clear up. I felt that yesterday he may have had an epileptic attack. I thought the doctor should check his blood sugar level for diabetes. My father had diabetes before he died. I also thought maybe he had a sort of allergy attack, as he is allergic to many plants."

Ahsen pointed out that Mrs. Jay had been reading physical symptoms into her son and because she had been doing it for so long, she had made him invent many illnesses. In a nonjudgmental way she was told that she had encouraged him to be shy, had given him the thought that many people were unkind to him, and had also given him the idea that probably he might even die.

The above-mentioned factors were all elicited through the eidetics and each time a point was raised for Mrs. Jay's consideration, an eidetic image was evoked to bring evidence to her and give her time to make up her own mind. As Ahsen demonstrated, any discussions held with Mrs. Jay which did not involve direct evidence from images tended to bog down in verbal controversy and led Mrs. Jay to sidetrack her emotional issues.

Following the above-mentioned eidetic procedures, Mrs. Jay was abe to go shopping, visiting places alone and without distress. The astonishing progress which she had made in the very first session had resulted in her overcoming the symptoms of chest pain, dizziness and severe palpitations. Symptoms of nausea, pins and needles and fear of other people similarly had been overcome along the way. Her treatment had centered around the initial overcoming of her main debilitating symptoms, followed by a series of progressive experiential "peak experiences" which permitted a new and different perspective and outlook to emerge. The insights which she had lacked due to adverse developmental conditions were clearly engendered in her through demonstrating an emotional causation within her own mind. It was not a treatment directed toward her overt behavior, which was never brought into discussion, but of purely subjective images and associated affects and it emphasized emotive and cognitive variables and other internal events, like her fantasy life. It was the case of a person riddled with subjective experiences involving guilt and self-doubt. This had resulted in her self-defeating attitudes generating overt symptoms.

A criticism of many subjective approaches is that overt behavior changes seldom ensue. In the case of Mrs. Jay, this criticism is certainly not upheld. It should be remembered that traditional behavior therapy had failed to make any significant inroads and that consequently the case was dismissed as "schizophrenic" and unamenable to psychotherapy. Furthermore, the patient's rich and significant fantasies had eluded all behavioral forms of inquiry. While Lazarus does not hold with many of Ahsen's theoretical points of emphasis, he must concede that the usual life-history, fear-checklist, Willoughby Personality Inventory and behavior analysis could not possibly have elicited the crucial data described above. In cases similar to the above he now makes use of imagery in the various ways and means described in this chapter. The net result is an increased therapeutic repertoire which enhances treatment outcome in many cases considered intractable by strict behavior therapists.

It is noteworthy that when, for technical reasons at Eastern Pennsylvania Psychiatric Institute, Mrs. Jay was transferred to Lazarus for therapy (six months after Ahsen had commenced treating her), the patient was most amenable and receptive to behavioral procedures. Now that the major internal sources of her anxiety had been ameliorated, the external factors maintaining various deviant responses were open to correction. This does not imply that all cases require a progression of treatment from "internal" to "external." In a broad spectrum therapeutic approach there is no reason why both approaches cannot be employed concurrently.

While Ahsen's use of imagery and fantasy techniques had almost entirely eliminated Mrs. Jay's somatic complaints and had rendered her less dependent and more mobile, she remained somewhat claustrophobic, socially reticent, unassertive, and afraid of travelling more than a few miles from home. She was also still deficient in feelings of self-worth. Furthermore, she tended to interact with her husband in a passive-aggressive manner and thereby triggered unnecessary tensions in the home.* Methods of assertive training, behavior rehearsal, desensitization, and a variety of rational techniques were all productive in achieving further gains. Several interviews with Mrs. Jay and her husband successfully modified the tension-producing elements in their home. It became obvious, after these joint interviews, that Mrs. Jay was deriving secondary gains from her husband's attention and over-concern. The couple was given a broad outline of operant principles of reinforcement, and the patient's husband agreed to reward a range of constructive behaviors that were pinpointed and listed during the interview.

Significant gains in Mrs. Jay's remaining areas of tension and uncertainty accrued soon after she weaned herself away from home several days a week and obtained employment as a part-time secretary.

A follow-up inquiry after one year revealed Mrs. Jay's progress had not only been maintained but had advanced beyond the point where therapy had been terminated. She has a full-time job, has taken several

---

* Editor's note: In fairness to Ahsen, it should be emphasized that he did not regard his own therapy as "complete" when he transferred the case to Lazarus.

long car journeys and two ocean voyages without any distress, and she is a generally more confident, relaxed and happy person. A second follow-up inquiry, two years later, revealed still further gains.

REFERENCES

AHSEN, A. *A Short Introduction to Eidetic Psychotherapy.* Published in India by Lahore Nai Matbuaat, 1965.

AHSEN, A. *Basic Concepts in Eidetic Psychotherapy,* New York, Eidetic Publishing House, 1968.

AHSEN, A. *Symptom Oscillation Test for Hysterias and Phobias,* New York, Brandon House, 1972.

LAZARUS, A. A. *Behavior Therapy and Beyond,* New York, McGraw-Hill, 1971.

6

An Holistic Approach to Behavior Therapy

MAX JACOBS, M.A. (Clin. Psych.), LL.B.

EYSENCK (1964) WRITES, "The most successful behavior therapists are likely to be those who have a wide grasp of the whole literature, and owe no allegiance to any particular school; the weapons in our armamentarium are not so numerous that we can afford to neglect any that may be there." It is the theme of this paper that effective behavior therapy depends upon the flexible and full use of the available techniques.

However, a perusal of the literature reinforces the point of view that behavior therapy is often mechanistic, concerned with specific techniques, rather than a "total" therapy, as if most patients suffered merely from monosymptomatic neurosis, which can be dealt with by a single procedure. Books on behavior therapy are often descriptions of various techniques, without any attempt to integrate these into a total therapy. We thus have books with such titles as *Behavior Therapy Techniques* (Wolpe and Lazarus, 1966) and *Conditioning Techniques* (Franks, 1964).

The writer in no way wishes to denigrate these excellent books, but only to point out the apparent stress on technique which is associated with behavior therapy.

Not only are monosymptomatic problems, in the writer's experience, rarely encountered, but even the most simple phobia can be viewed in terms of "classically conditioned" autonomic anxiety responses (intervening variables), "operantly conditioned" avoidance behavior and "catastrophic" cognitions about the phobic situation. It follows from this analysis that all three aspects should be dealt with by the behavior therapist. But Wolpe's (1958) technique of systematic desensitization which is most often used in the treatment of phobic conditions (a Classical Conditioning Paradigm) concentrates treatment only on the first aspect. The Skinnerians stress instrumental learning, employ extinction techniques and treat the second aspect, whereas, Ellis (1962) devotes his efforts to cognitive reorganization.

The writer's approach to behavior therapy, which he has arbitrarily labelled "holistic," is to treat, wherever possible, simultaneously the autonomic anxiety, the overt motor responses and the cognitions which go to make up the patient's neurosis. These may be paraphrased as the way the patient "feels, acts and thinks." The patient's anxiety is treated by procedures such as desensitization or deep relaxation; operant techniques are used to modify or condition new motor responses; and the patient's cognitions are modified by such cognitive reorganization techniques as Ellis' Rational Therapy (Ellis, 1962) and Frankl's Logotherapy (Frankl, 1970).

A monistic view of neurosis and its treatment, e.g. the treatment of only one of the above aspects of a phobia, cannot be justified by recourse to learning theory, and behavior therapy techniques are far from adequate and often tenuous (Buchwald and Young, 1969, Lazarus, 1971).

In addition, many behavior therapy techniques cannot be said to be clearly based on any particular theory at all. Rachman and Teasdale (1969) discussing aversion therapy write: "The connections among aversion therapy, psychological theory and verified experimental data are tenuous." Feldman (1966) comes to a similar conclusion. Buchwald and Young (1969) point out that an adequate explanation of how reciprocal inhibition works is nonexistent.

Therefore, if the behavior therapist cannot rely entirely on "learning theory" to justify his choice of technique in treatment, he should base his treatment on the test of effectiveness. This implies that the behavior therapist should not confine himself to a narrow range of treatment methods, but should make use of all methods of behavior modification which have been found effective.

It has been submitted that total treatment requires the modification of autonomic anxiety, motor responses and cognitions. This 3-factor model can be usefully employed to analyze most of the problems dealt with by the therapist, particularly phobias, obsessive behavior, and homosexuality. The use of this model will be described below.

Not only should all three aspects be dealt with, but as many techniques as possible should be brought to bear on the problem. The writer in an earlier publication (Jacobs, 1969) discussed the use of emotive imagery (Lazarus and Abramovitz, 1962) concomitantly with the usual desensitization paradigm in order to strengthen the anxiety inhibitory effects of the procedure. Instead of having items of the hierarchy presented in the usual way, emotive images are produced, e.g., the following two items from a claustrophobic's hierarchy:

"Picture yourself standing in the center of a crowded room at a cocktail party; you are talking animatedly to a very attractive, interested female; you have a drink in your hand and are enjoying yourself." (The emotive images are the attractive female, the drink and the fact that he is enjoying himself.)

or

"Picture yourself in the elevator, going up to the fifth floor. You have just met an old friend in the elevator, whom you are very pleased to see. You are leaning against the elevator and are feeling calm and relaxed." (Emotive images of excitement and pleasure at seeing an old friend, relaxed posture and feeling.)

This method was used with 29 phobics and the results appear, although tentatively, to indicate the increased effectiveness of this approach over that of the usual desensitization procedure.

CASE 1. *Phobic.* Mrs. K. a married woman, in her late thirties. Her presenting problems, of at least 15 years standing, manifested as severe claustrophobia. The phobia extended to flying in aircraft, travelling in elevators, being in trains, buses, cinemas, restaurants, theatres, department stores and other closed, confined spaces. She was even unable to wear jewelry or close-fitting clothes around her neck. She attempted to avoid the above situations whenever possible, but if she was compelled to be in any of them she would panic, severely hyperventilate, feel swollen, develop tachycardia, severe stomach cramps, and tension headaches. Her phobias became exacerbated after the death of her mother in a foreign country three years prior to treatment when she had to fly to her mother's funeral. The problem was particularly debilitating since Mrs. K., who lived in Britain, was an actress and was often required to fly abroad in order to act on stage and television. Further, her aged father resided in South Africa and she wished to visit him from time to time and would have to fly to see him. The patient presented herself for treatment eight days before being due to leave South Africa, where she was holidaying, to return to Britain. She had recurring nightmares of being buried alive and during the first case-history taking interview, it emerged that in the phobic situations she feared she would choke or die (since she felt both short of breath and dizzy as a result of hyperventilation). Another area of difficulty for the patient was that she became very tense when about to appear on stage, lest she forget her lines (needless to say, she had never done so in many years of acting).

Now, if phobic anxiety is to be viewed simply as conditioned anxiety responses to specific situations and stimuli, I would have treated the patient by Wolpe's method of desensitization. Carefully calibrated hierarchies would have been drawn up to desensitize the patient and she might have been admonished not to expose herself too hastily to real life phobic situations unless she could handle them, lest she resensitize herself. Such an approach would deal with the "autonomically conditioned" anxiety, but would pay little attention to the patient's "voluntary" avoidance behavior and cognitions. Furthermore, it became immediately apparent, during the taking of the case history, that the patient reacted in an all-or-none manner to all phobic situations and that it would be impossible to construct hierarchies.

The course of treatment is detailed below and, as can be seen, therapy was directed particularly at the behavioral and cognitive aspects of the phobia.

1st session: The case history was taken. Patient's husband was present during the whole interview. The patient was told that the shortness of breath and giddiness she experienced in the phobic situations were due to overbreathing and she was reassured that no physical harm could befall her in the phobic situations. She was shown how to control hyperventilation by breathing into a paper bag or holding her breath. She was then made to hyperventilate, whereupon she began to panic and weep. She was immediately told to hold her breath. The symptoms ceased after she had done so. Her reaction was one of amazement and delight at discovering that these sensations which had so terrified her were due only to overbreathing and that she could control them. She stated, "Why has no one told me before that it was only my breathing? I actually thought I was physically sick." It was again stressed to her that she could from now onwards control those symptoms and that since she now knew what it was (overbreathing, not a terrible disease) she had no cause to fear them. A learning theory model for the acquisition and maintenance of her phobias was discussed with the patient and her husband (at which stage she remembered that she thought her phobia had started when, as a child of about 6 years of age, she had often been locked up in a cupboard as punishment by a nursemaid). She was told that if she became anxious in a situation and then ran away from it, and subsequently avoided it, she would develop a phobia. Conversely, she was told that if she would expose herself to her phobic situations and make herself remain in them (no matter how bad she felt initially) until she became calm, she would soon overcome her fear. Thus, during this first session the patient was reassured, given a new response to diminish the hyperventilation symptoms, was shown that these symptoms were non-dangerous but controllable (a cognitive reorganization), and instructed not to avoid phobic situations, but, with her husband's help, to seek them out and remain in them for as long as it took for her to become absolutely calm in them. (This might be called *in vivo* desensitization, but the writer feels that the crucial element is the elimination of avoidance behavior habits by non-reinforcement and the learning of new non-avoidance patterns, which will be reinforced by the mere sense of achievement). The patient was also told that if she succeeded in placing herself in and remaining in a phobic situation, she ought to boast of it to as many people as possible. It is clear that this approach is very different from the use of gradual, careful exposures to the phobic stimuli which is the approach usually adopted.

2nd session (the following day): The patient came without her husband and reported feeling much more confident. She had already been in an elevator with her husband and had had little difficulty. She was praised for this by the therapist. The first half of the session was devoted to a Rational Therapy approach in attempting to effect a cognitive reorganization. The patient was made to logically examine her "catastrophic" ideas, i.e. she had for all the years of her phobia thought, "It

is awful and terrible to be in an aircraft elevator, cinema, etc., I hate it."
She was made to replace these thoughts with, "So what if I am in an
aircraft, elevator, etc., it can do me no harm," "It's fun to travel by air,"
"So what if I forget a line on stage, I've never done so yet, nothing will
happen, why should I be perfect?" She was then taught thought stopping
(Wolpe and Lazarus, 1966) and told to use this to block out any
"catastrophic thoughts." Frankl's (1970) technique of paradoxical intention was then brought in to further attack her cognitions and behavioral
responses to the phobias. She was told that whenever she began to feel
anxious in any of the phobic situations, instead of trying to fight and
suppress the symptoms and thoughts which troubled her (e.g. feelings
of dizziness, loss of control, thoughts of death and suffocation), she was
to say to herself, "I know there is nothing physically wrong with me,
I'm only tense and hyperventilating, in fact I want to prove this to myself
by letting these symptoms become as bad as possible." She was told to
try to suffocate or die "right on the spot" and to try to exaggerate her
physical symptoms.

She was then taught a brief modified form of Jacobson's (1938) progressive relaxation. She was told to practice it and to apply it in the
phobic situations to remain calm, but it was stressed that she should
not try too hard to relax or fight the tension. While under relaxation,
desensitization was begun. She was asked to imagine flying back to
Britain. Lazarus and Abramovitz's (1962) technique of emotive imagery
was used simultaneously as part of the scene in order to increase the
anxiety inhibition effects. Thus, the scene was presented as follows:

"You are in the aircraft, you are completely relaxed, you are having
a drink, smoking and having an interesting conversation with your husband. You're sitting back in your seat and looking forward to the delicious
meal which the air hostess is about to serve." The patient was attached
to a GSR monitoring machine. At the third presentation, the machine
showed no response and the patient reported no anxiety. During the first
two presentations, the patient was not asked to stop imagining the scene
as soon as she reported anxiety or when autonomic reactions were shown
on the machine; but she was asked to continue imagining the scene
(while continuously being given suggestions of relaxation) until both the
machine and the patient indicated that the anxiety was becoming easier.
The rapidity of desensitization is attributed to the therapy carried out
prior to desensitization, in particular the teaching of new responses and

cognitions to the patient and the feeling that she could both understand and control the anxiety.

I feel that it is of the greatest importance that the patient realize that he is in control; that he perceive that he is not subject to mysterious uncontrollable forces, but that he has a choice and can choose his reactions to situations, circumstances and stimuli. In this respect my thinking has been particularly influenced by such "existential" writers as Frankl (1970), Sartre (1966), Vizinczey (1969), and by the work of Ellis (1962). Therefore, my patients are taught that it is not situations themselves which are "bad" or "catastrophic," rather it is the way they are perceived and reacted to that usually causes difficulty. For example: a patient with a panic reaction to tachycardia, because he fears dying of a heart attack, would be shown that it is his misperception of the tachycardia as dangerous and awful that is his problem and he can choose to react differently.

Before the patient left the consulting room, she was instructed to seek out all the previous phobic situations, such as elevators, crowded stores, cinemas, restaurants, initially with her husband, then alone; place herself in them and to do the following: to relax as taught, hold her breath if she hyperventilated, to tell herself to let it come, "I don't care, I can handle it, let it do its damndest I want to prove that nothing happens." Perhaps most important of all she was to remain in the situations until completely calm.

3rd session: She was seen two days later and reported that she had carried out her instructions, that she had been in a cinema and restaurant, had travelled innumerable times in elevators alone, and had been in several buses and crowded stores. Although there had been some initial anxiety in the bus and store situations, this had soon dissipated. She expressed disappointment that the cinema was not more crowded, but she had made a point of taking a seat in the middle of a row, not on the aisle. The husband confirmed her improvement. She was again praised for her determination. The session was devoted to further training in relaxation and desensitization to the aircraft phobia, which had been her major fear. During desensitization presentations, no anxiety to the scenes was reported by the patient or indicated on the GSR machine.

4th session: The patient was seen four days later, just prior to her departure, by plane, for Britain. She had maintained her improvement and was feeling no anticipatory anxiety whatsoever regarding the flight she was about to undertake. She reported, and her husband confirmed, that she had been in elevators, buses, crowded stores, in a restaurant and cinema, etc. without any anxiety or fear. She had had none of the psychosomatic symptoms, tension headaches, stomach cramps, tachycardia, had not hyperventilated or swollen up. The rest of the session was spent discussing the lessons she had been taught.

The patient wrote to me, the letter being received two weeks after she had left South Africa. She reported that she had had no difficulty at all during the flight home and that she had been completely free of her phobias. She had also been travelling on London subway trains—which she had not done for many years. Her latest report—now some four months after treatment—indicates that she is maintaining her improvement.

CASE 2. Mr. T., 39 years old, was referred for the treatment of an extremely debilitating obsessive-compulsive neurosis. His neurosis was of 12 years standing. He had undergone various treatments, such as psychoanalytically oriented therapy and E.C.T., both to no avail. He had been spending at least 50% of his waking time in carrying out various ritualistic and checking behaviors so that he was finally unable to work and had to resign his job as an advertising manager. These rituals consisted of (to mention a few): counting all his clothes in his cupboard, (shirts, socks, suits etc.) at least 12 times every morning and evening; constantly examining the clothes he wore in case they were stained or marked (this would take up to half an hour at a time); checking the walls and furniture of his house to see whether they were marked or dirty; checking his car before he could drive it to make sure that it was absolutely clean and that the tools in the trunk were arranged in a certain order; inventing elaborate codes to remind himself not to forget to check; he would have to check through his wallet at least twice a day (for at least 20 minutes at a time) to see and count that it contained all that it was supposed to; checking and arranging the contents of the drawers of his office desk in a certain order. He was unable to tear himself away from light switches, door handles etc.; he felt compelled to constantly remind himself of all outstanding debts he owed and kept repeating certain codes to himself in order not to forget. In addition, he felt compelled to write down every single task he had to do, no matter how minor, and to keep constantly referring to this list. He then constructed a second identical list to check on the first. When the task was completed, it had to be deleted in a particular manner. He also suffered from obsessive-compulsive ruminations such as thinking he would do ridiculous things in public. He had also over the previous 7 years developed an obsession and fear about choking, so that he found it difficult to eat or drink as he became extremely anxious and in trying to force himself to swallow had produced a state of globus hystericus. He found it difficult to cross a road as he thought he might choke when halfway across it. His only help lay in alcohol.

According to an holistic theory, the obsessive behavior would be conceptualized as a learned habit, reinforced because it reduced basic autonomically conditioned fear and also anxieties caused by "catastrophic" cognitions. Most writers (Walton and Mather, 1963; Eysenck, 1960; Haslam, 1965; Wolpe, 1964) stress treatment of "underlying anxiety or autonomic drive"—but this appears too narrow a view (Jacobs, 1967). It would in this case have meant desensitization to innumerable hierarchies (dirt on walls, untidyness, forgetting to pay bills, drinking, eating, crossing roads etc.). Since the patient's compulsive behavior was making life intolerable for himself and his wife and was preventing him from working, it was decided first to concentrate attention on the elimination of these compulsive habits.

The first session was devoted to case history and the giving of reassurance. The next two sessions were devoted largely to discussing the various obsessions, which were listed by the therapist. The patient was then (during the third session) instructed to cease carrying out all the obsessive behavior. He was told that it would be difficult at first, but that if he resisted the desire to carry out the obsessive behavior, it would weaken as the habits weakened (the paradigm of extinction through nonreinforcement had been explained to him). Each obsession which had been listed was dealt with and he was given very specific instructions as to what to do, e.g. obsession 1 on the list was "counting shirts in my cupboard every morning and evening"—he was told to go to his cupboard only to take a shirt out and never to count. His attitude was, "I will do it if you tell me to."

When he came for the next treatment session, he reported that he had been able to desist from carrying out his obsessive acts although sorely tempted to and initially made anxious by nonperformance. He had, however, rapidly found a diminution in the desire to carry them out and was already feeling much better. He delivered over to the therapist all the lists and codes he had previously so carefully made and which governed his life. These were destroyed in front of him. He was then instructed to deliberately set about doing the very things he had so feared and which his obsessions were meant to obviate, until they no longer bothered him. Thus he was instructed to mark the walls or furniture, to deliberately make small stains on some of his clothes, to untidy his desk and car. It was felt that this would be *in vivo* desensitization of the anxiety caused by these stimuli.

The next session was devoted to cognitive reorganization. In particular it was felt important to correct his "internalized sentences," which themselves were a major cause of anxiety maintaining his obsessive behavior. Thus he was asked, "So what if your suit has a stain on it, or you forget to pay a bill, etc."? His "catastrophic sentences" were constantly challenged until he was made to state that it did not matter that the wall had a small mark on it, that it was not the end of the world if he lost a shirt, etc. He was also taught thought stopping to control his obsessive-compulsive ruminations.

At the next session he reported a very strong diminution in all the obsessive behavior, save that of his choking obsession, in spite of the fact that he had not been avoiding crossing roads or eating and drinking. He had, in fact, found it very difficult to eat and (as he had done for many years) he had avoided lunch and taken a great deal of time over breakfast and dinner (which he was only able to consume after vast quantities of beer). He was relaxed and desensitization was begun.

It should be noted that finely calibrated hierarchies were not drawn up. Instead the situations in which the choking response was present were listed (there were six such situations) and the patient desensitized to these. The GSR monitoring apparatus was also used as described above. It would have been extremely difficult to construct hierarchies as the patient tended to react in an all-or-none manner and the amplitude of his choking responses seemed to be equally intense, whenever it occurred. Further, it has been my practice to commence desensitization to situations as high up on the hierarchy as possible. This means that desensitization is begun not with the item of lowest anxiety evocation, but rather to the item of highest anxiety tolerable to the patient. Of course, cognizance is taken of the possibility that if the anxiety is too overwhelming desensitization might not be possible (but cf. Stampfl's Implosion Therapy). However, using the GSR machine and the patient's subjective reports, it is usually possible to assess, after a few presentations, whether the anxiety response to the particular visualization is being reduced. If not, a lower item is presented. In this way, desensitization can be both speeded up and simplified.

The patient was also instructed to practice relaxation whenever eating, drinking or crossing roads. Using the technique of paradoxical intention, he was (after the desensitization) given a glass of water to drink and told to try as hard as possible to make himself choke—which he was quite unable to do. He was instructed to try to choke at least 3 times a day. It can be seen that although the autonomic anxiety factors in this "choking obsession" were particularly strong and had been treated by desensitization, the behavioral aspect was also treated (he was instructed not to avoid eating, etc., as he had done, and by carrying out paradoxical intention thrice daily he was indeed changing his behavior). In addition the paradoxical intention implies a different attitude of "let it happen." He was, of course, reassured that it was impossible for him to choke.

The next few sessions were devoted to further anxiety reduction techniques and the use of paradoxical intention. The patient was also invited to lunch with the therapist on each visit as an *in vivo* desensitization. By the 12th session the patient was able to report the complete disappearance of his former obsessions. He no longer had difficulty in eating, swallowing, drinking, crossing roads, had no desire to carry out any of his rituals, checking, etc., and was not troubled by his obsessive compulsive behaviors. The patient subsequently began work again and at present, after a three-month follow up, has remained completely well.

CASE 3. Mr. N., 37 years of age, desired to overcome homosexuality. He had been receiving psychoanalytically oriented psychotherapy for some years without apparent change. He had been married for 12 years, was the father of three children but had no desire for sexual relations with his wife. He most often avoided this, and only had physical contact "out of duty" to her. He was otherwise happy with her as a person. He had married in order "to cure himself." He was a school teacher and obsessed with thoughts of indulging in mutual masturbation with his male pupils. He would very frequently have homosexual relations with males whom he picked up in bars and at parties. He also frequently masturbated with homosexual fantasies. He had two years previously declared his homosexuality to his wife and the marriage was in the process of breaking up (the wife had promised to remain with him for as long as he was receiving therapy).

An holistic approach is particularly useful in the treatment of homosexuality. A perusal of most reports in the literature, describing the use of various aversion therapies, indicates that the therapists are conditioning aversion or avoidance to only the external manifestations, behavior and stimuli associated with the homosexuality, but that the internal homosexual drive or desire is left untouched, as is the patient's attitude to women and his thoughts and fantasies about hetero- and homosexuality. This comes from seeing homosexual behavior as a conditioned response or habit to external stimuli, rather than as a response to an inner need, desire or tension. It is much the same as forgetting the fact that a conditioned salivary response to a bell can only occur if the experimental animal is hungry or wants food.

An holistic theory would propound that there are three aspects of homosexual behavior: the first an autonomic drive or desire, the second homosexual acts and habits, and thirdly the homosexual fantasies. If only the second aspect is treated, e.g., an avoidance response conditioned to certain classes of men and specific sexual acts, it is quite possible that the patient may still become aroused by other classes of men or male sexual stimuli as his basic drive or desire remains strong. It is noteworthy that aversion therapists have generally obtained poor results in treating homosexuality (Feldman, 1966).

Using a 3-factor approach, the writer adopted the following aversion/ avoidance conditioning procedure for treating homosexuality. At each therapy session the patient is given 10 conditioning trials (using a classical conditioning paradigm to "suppress" the autonomic drive), 10 trials (using an operant avoidance conditioning technique, as described by Feldman and McCullough [1965], to condition an avoidance/aversion response to the external homosexual acts and stimuli) and 10 conditioning trials (using the patient's fantasies as the CS) to deal with the cognitive aspect of the problem. In the first instance, the electrodes of the transfaradic unit having been attached to his forearm, the patient is asked to visualize homosexual acts (which for him are most arousing) and may be shown pictures of naked men, whom he finds to be arousing. When and only if the patient becomes aroused, excited, "worked up" or reacts to his visualizations, he signals to the therapist, whereupon an unpleasant shock is delivered to his forearm and maintained until the patient signals a complete disappearance of the arousal or desire. The procedure is repeated 10 times. Then, with an approach based on Feldman and McCullough (Jacobs, 1969b) the patient is given 10 conditioned avoidance trials. Briefly a picture of naked men or even the words "think of homosexual sex" are projected onto a screen, which the patient is observing. Exactly 8 seconds thereafter, a shock is delivered to the patient's forearm if he does not attempt to avoid the shock by pushing the switch on a control box in front of him. If the patient receives shock, by pushing the switch he removes the picture from the screen and terminates the shock. If he pushes it before the 8 seconds have elapsed, he is allowed to avoid 40% of the time (i.e. as soon as he switches off, the picture disappears and he knows he will not receive shock), he is delayed 40% of the trials (i.e. the picture does not disappear immediately, but after 4 seconds, although he does receive a shock) and on 20% of the trials he is not allowed to avoid and is shocked (i.e. in spite of his switching off, the picture remains illuminated and he is shocked 4 seconds after attempting to avoid). In order to treat the "cognitive" aspect (the patient's usual homosexual fantasies), a stimulus card with the word "fantasy" is used as the CS in the apparatus instead of the pictures of naked men. On being presented with this stimulus, the patient is instructed to bring to mind his usual homosexual fantasies and is shocked until the fantasy disappears.

Mr. N. was treated as follows:

Session 1: Devoted to case history. N. seemed well motivated and was given reassurance.

Session 2: N. and his wife were counselled as regards improving their sexual relationship. In particular it was stressed to Mrs. N. that she should try to understand her husband's problem and that she could help him overcome it by reassuring him that she did not demand any particular criterion of sexual performance from him. Mr. N. had always been tense when love-making with his wife as he had felt that he had to prove his masculinity to her and at least satisfy her. Wolpe's (1958) method of *in vivo* desensitization for impotence was explained to them and they were encouraged to have some form of sexual contact as often as possible. They were told to have long love-play periods and that Mr. N. should only do what gave him pleasure; they were to experiment sexually and not to have intercourse unless N. had a strong desire for it. Mrs. N. agreed to cooperate, to make no demands on her husband and to "let her hair down." N. was told not to try to do well. They were both reassured that the patient was merely suffering from a strong "bad" sexual habit rather than a disease and that with mutual help and understanding he would be able to overcome it. The wife was told that she had to help him learn to like sex with her.

Mr. N. was very strongly instructed not to masturbate (he masturbated at irregular intervals) with male-homosexual images and fantasies; but was told to force heterosexual fantasies into his mind whenever he masturbated. He was also taught thought stopping in order to block out homosexual fantasies whenever he thought of them. The writer feels that unless these steps are taken the patient will merely re-establish his homosexuality in the real life situation in spite of any treatment procedures. The elimination of homosexual thoughts and the substitution of female thoughts is considered essential in the successful treatment of the problem. This is regarded by the writer as part of the cognitive aspect of the problem.

The following 4 sessions (at weekly intervals) were spent in carrying out aversion and avoidance conditioning, as described above. After 2 such sessions, the patient reported a "complete loss of interest in my own sex." He and his wife had been carrying out the instructions given to them and he was able to report a great improvement in his sexual relationships with his wife (confirmed by her); in particular he was both discussing and enjoying sex with her much more than he had ever done. By the 4th session he stated that he felt "completely cured." There was no desire for homosexual activities, he no longer felt attracted to men (he was able to walk in the street without being attracted to any of the male passers-by) and he no longer had homosexual thoughts, fantasies or dreams. His sexual life with his wife was "good." They were having intercourse 3-4 times a week and he was obtaining full satisfaction. Therapy was terminated at this point. The patient was last seen, some 7 months after this date, for a follow-up visit with his wife, when they both stated that he had maintained his improvement.

The rapidity of treatment in the three above cases is attributed to the application of the "holistic" approach. Effective therapy should be rapid; slow improvement, as typified by psychoanalysis, is slow precisely because it is inefficient. For illustrative purposes I have selected three cases with a traditionally negative prognosis who nevertheless responded to direct therapeutic retraining quite spectacularly. The reader should not be misled into assuming that the writer claims such dramatic results for all of his cases. The point at issue is that a direct (and, in the writer's opinion, total) attack on target symptoms employing the "holistic" notion that feelings, thoughts and specific behaviors require specific attention is often extremely rapid and effective. One element in accounting for such rapid and seemingly straightforward gains in the three cases was their respective readiness for change. They had each reached a stage of life where they genuinely desired to effect fundamental changes. Nevertheless, it is my belief that a narrow behavioral approach or a purely interpretive therapy could not have achieved similar results despite the patients' apparent readiness for change. A further possible factor was the stress conveyed to the patients that they themselves could control, or choose to control, their symptoms by a change in their reactions, both motor and cognitive, to their problems.

Many therapists, when confronted by seemingly intractable phobic patients, obsessive-compulsive neurotics or homosexuals, convey an attitude of semi-hopelessness. Perhaps the writer's very firm belief that change (often rapid change) may be expected is a major contributing factor to his therapeutic results. It is hoped that this chapter will lend other therapists the temerity to apply direct, frontal and holistic behavioral methods to some of their more refractory cases.

More recent follow-up data is available for each of the three cases described. Case 1: I saw Mrs. K. and her husband (on a visit to London) 15 months after the termination of treatment. Both confirm that she has remained completely free of her previous symptoms. Case 2: Four months after cessation of treatment Mr. T. became depressed and was diagnosed as suffering from "endogenous depression." He did not respond to anti-depressant medication and was hospitalized. I saw him in hospital and he reported that he had remained free of his previous obsessions until he became depressed. As his depression deepened, he developed a host of debilitating obsessions, different from those for which he had been treated by me. In addition, his previous phobias had remained absent. Case 3: Twenty-two months after termination of treatment, Mr. N. reported that he had had no homosexual desire or fantasy whatsoever. His wife confirmed that intercourse was taking place frequently and "very satisfactorily."

REFERENCES

BUCHWALD, A. M., & YOUNG, R. D. (1969) Some Comments on the Foundations of Behavior Therapy, in Franks, C. M., *Behavior Therapy Appraisal and Status*, New York, McGraw-Hill.

ELLIS, A. (1962) *Reason and Emotion in Psychotherapy*, New York, Lyle Stuart.

EYSENCK, H. J. (1960) *Behaviour Therapy and the Neuroses*, Oxford, Pergamon Press.

EYSENCK, H. J .(1964) *Experiments in Behaviour Therapy*, Oxford, Pergamon Press.

FELDMAN, M. P. (1966) Aversion Therapy for Sexual Deviations: A Critical Review, *Psychol. Bull.* 65:65.

FELDMAN, M. P., & McCULLOUGH, M. J. (1965) The Application of Anticipatory Avoidance Learning to the Treatment of Homosexuality. 1. Theory, technique and preliminary results, *Behav. Res. Ther.* 2:165.

FRANKL, V. E. (1970) *Psychotherapy and Existentialism*, London, Souvenir Press.

FRANKS, C. M. (1964) *Conditioning Techniques in Clinical Practice and Research*, New York, Springer.

HASLAM, M. T. (1965) The treatment of an obsessional patient by reciprocal inhibition, *Behav. Res. Ther.* 2:213.

JACOBS, M. (1967) The Treatment of Obsessive-Compulsive Neuroses by Behaviour Therapy, *S. Afr. Med. J.*, 41:328.

JACOBS, M. (1969) Possible Aids in the Practice of Reciprocal Inhibition, *Medical Proceedings*, Vol. 15:365.

JACOBS, M. (1969b) The Treatment of Homosexuality, *S. Afr. Med. J.*, 43: 1123.

JACOBSON, E. (1938) *Progressive Relaxation*, Chicago, Chicago University Press.

LAZARUS, A. A. (1971) *Behavior Therapy and Beyond*, New York, McGraw-Hill.

LAZARUS, A. A., & ABRAMOVITZ, A. (1962) The use of "emotive imagery" in the treatment of children's phobias, *J. Ment. Sci.* 108:191.

SARTRE, J. P. (1966) *Existential Psychoanalysis*, Chicago, Henry Regnery Company.

VIZINCZEY, S. (1969) *The Rules of Chaos*, London, Macmillan.

WALTON, D., & MATHER, M. (1963) The application of learning principles to the treatment of obsessive-compulsive states in the acute and chronic phases of illness, *Behav. Res. Ther.*, 1:163.

WOLPE, J. (1958) *Psychotherapy by Reciprocal Inhibition*, Stanford, Stanford University Press.

WOLPE, J. (1964) Behaviour therapy in complex neurotic states, *Brit. J. Psychiat.* 110:28.

WOLPE, J., & LAZARUS, A. A. (1966) *Behavior Therapy Techniques*, Oxford, Pergamon Press.

7

Personalistic Family and Marital Therapy

PHILIP H. FRIEDMAN, Ph.D.

THE LITERATURE ON BEHAVIORAL APPROACHES to family and marital therapy has been primarily confined to discussions of behavioral problems with children (Bernal, 1969; Hawkins et al., 1967; Lindsley, 1966; O'Leary, et al., 1967; Patterson, et al., 1968, 1970; Tharp and Wetzel, 1969; Wahler, 1969; Wahler, et al., 1965; Werry and Wollersheim, 1967) or between married couples (Knox and Madsen, 1969; Lazarus, 1968; Liberman, 1970). The approach has mainly consisted of attempts to modify behavior patterns in dyads with only occasional limited attempts to see the family as a complex social system composed of triads, tetrads, etc., with each component of the family system interacting with each other and having continuous feedback effects on the other components of the family system. The theoretical orientation for selecting techniques and conceptualizing problems has been predominantly learning theory and, more narrowly, operant learning theory. Consequently, a relatively restricted range of available interventions in families has been used. Depending upon the referral problem, the concern of the behavior therapist has usually been the deviant behavior of the child, or the disturbed or maladaptive behavior of one or both spouses. The major exception to the above statements has been the recent articles and book by Arnold Lazarus (1967, 1971).

The orientation of the present author is somewhat different from most of the above authors. A broad and flexible approach to intervention techniques is espoused. Therefore, a wide variety of behavioral interventions are used drawn from therapists of many different theoretical orientations. The conceptualization of family and marital problems is an evolving one based empirically on the author's observation of families and also on the groundwork provided by many other observers of family malfunction (Ackerman, 1966; Beels and Ferber, 1970; Framo, 1970; Haley, 1963; Minuchin et al., 1967; Nagy and Framo, 1965; Satir, 1964; Watzlawick, Beavin and Jackson, 1967; Zuk, 1966, 1969). The author, for example, has observed the maladaptive influence of members of three generations of one family toward the disturbed behavior of a child, a spouse or a grandparent. Moreover, the author has observed that, when one member of a family is referred for a behavior problem, between 60% and 80% of the family members demonstrate behavioral problems of their own within two family interaction sessions. This means, for example, that when a family of five is referred for treatment because of a depressed wife or a highly aggressive son, an additional two or three family members are observed to have behavioral difficulties within two sessions, such as underachievement in school, psychosomatic problems, (ulcers, stomach pains, muscle spasms, asthma) impotence or frigidity, suicidal thoughts and feelings, alcoholism, poor peer relationships, difficulty in holding a job, inability to give affection or assert oneself, etc. This suggests, furthermore, an orientation which shows concern for the problems, worries, and dysfunctional or maladaptive behavior of all family members. An attempt is made to improve the behavioral relationships of all members of the nuclear and extended family with each other and often with friends, work associates and neighbors.

The personalistic family therapist uses not only a broad spectrum of behavioral interventions, and a system oriented three generational conceptualization of family problems (Bowen, 1966; Haley, 1967) but also tries to develop a personal relationship with each family member which respects his individual behavioral style, values, beliefs, and cognitions.

He may try to modify each family member's attitudes and the family based attitudes and myths but he does so with compassion and empathy. He considers it an asset to reveal many of his beliefs, desires, feelings, strengths and weaknesses to the family. His purpose is both to serve as a model to the family and to share his role in his own family with them.

WHAT IS THE FAMILY PURCHASING? WHAT IS THE THERAPIST SELLING?

The most obvious answer to the first part of the question is that the family is purchasing a contract with the family therapist to alleviate the symptoms, behavior problems or malfunctions of the person labelled by the family as the patient. Some parents will indicate that no one besides the labelled patient has problems, or dysfunctional or annoying behaviors. However, the therapist and his assistants, if he has any, make observations of their own as to the problems, concerns and interpersonal maladaptive behavior patterns in the family. In many cases the perceptions of the family members and the therapist differ when it comes to defining the basic difficulties in the family. For example, in Family A the parents indicated that their 15-year-old son was frequently truant from school and underachieving but that there were no difficulties with their youngest son or themselves. The therapist, with the help of the 15-year-old son, observed that the parents fought constantly, that the husband ignored his wife's complaints for more affection, a different house and greater occupational efforts by her husband. In addition, the wife had frequent stomach distress and appeared notably depressed. The therapist perceived a marital struggle in these parents in which the mother and father were mutually disappointed that their respective spouse hadn't lived up to their expectations. Also, Mrs. A felt extremely competitive with her brothers who lived nearby but ignored her and Mr. A felt abandoned by his father.

In Family B, the parents also identified the children as the problem. The 12-year-old boy was depressed, confused and underachieving in school while the 11-year-old was having temper tantrums, hitting children at home and in school and threatening to throw himself out the window. These two boys fought constantly with their three brothers and one sister, ranging in age from 4 to 13. The parents spoke with outrage about their own parents but denied any difficulty between them, which the children initially agreed with. The therapist perceived, however, that Mr. B was deeply hurt that his wife failed to appreciate the highly skilled and theoretical nature of his job and that he was blamed for being aloof and uninvolved in family life. Mrs. B was resentful of the lack of affection she received from her husband and of being constantly misunderstood by him.

In Families A and B the family may want to purchase less than the therapist wants to sell them. The therapist may want to sell the parents an improved marital relationship, a different set of interpersonal behaviors with their own parents and a new pattern of behaving with their children. The therapist must first decide whether to adhere to a "limited contract intervention" such as selling the family only behavioral changes in the children. It is the author's belief that it is advantageous to the family members in the long run for the family therapist to be concerned about and try to sell all the family members a comprehensive regimen aimed at alleviating their own problems and modifying their broader behavior patterns even if the family members do not acknowledge that they have problems in these other areas. Moreover, even if the family therapist were to accept a more limited goal, he might believe from empirical observation that change in the labelled patient will not be as effective, rapid or as durable unless parts or all of the three generational system of family behavior patterns are modified.

Whom does the family therapist see during therapy sessions? What constellations of family members are seen during family treatment? Broadly speaking, the family therapist will see children, parents, grandparents, unmarried siblings living away from home, married siblings and their spouses, relatives, boy friends or girl friends, neighbors, school teachers, counselors, principals, theologians, and welfare workers at various times with different families. He may see an individual, the married couple, the siblings, the nuclear family, and the three-generational family including children, parents and grandparents. He may see any of these constellations of family members alone or with other couples or family groups. For example, while the author may see two or three families simultaneously, including parents and children, Patterson (1970) sees couple groups and Lindsley (1966) sees parent groups, i.e. fathers. Moreover, various combinations of family members may be seen at different times. For example, in Family C, the 28-year-old divorced daughter was seen alone for several months, then she and her sister were seen together, and then she was seen with her mother and father for a few months. In family D, the wife was seen alone for six sessions and then the wife and husband were seen for 14 sessions with a child included on occasion.

In Family E the husband was seen alone once. Then the husband, wife and two children were seen twice and finally the husband, wife, two children and grandmother (who lived with them) were seen for 15 sessions. In most cases, however, the nuclear family consisting of mother, father and children are seen regularly in family sessions.

The decision as to who should attend family sessions and when and where they should take place is a complex one. The personalistic approach respects the desires of family members. However, family members may not only differ as to the problems they perceive in the family, they may also differ as to who should be present in family sessions, and when and where they ought to take place. The therapist may agree with one, two, all or none of the family members concerning these decisions, depending on his assessment of the family difficulties. In addition, grandparents, relatives, friends, neighbors, school counselors, teachers, welfare workers, judges and other professionals may all have their own views as to which family members should attend meetings. Moreover, a grandmother may be willing to meet with the family and therapist in the parent's home but not in the therapist's office.

The only rule that can be given is that the family therapist must decide for himself as to what seems most likely to help a particular family and then negotiate with the family members and other members of their ecological environment. The personalistic family therapist respects the differing views of the family members, their ecological network and his own professional judgment and competence. Eventually, through negotiation, persuasion and discussion, a contract is made between family members and the therapist as to who should attend sessions, when, where and how frequently. This negotiated contract between therapist and family is similar in many ways to the contracts between teachers and children and parents and children discussed by Homme (1969), Patterson et al. (1968) and Tharp and Wetzel (1969).

PERSONAL RELATIONSHIP WITH EACH FAMILY MEMBER

Although a personal relationship with the labelled patient is taken for granted, it is just as important for the family therapist to show concern and empathy for other family members because they also may be in emotional distress and may exhibit maladaptive family behavior patterns. Even if other family members do not demonstrate these difficulties, the therapist nevertheless displays compassion and concern to the entire family. It is particularly important that he do so in the initial interviews because later he may want to confront a family member with the consequences of his behavior on another family member. This confrontation is likely to be perceived as moderately aversive to the family member unless the therapist has preceded it with empathic statements that are reacted to in a positive way. For example, in one family a 30-year-old Negro mother came in with her three children. The 17-year-old daughter had just been released from the hospital after attempting suicide by taking an overdose of sleeping pills. The 15-year-old daughter was roaming around the room, ignoring the conversation, complaining about coming, and writing on the blackboard. The mother revealed that she had been pregnant at age 12 and 14, never married, put herself through high school and 2 years of college while working at a bar and worked 16 hours a day. Her urgent tone of voice, and tense facial expression indicated that she was overburdened and under tremendous stress herself. These nonverbal behaviors as well as the frowns and grimaces she made to her 15-year-old daughter were used by the therapist as cues that the mother was depressed and needed some relief from family pressures herself. When this was pointed out to her in a quiet reassuring tone of voice, the mother cried and reached over to touch the therapist's arm. After crying, her facial expression and verbalization indicated that she felt considerable relief.

In the second interview the therapist pointed out to this mother that due to her resentments she never really listened to what her 17-year-old daughter had to say, and that her 15-year-old daughter appeared to be no less defiant and distressing to her than the 17-year-old. Moreover, the therapist noted that the mother herself failed to speak up and tell her own sister, who was older than she and lived upstairs, that she was annoyed with her or that she wanted her sister to stop interfering in her family's affairs. It was pointed out to the mother that she presented a poor model to her daughters if she wanted them to communicate frank and open feelings to her. When the consequences of the mother's behavior were pointed out to her, she initially reacted as if she had been presented with a mildly aversive stimulus. However, if the therapist had not preceded these statements with some empathic and positively reassuring ones she would most likely have perceived them as moderately to extremely aversive and might have withdrawn emotionally and behaviorally from any constructive interaction with her daughters.

The personalistic family therapist uses a wide variety of therapeutic approaches, techniques and strategies with families. Moreover, he tailors the techniques to meet the unique needs of each family.

Relabeling, Cognitive Restructuring and Reconceptualizing Family Behavior Patterns

The family therapist tries to be a perceptive observer of family interaction. He uses a wide range of cues, both verbal and nonverbal, of all family members to organize what he observes into a coherent pattern. Through his previous empirical observation of many other families and the observation of other therapists, he skillfully learns to elicit behavior patterns and affects that would ordinarily be unobservable in the clinical setting. He is particularly attuned to sequences of behavior patterns between three or more family members that occur repetitively.

Eventually the family therapist labels the interactional sequence for the family. His goal is to help the family members to focus on the sequential patterns of behavior occurring in the family. Through repeated labeling by the therapist and other procedures such as charting, graphing and audio and videotape playback, the family members learn to discriminate what is happening in their family from a random series of events. In many families they develop a more accurate, less distorted set of perceptions of family interaction. This new capacity to discriminate more accurately enables them to begin to engage in a new set of behaviors in reaction to the behavioral cues put forward by other family members. In doing so they also emit a new set of behavioral cues. This is the beginning of a more adaptive and satisfying pattern of behaving in the family for all members.

For example, in one family a fairly typical sequence of family interaction occurred whenever the mother was talking about something of concern to her. Then the father would interrupt her. The mother would look irritated and tell him to stay out of the conversation because she had not finished talking. The husband would show a hurt and resentful expression on his face, and turn away from her. He would then look at the 11-year-old "aggressive son" referred for treatment, snap his fingers at him and in a harsh tone of voice demand that the son stop what he was doing and move rapidly over to the couch and sit near his 13-year-old brother. The 11-year-old son would sulk and resentfully comply. Then he would look at his 13-year-old brother scornfully, and lightly hit him on the arm. This provocation would set off the 13-year-old who would hit his brother back. Within 30 seconds the two brothers would be hitting, clawing and screaming at each other. The parents would then temporarily unite. The mother would get very upset and turn to her husband to discipline the boys. He would scream at them and harshly punish one or both of them. The mother would turn on her husband and criticize and insult him for being so ineffective and punitive with the boys. This sequence would occur with minor variations many times. After this sequence was pointed out to the family, the 13-year-old mentioned that at home his mother often insulted his father, who "buries his anger toward her and then takes it out on us." By labelling this sequence on a number of occasions, the therapist taught the parents that the disruptive, aggressive behavior of their sons was a consequence of their own maladaptive behavioral patterns. The next step was for the parents to learn how to resolve their own marital problems so that their anger at each other was not directed at their children.

In another family the grandmother would criticize her 29-year-old married son, who lived with her, for being irresponsible, that is, not working regularly. Whenever the son expressed hurt or annoyance at his dead father, his mother started blaming her son for his irresponsibility, and heavy drinking. He in turn criticized his wife for being inadequate as a mother because she was always so tired, didn't help out around the house and let his mother discipline and comfort their one- and three-year-old children. The son's wife would then meekly criticize the grandmother for being too domineering with her and disapproving of her son. As the sequence continued the grandmother would defensively state that her son, who was adopted, was given the best home environment anyone could reasonably expect. The son would point out that his mother wasn't very affectionate or approving of him and that his father drank heavily as far back as he could recall. This would be denied vigorously by his mother. She would then withdraw all affection from her son, nonverbally as well as verbally, calling him ungrateful and a liar. The son, would become increasingly infuriated at his mother and wife, and would withdraw and pout. Subsequently he would drink heavily and be criticized by his mother and wife for it. He would then drink even more heavily and go out and smash up the car. This repetitive behavioral sequence was described and labelled by the therapist, and the behavioral pattern leading to the son's heavy drinking and car accidents were reconceptualized for the family. In this way the family therapist helped the family members reconstruct the chain of behavioral events leading to extremely maladaptive behavior in one or more members. This cognitive reconstruction permitted the therapist, and later the family members, to constructively intervene into the dysfunctional chain of events at an early stage.

Sometimes what appears to the family to be maladaptive or annoying behavior is labelled by the therapist as adaptive or considerate behavior. For example, in one family, whenever the mother talked about the struggle between her husband and herself for attention and the right to make decisions, the 17-year-old daughter and later the 14-year-old daughter would interrupt, make loud noises, say something mean to her siblings or parents, or hit someone. When the parents were alone they could openly disclose to one another how they each felt threatened by any assertive behavior exhibited by either one of them toward the other or with their children. The parents could also discuss how they retaliated or withdrew in response to it. They were obviously somewhat uncomfortable discussing this area of their marital relationship when alone with the therapist and even more so when the 3 children, 2 girls and a 6-year-old boy, were present. However, whenever the parents began to seriously discuss their behavior and feelings toward each other in front of the children, the annoying, disruptive behavior of the children would intercede and distract the therapist and parents from continuing to discuss the marital problems. The so-called maladaptive behavior of the two children was labelled as considerate of the wishes of the parents not to discuss their marital problems. Consequently, it was pointed out that the alarming behavior of their children served to reduce anxiety in the parents. Although the parents initially protested against the therapist's formulation, in ensuing weeks they reported that on numerous occasions they noticed that they did not have to confront each other with their feelings because of the disruptive behavior of one of their children. Although they felt relieved when this happened, because a marital struggle was avoided, they became progressively aware that this was an unsatisfactory way to resolve their difficulties with each other.

In another family, the 50-year-old husband's vulgar language, temper tantrums and abusive behavior at home were labelled bizarre, dangerous, and almost psychotic by his 45-year-old wife who wondered whether he should be hospitalized. The therapist, however, observing that the wife was silently angry at recent events in the family and markedly depressed, labelled the husband's behavior as considerate and adaptive to his wife's need not to express her anger or to openly face up to her depression because of the anxiety it would generate in her. The husband became noticeably less tense and the wife more uncomfortable when this reconceptualization was presented to the couple. Placing the husband's behavior in a new frame of reference (Haley, 1963) in itself helped to reduce his abusiveness and vulgarity. Also the marital couple's new cognitive set toward the husband's behavior permitted them to explore further their behavior and feelings toward each other and to experiment with more effective ways to deal with marital stresses.

Behavioral Feedback and Interpersonal Consequences

The personalistic family therapist uses a variety of methods to give family members feedback on how they interact with each other. He attempts to help each family member perceive the consequences of his own behavior on the other family members as well as the effects that other family members have upon him. Furthermore, it is also useful for family members to learn to evaluate their reactions, internally and externally, to the ongoing interaction between two or more other family members. The therapist can provide his own verbal and affective feedback to the family by his comments, gestures and facial expressions. Moreover, he can arrange for feedback to be presented via roleplaying, audiotape, videotape or frequency charts.

In order to provide feedback, the therapist may not have to relabel a behavior sequence, but just point out to a mother that although she says she wants her daughter to speak up more, her tone of voice when she says it is harsh and aversive. Or a husband may be told that the way he verbally expresses affection to his wife is unconvincing because of the frown on his face, the sarcastic tone of voice and indirect body posture. Thus, one major area of feedback occurs when the therapist points out the discrepancy between a family member's verbal statements and his non-verbal behavior.

Another opportunity for the therapist to provide feedback occurs when one family member behaves inconsistently toward another family member. For example, a father may comment on how attractive his daughter's dress is but ignore the talented art work which is more important to her than her dress. A wife may approve of her husband's occupational endeavors but criticize his sexual performance even though she says she always says positive things about her husband. A mother may request that her daughter express her feelings and opinions but change the topic or disagree with her as soon as she does. In addition the therapist may give feedback to any family member who inaccurately labels his own behavior or affect. Thus, in one family a mother talked about her own father whom she visited over the weekend. She said she enjoyed the visit and felt good about her talk with her father. However, her facial expression looked very sad and unhappy. When she was provided with this feedback, she initially denied being sad. Later she admitted that she felt like screaming at her father because she was so mad at him for criticizing her children, although she could never tell him this. Interestingly, the 7-year-old daughter had asked for permission to scream at the beginning of the session.

The goal of providing feedback of this sort is to increase the congruence between a family member's verbal and non-verbal behavior and between his verbal behaviors toward a family member at two different times or in two different situations. Lack of congruence in a family member's behaviors decreases his ability to be perceived as predictable by other family members. This causes confusion and conflict for other family members and elicits stressful reactions in them. Furthermore, it makes it almost impossible for them to respond consistently in return.

Feedback can also be given via roleplaying procedures. In one family, for example, the children were asked to play the roles of their parents while the parents played the roles of the children. In their new role the children screamed at their parents, chided them and hit them for misbehaving. The parents perceived for the first time how punitive they appeared to their children and how intensely their children felt about it. By playing the role of their children, the parents could see themselves withdrawing and not wanting to speak up, just as their children did when they screamed at them. The children also learned how difficult it was for their parents to put them to bed at night when they giggled and fought with each other. In this case, both the parents and children learned something about the consequences of their behavior on each other. Also the parents and children learned something about the consequences of each other's behavior on themselves. When each played his own role, the parents discovered that the children's foolishness in the bedroom could easily get them irritated at each other and provoke a fight between them. The children learned how exasperating it was to them to have their parents make such indecisive, sporadic attempts to back up their requests for a change in behavior by the children.

Feedback can also be administered by audio or videotapes. In one family a 37-year-old mother saw herself in the videotape and responded with disgust. "I look just like my mother and hate it," she remarked. In another family, the father saw himself on videotape and said that he never realized before just how timid, frightened and withdrawn he looked when amongst his family. After seeing himself, he became extremely motivated to change his behavior. Roleplaying and videotape feedback can be combined. In one family the father was seen alone for a session and a scene was roleplayed in which the 50-year-old father had a conversation with his own father, a 92-year-old man who would be visiting him that weekend. The father was attempting to express his desire to have his own father refrain from constantly prescribing medical remedies for his son's walking difficulty. When the taperecording of the roleplayed sequence was played back to the father, he remarked that he was much more hesitant and ineffective when talking to his father than he had imagined.*

Feedback can also be provided by charting or graphing the number of times a parent engages in a certain behavior to a child or to a spouse. In one family, for example, the 13-, 12-, 11- and 9-year-old children were asked to keep individual records of the number of times each parent praised them or said something positive or reassuring to them for some behavior they did. The four boys were also asked to count the number of times each parent praised the other parent. The data a week later indicated that for the first two days the boys received no more than three compliments apiece from their father and one to six from their mother. They also indicated, (by writing it down), however, that most of the compliments were bribes or had been said sarcastically. The boys were so discouraged by the minimally positive feedback that they stopped recording after two days. However, they did report unanimously that they saw no instance of their parents complimenting each other except when their father told their mother that he liked her cooking. This information from the boys led to a discussion of the parents' inability to express affection and praise to each other or to their children and how they might try to change their behaviors.

In other situations the therapist may keep a record of how many times a mother praises her son when he behaves properly, or how many times she ignores his temper tantrums, or hits him or screams at him

---

* Editor's note: For a comprehensive treatment of the use of videotape, see, *Videotape Techniques in Psychiatric Training and Treatment*, M. M. Berger, Editor, New York: Brunner/Mazel, 1970.

for misbehaving. The therapist then shows her the frequency chart or graph, which serves as feedback to her of her behaviors in certain situations. The information received from the feedback can later serve as a cognitive cue to the parent to behave differently.

One difficulty that can occur when a family member counts the behaviors of another family member in response to them is that the recorded frequency of positive feedback may be so low that it is aversive to the family member recording, and he may engage in some withdrawal or retaliatory behavior before the next session with the therapist. For example, a 29-year-old husband agreed to stop drinking if his wife recorded every day that she did not smell alcohol on his breath, and his mother (who lived with him) and his wife gave him some praise each day for not drinking. The husband was going to record the number of times his mother praised him. This contract was agreed to by the husband, wife and mother and negotiated by the therapist. The contract broke down when the wife failed to record the number of days the husband did not drink and the mother failed to praise him. When the husband recorded no checks for praise from his mother, he was extremely upset, and angry at her. He left home, got drunk and got in trouble with the law, all before the next meeting with the therapist. This was a considerable setback to the progress which had already been achieved in this family. It was not until after the husband was released from jail that the meaning of the mother's and wife's neglect was able to be discussed with the family.

Feedback can also be given to other families in multiple family therapy and, of course, by one family member to another. For example, a mother upon observing a mother from another family screaming at her 7-year-old son when he fell backward off a chair said to her, "I scream and holler at my children when I'm frightened, too." Not only did this statement provide feedback to the mother who screamed and to all members of her family that she was really scared and not angry, but it also provided feedback in a way that could be easily accepted.

DIRECT INTERVENTIONS

The family therapist directly intervenes into the ongoing maladaptive family behavior patterns in a number of ways. One way he does so is by interrupting a sequential chain of family behaviors at an early stage and by indicating the insidious ways in which repetitive behaviors can become self-defeating. He may ask the family members to change the pattern by engaging in a new set of behaviors. He may change the sequence himself by redirecting the conversation to another family member or back to the family members who are the initial links in the chain. For example, in one family the husband was angrily telling his wife that he wanted to be number one in the family when it came to receiving the attention and companionship of his wife. He felt his two daughters were favored by his wife. His wife complained that he was "nasty" to her and to her daughters and she did not like the way he treated them. The 28-year-old depressed daughter, who often asserted that her parents were incapable of changing, burst into the conversation by blaming her mother for not being sufficiently devoted to her father. Typically, mother and daughter would start a verbal battle at this point and the father would be ignored. The therapist intervened by stopping the daughter from continuing, pointing out that the present battle was between her parents, that she was taking attention away from her father, and that the parents should continue the conversation in order to work out their marital problem. As it turned out, the father indicated that he was nasty to his wife and daughters because he felt neglected by his wife. Since the daughter's depression was partly based upon her feeling that it was hopeless to imagine her parents changing in any way and her marked irritation at her father's nastiness, the successful resolution of the parents' marital problem was beneficial not only to them but eventually to the daughter as well.

In another family, the mother would constantly talk about the inability of her husband to communicate with their 15-year-old daughter. However, on the numerous occasions when the therapist would ask the father to talk to his daughter, the mother would not even permit the father to say one word before she would start talking for her husband or for her daughter. It was necessary to stop the mother from continuing in order to permit the father to talk to his daughter. In another family, the 17-year-old wife would constantly criticize her 18-year-old husband from whom she was separated because she objected to his using drugs, to his going out with the boys all the time, and to his not wanting to take back their three-week-old child from a foster home. The therapist intervened by interrupting the wife when she started her attack again and by asking her to list all the positive qualities she saw in her "hippie" husband. She stated that he was a hard worker and economically dependable, sexually exciting and capable, and affectionate with her and with most children.

The therapist then asked her to give reasons why her husband might be reluctant to keep the baby and why he might prefer to give it up for adoption. She was able to say that her husband might be scared of the responsibility of having a child and unsure of whether he could be a good father. As a result of the wife being helped to focus on what she liked about her husband and upon what he might be afraid of instead of blaming him and condemning him, this young couple was able to reexpress the warmth and affection they felt for each other. Three weeks later they had reunited, and retrieved the baby from the foster home. Additional therapy taught the wife how to become even more perceptive and empathic concerning her husband's feelings and emotions.

In one family, a mother would frequently attack her 11-year-old daughter for being an irresponsible liar and thief and constantly starting fights. The mother usually labelled her daughter the "bad one" after the mother completed a long vitriolic harangue against her own punitive, irresponsible father. Her father had always ignored his daughter. Moreover, the mother's outbursts usually followed a visit to her own parents who lived nearby. It was necessary to interrupt the mother when she started castigating her 11-year-old daughter in order to redirect her back to talking about her intense anger toward her own father (the maternal grandfather). Later it became apparent that the maternal grandmother was an accomplice to the maternal grandfather's physically abusive behavior. When this became evident, the therapist intervened by redirecting the mother's comments toward her own mother. The stored-up anger that the mother felt toward her own mother (the maternal grandmother) was then expressed but with considerable anxiety. The mother was then encouraged to express her feelings directly toward her own mother and father rather than taking it out on her 11-year-old daughter.

In another family, a 55-year-old, overweight, mildly depressed mother on social security complained that there was no communication between her and her three sons, ages 23, 18 and 13. The mother's husband had died 10 years earlier and the mother appeared overburdened trying to raise and guide her active, highly talented and intelligent sons. In the initial sessions, however, the mother talked constantly and rapidly, hardly permitting any of her sons to talk. The therapist consistently stopped her and gently reminded her that her sons had something to say. The mother became easily upset, however, when any of her sons spoke up and complained that she was overprotecting them by restricting their hours out, fussing too much about what and when they ate, and with whom they associated. The mother would then complain about not having a husband around to guide her sons. Eventually, through the therapist's intervention, the 13-year-old would start talking about how he missed his father, whom he had hardly known, and about how rough it was for his mother without a husband. He would talk so rapidly and emotionally that it soon became almost impossible for his older brothers to talk. Consequently, the 13-year-old had to be stopped from talking so that his 23-year-old brother could talk. His 23-year-old brother would then talk resentfully about the way in which his mother held him responsible for his father's death. His mother and younger brother became upset when he expressed these feelings and attempted to cut off his communication to them. The therapist had to intervene on these occasions to maintain an open flow of communications among all the family members. It was not until the 23-year-old was absent for a few meetings, beginning with the tenth session, to coach the track team, that the 18-year-old son spoke up and expressed a range of opinions and feelings about various family members.

The foregoing examples illustrate the need for the therapist to intervene not only in the parent-grandparent subsystem, the marital subsystem, or the parent-child subsystem, but also in the sibling subsystem. Moreover, the therapist should be alert to the fact that family members can get anxious when other family members openly communicate their feelings and beliefs. When this occurs, family members will often try to reduce their own anxiety by cutting off the direct, forthright communications they verbally proclaim to desire. The therapist's judicious interventions help open these channels of communication, thereby fostering confrontations that lead to open, honest and more authentic relationships.

INDIRECT INTERVENTIONS

Assertive Training, Emotional Freedom, Sexual Liberation and Family Relationships

The family therapist can employ an indirect intervention when the behavior to be changed cannot be directly observed. This may occur for ethical or practical reasons. Sexual problems are one area where this is prominent. For example, a husband complained that, in addition to other marital and family problems, his wife was often frigid and he experienced premature ejaculation. Further exploration of this couple's sexual difficulty revealed that the previously observed maladaptive marital interactions had affected the couple's sex life as well. Both spouses vied for control over each other. When either spouse asserted himself by making a decision for the family or couple, the other became threatened. This applied to vacations, weekend activities, meals, and activities with the children, as well as sexual relations. The husband indicated that he did not like his wife reading in bed when he was sexually interested in her. He was afraid to do anything, however, because he felt that "she has a right to read if she wants." Moreover, on the few occasions that he meekly complained about her reading, she would get upset and say that she was tired and just wanted to read and go to sleep. The husband rarely told his wife that he was sexually excited and desirous of having sexual inter-course with her on these occasions. The wife, on the other hand, would tend to read in bed at night whenever the husband had asserted himself during the day with her or the children. She felt threatened by the control she perceived he had over her and the children and she withdrew from him. She then asserted herself in retaliation by stubbornly reading and refusing to get sexually involved. The husband felt resentful when she read because he could not satisfy his sexual desires. This pattern would occur for three to four weeks at a time. When the couple would finally have sexual relations, the wife stated that she felt obligated to first satisfy her husband. It was her "duty as a wife and woman." Conse-quently her husband would become highly sexually aroused when she manipulated his penis, while she remained relatively unaroused. They would then have intercourse and the husband would naturally ejaculate quickly. His wife indicated she did not relax until her husband had an orgasm. Then she was able to relax and let her husband masturbate her to orgasm.

In this situation the wife, who was involved in women's liberation activities, felt extremely guilty when asking her husband to engage in sexual foreplay with her for an extended period of time until she could become sexually aroused. Politically and socially this woman sought liber-ation for females. Sexually, however, she was afraid to liberate herself from oppressive sexual attitudes. The therapist pointed this out to the couple and openly disclosed his own values and attitudes toward sex. He indicated his belief that the wife had a right to request or strongly urge her husband to engage in considerable sexual foreplay with her. He pointed out that a woman has no obligation to satisfy her husband's sex drive first even if in her family women were expected to serve a domineer-ing father. He told the husband that he should tell his wife when he was sexually interested in her and should take the book away from her if necessary. (Interestingly, the 17-year-old daughter had previously frustrated the father in monthly meetings with the three children by reading a book and not participating in the family discussion). He told the wife to discuss with her husband the behaviors he engaged in that were threatening to her. Moreover, he suggested that the wife should stimulate her husband less during foreplay activities so that he would not be as likely to ejaculate as rapidly during intercourse. The result was a remission of the premature ejaculation, an increased frequency of sexual intercourse, an increased number of orgasms by the wife during intercourse, a greater ability to discuss intimate problems, and a raise in self-esteem and pleasure by both husband and wife. Moreover, the wife said she became sexually aroused when her husband would take the book away from her even if it did make her slightly anxious. "He's more of a man when he does that," she said. She respected her husband more for being sexually more assertive. He, in turn, was pleased that she got sexually aroused more often and more intensely.

Since the therapist obviously could not observe the couple having sexual relations, the suggestions and instructions he gave them served as indirect interventions. He could intervene directly on the values and beliefs that the couple expressed toward sex but only indirectly on their sexual practice. The therapist had at an earlier meeting successfully encouraged the husband to take a book away from his daughter, and had successfully encouraged both the husband and wife to openly discuss other behaviors that threatened each of them. These direct interventions served a useful function in augmenting the execution of the indirect interventions.

In another family, a direct intervention was followed by a crucial indirect intervention. In this Negro family, the wife was seen five times individually for hypochondriacal complaints and depression. She had received hypnotic relaxation instructions for three sessions when she came to her next meeting extremely overwrought. While deeply relaxed she was asked to state at the count of ten what she was upset about. She said she was angry at her 6-year-old son's school teacher. After listening to her account, the therapist advised her to talk to the boy's teacher. Two days later she frantically called up to ask if her husband could be hospitalized. A conjoint appointment was scheduled during which the wife expressed considerable frustration with and resentment toward her husband. Over the course of a few weeks the husband in turn had numerous complaints to make about his wife, the most prominent of which revolved around her sexual inhibitions and unwillingness to sexually approach him. The wife wanted more help around the house, more time alone with her husband, outings together at the movies or weekend trips, and an unequivocal statement from her husband that he was faithful to her.

Over the course of 15 sessions the therapist engaged in numerous direct interventions to increase self-expression in both the husband and wife. He openly discussed sexual attitudes and values with the wife in the husband's presence and helped the couple negotiate for desirable behaviors from their spouse. The key intervention, however, was indirect since the wife had to be willing to sexually approach her husband, and engage in intense vocal sounds and rhythmic body movements before and during sexual intercourse. As the wife began to receive the attention and help she wanted from her husband, she started to become sexually less inhibited. He then paid more attention to his wife and was more helpful. Her sexual inhibitions were further reduced and her anger toward her husband abated. In addition, her depression lifted and she stopped having hypochondriacal complaints. Thereafter, the wife spoke proudly of her husband and he was delighted with his wife's sexual freedom.

THE USE OF TASKS AND ASSIGNMENTS

The personalistic family therapist assigns tasks to family members to help them assert themselves in family interactions, free themselves from emotional conflicts and develop improved interpersonal relationships with family members. In the two previous families discussed, this was done by assigning tasks centering around sexual problems and affection. Task assignments, however, can center around almost any conflict area. Often tasks are assigned that require one or more phone calls, letters or personal visits between family members, especially between parents and grandparents. Thus, a 50-year-old married man was encouraged to write a letter to his elderly father expressing hurt and annoyance at the constant demanding comments made by his father. A 45-year-old depressed woman was persuaded to write a letter to her mother inquiring about the problems encountered by her mother in her life. She was surprised to receive a letter, in return, particularly one that stated that perhaps the mother's mother hadn't given her daughter enough affection when she was a child.

A 30-year-old man and his wife were both assigned the tasks of making telephone calls and personal visits to their parents who lived within an hour's ride. The husband had never told his mother how much he cared about his stepfather whom she constantly berated, and his wife had never told her father to stop disciplining her own children harshly, and criticizing her for expressing her own beliefs. Both spouses successfully completed their assigned tasks with increased feelings of self-esteem. The wife, however, was unable to tell her father that she knew she was adopted even though he had never told her.

Frequently, a husband is assigned a task that a wife ordinarily does. For example, the husband is told to put the children to bed at night, to spend weekends playing baseball or working with the teenage boy, or to make a phone call to the child's teacher. In these cases the wife's task is to let her husband take the lead. This is often as difficult for the wife as being the leader is for the man. At other times, the couple may be assigned the task of going out alone together for dinner or a movie. A woman might be assigned the task of taking a vacation, or getting a job, or cooking dinner a certain way, or enrolling in an art appreciation course. After extensive discussion a husband might even be assigned the task of buying a new house long desired by his wife or a wife might be encouraged to get her tubes tied to prevent pregnancy.

Other assignments that can be made are reading certain books such as *The Intimate Enemy*, (Bach and Wyden, 1969) *Between Parent and Child* (Ginott, 1965) or *Living With Children* (Patterson and Gullion, 1968). These books give numerous examples of marital and parent-child problems and many clear-cut behavioral prescriptions on how to deal with them. In this sense they serve as verbal models for family members. One father, for example, after reading *Between Parent and Child* stated, "I never knew you could tell your children you were angry with them. I'd like to try that." A mother, after reading *Living With Children,* said she did not realize one should reward children for good behavior. She always thought children should just behave a certain way because they were supposed to. A young divorcée, after reading *The Intimate Enemy,* indicated that she would never have thought of talking about sexual conflicts with her husband, let alone having constructive fights for more sexual enjoyment. Other books that can be assigned include *The Angry Book,* (Rubin, 1969) or any of the various books by Albert Ellis such as *Sex Without Guilt,* (1965).

PERSONALISTIC ASPECT OF TECHNIQUES AND INTERVENTIONS

No technique nor intervention is administered in a vacuum. Every time the family therapist engages in the cognitive restructuring of a family behavior sequence, or provides feedback to family members, or directly intervenes into an interaction pattern or assigns a task to a family, the family members react in very personal and highly idiosyncratic ways. Many of the reactions of the family members to the therapist on these occasions replicate long standing patterns of behavior in the nuclear or extended family (as previously observed by the family therapist). Other reactions of the family members to the therapist's interventions reflect their own uniqueness. Moreover, the family members sometimes react as a family unit, sometimes as individual family members and sometimes as family subgroups. The personalistic family therapist tries to deal with the family's reactions in a number of different ways and his behavior serves as a model for the family.

One family was given feedback by the therapist on the role of the children in protecting the parents from focusing on their marital problems. As previously mentioned, whenever the parents started talking about their difficulties, first the 17-year-old girl and later the 4-year-old girl started interrupting, making noises, screaming or hitting. The week following the session in which these interactions were identified, the mother entered the room with a particularly sullen expression on her face. Although only her husband was present she was noticeably reluctant to talk. Her husband, who was usually the less talkative of the two, started discussing at some length the outburst by his 4-year-old girl before, during and after the previous week's session. He said she had been acting up for 2½ weeks. He was puzzled since his 17-year-old daughter had been much calmer for the past month.

After mentioning how upset and guilty she was that her 4-year-old daughter was being so vindictive, the mother said that she blamed herself for being a bad parent. She said she was mad at herself and at her daughter. When she was asked if she was mad at anyone else, she said in a soft, methodical voice that she was furious at the therapist for having told her and her husband the previous week that their daughters were being considerate of their needs by protecting them from discussing their marital problems. She said she had thought a great deal about that statement during the week and realized how true it was. However, she was angry at the therapist for confronting her with this information.

"All these years I tried so hard" she related. When asked why she had not said something the previous week, she stated that it was very difficult for her to tell anyone she was angry, especially men such as her husband or father. The therapist had observed in earlier sessions that this woman had difficulty in expressing both hurtful and angry feelings toward her husband. Naturally, this had been one of the focuses of family sessions. Her husband, who had an equal or greater difficulty in expressing angry feelings, then volunteered that he, too, was mad at the therapist because family therapy was making him aware of problems that had not previously been evident (i.e. in his 4-year-old daughter).

On other occasions, the therapist might have only supported their expression of strong feelings and pointed out how uncomfortable they felt about telling the therapist, as well as each other, their parents, friends, and coworkers that they were angry and upset with them. This time, however, the therapist chose, in addition, to tell the couple that since he cared a great deal about them he did not want them to blame themselves, since they were doing the best they could to resolve the family problems. Moreover, the therapist indicated that his feelings would also have been hurt if he had received the same feedback about his own family. In this way the therapist tried to convey that he had emotions too, in relation to the couple, and that he could talk openly about them. He thus tried to serve as a model for the open communication of feelings. He did, however, also discuss with the parents the fact that this aspect of their interpersonal problem, i.e. their failure to openly express feelings, extended into their behaviors toward the therapist. They were encouraged to express strong feelings to the therapist when they experienced them, even at the risk of hurting his feelings. He indicated that he "could take it." In subsequent weeks the parents made noticeable progress in openly communicating hurtful and angry feelings with each other and the therapist.

In another family, the therapist had seen a young female divorcée individually for some months and in the course of therapy felt progressively provoked and irritated by her subtle, sarcastic jibes, and demands for more and more specific advice and therapeutic time. Every specific program planned for her she dismissed in a wailing tone of voice as inadequate and as not benefiting her. Eventually, the therapist gave her feedback on these behaviors and indicated how they were irritating him and making him very angry. It was also mentioned that similar behaviors seemed to be responsible for the fact that she had difficulty in maintaining a satisfactory heterosexual relationship.

When her parents and sister were included in the therapy sessions, it became obvious that many of these behaviors also irritated them. However, although her parents and sister had many charming, positive qualities, it soon became apparent that they also made excessive demands for attention on each other and the therapist. They would make subtle but nevertheless sarcastic comments to the therapist, and would insist on specific suggestions which were then not followed. In the early family sessions the therapist pointed out how the family members engaged in these behaviors with each other and how it created angry and hurt feelings among them which often led to an outburst or resulted in depression. After the eighth family session, the therapist told the parents that they were irritating him with their provoking, sarcastic, demanding behaviors. He was explicit in what bothered him. Previously, he had joked and laughed with them, and referred on a number of occasions to the enjoyable aspects of their family. In many ways they were a very likable family. Consequently, the therapist's very personal feedback to the family was cushioned by his prior positive and empathic statements. The therapist's intention was both to reveal something about his own feelings in relation to the family and to convey the seriousness with which he thought this family behavior pattern was disturbing to others and maladaptive as a manner of getting along within or outside of the family system. Eventually the family members learned to be less demanding and sarcastic with each other and the therapist and more concerned with and empathic to each other's needs.

In a third family, the therapist was so emotionally moved by the sorrow of the father and sons that he openly cried on two occasions. On the first occasion the father was talking in a roleplayed situation to his father (played by his son) about his natural mother who had died six weeks after he was born. His longing for her was so great that the father started crying for the first time in 30 years. Three of his sons, ages 11 to 13, then started crying. On the second occasion, a week later, the 12-year-old depressed son started talking about how upset he was that his father had experienced so many painful feelings during the week as a result of talking about his dead mother. The son cried profusely over the fact that his father had been so depressed and blamed himself for bringing his family into therapy. The father displayed more physical affection to his sons at the end of each session than the therapist had ever seen him show. Moreover, the father indicated that he saw the therapist crying. A discussion followed in which the father indicated that he never knew that anyone cared about him or his children so much. Until those two meetings the father had doubts as to whether the therapist only cared about him in the usual way a professional is concerned about his client or whether he was concerned about him as a person. The fact that the therapist was moved to tears proved to be an important ingredient in the build up of the therapeutic trust with this particular family.

When a family therapist assigns a task to a family, the task may or may not be readily accepted by one or all family members. The therapist may feel strongly that the task is an important one for the family member or members to carry out. However, family members may openly refuse to carry out the task or may verbally accept the task but still not carry it out. The reactions of the family therapist to this set of circumstances can be dealt with effectively in a personalistic way.

In one family the therapist suggested that a 50-year-old man, who was being seen with his wife and children, write a letter to his father telling him how he had always felt neglected by his father who had paid more attention to his younger sister when they were teenagers. In particular, his father used to take long walks with his sister while sending him on errands. His symptom, an hysterical limp, made it impossible for him to walk adequately, and had developed during his teens. He had always felt hurt by his father's neglect and sibling favoritism and resented both his father and sister for it. He had never told his father about these feelings, particularly since his sister died in a tragic car accident. He felt both guilty and relieved at her death; he had never cried over her death.

When the task to write to his father was assigned to this man, he initially agreed, saying that it was a good idea. In the following weeks it turned out that he resisted complying with the task, particularly since he perceived it as a demand by the therapist. He said he did not like to do anything under pressure because his father had always made demands on him and he had always complied like an obedient child. He was encouraged to tell the therapist openly and directly when he disliked any of his suggestions and particularly to state if he was annoyed at the task assigned. In the following weeks the man was able to state more directly his annoyance at suggestions made by the therapist. The therapist made no further mention of the letter. Two months later, however, the man indicated that maybe it would be beneficial for him to write a letter to his father as previously discussed. His wife volunteered to help him write the letter. It was necessary in this case to allow a sufficient amount of time to pass so that the initiative for the task came from the client. This was especially important for this man whose usual style of asserting himself was by resisting the desires or requests of other people. If the therapist had insisted on his writing the letter, he would not have done it and therapy progress would have been retarded by the resentment accruing from the client toward the therapist. It is also important to note that many suggestions made or tasks assigned by the therapist will be complied with only after a delay of from a few weeks to several months.

It is of some interest how the information about this man, his father, sister and symptom development was obtained. The mother was talking about the death of her mother at the age of three and how she had never seen her father cry when her mother died. The therapist then described a personal experience that had recently had a profound impact on him, the memory of which had been elicited by the wife's comments. He discussed a recent conversation he had with his father who told him about the tragic death in an automobile accident of his younger brother when he was 22 years old and his brother was 7 years old. The therapist's father, who by family reputation never showed his emotions, cried profusely on that occasion, and his son, the therapist cried with him. The only other time the therapist had ever seen his father cry was when his grandfather had died.

The therapist was looking at the mother while telling the story but he noticed that the father became very emotional while the story was being told. When the father was asked what was upsetting him, he stated for the first time how upsetting his sister's death and his feelings toward her had been to him. Previous interviewing had revealed only minimal information about his sister, his father and himself and the affect attached to this triangular family involvement. The personal self-disclosure by the therapist had positive ramifications well beyond the intended goal, which was to share a related experience with the mother. It released in the father some strong affects and some important information about his past life which still bothered him in the present. This led to the assignment of a task, writing a letter, designed to eventually establish a new set of constructive emotional communications between this man and his father.

In another family, the therapist assigned an overweight, depressed, widowed mother of three sons the task of taking a vacation for herself and getting involved in more activities from which she would derive personal pleasure. The mother, who spent almost all her time around the house or in the community doing things for others, constantly complained about being overworked but resisted complying with the therapist's suggestion. She insisted that her sons, ages 13, 18 and 23, should do more to help her around the house but all indications, including actual charts of their work, showed that the boys helped a great deal. In this case, the therapist persisted and for almost two months he urged her to get involved in some activities for her own enjoyment. She did make an occasional trip to the swimming pool and spent one evening out with some woman friends, but she always found some reason or other for not taking that long-desired vacation.

The therapist inquired about the mother's own family and found out that her parents placed a high value on dutiful, constant work on behalf of the family. Thus, to take a vacation would, in the eyes of this woman, have been disloyal to the family's values. After acquiring this information, the therapist switched tactics somewhat and put pressure on the sons to encourage their mother to go on a vacation and to verbally and physically express affection to the mother so that she would not have to work constantly to feel loved. Again the therapist persisted in his approach with only minimal success for a few weeks. The 18-year-old son did express some affection to his mother which initially embarrassed her. However, it was only after the 23-year-old son entered the service and the 18-year-old son went to work in Maine that the seeds of the therapist's efforts began to bear fruit. The two oldest sons wrote their mother frequently and comprehensively about their activities and showed obvious concern for their mother's wishes in making important decisions. The 13-year-old son agreed to go on a 10-day vacation to the shore with his mother, accompanied by a friend and his parents. The mother seemed very pleased by these events, was no longer depressed and looked much more attractive and cheerful.

In another family, the mother appeared to be markedly depressed over the fact that she did not feel loved by her parents. She was an adopted child but her parents had never told her that she was adopted. She had accidentally found out about this when she was 13 years old. Her own daughter also complained that she felt unloved. The mother complained that her daughters would not talk to her when things bothered them. It was pointed out to the mother that she did not serve as a good model for her daughters since she never told her parents, whom she frequently visited, her true feelings. The mother was assigned the task of telling her parents that she knew she was adopted, felt unloved by them and bewildered as to why she had never been told of her adoption. The mother was very reluctant to carry out this assignment and resisted doing so for the next two weeks. The therapist initially employed verbal persuasion. However, in subsequent weeks the mother still did not respond to these pressures and was getting obviously annoyed at the therapist for inquiring about it. The therapist then asked the mother if she felt that he was picking on her, since she looked so perturbed. She admitted feeling irritated by the therapist's insistence since she did not wish to tell her parents about the adoption. The therapist agreed not to mention it anymore. The therapist's empathy with the mother's irritation and willingness not to pressure her further appeared to facilitate the mother's openly revealing for the first time that she was extremely angry at her husband because of the arbitrary demands he placed upon her. A very important series of discussions between the mother and her husband followed, centering around their marital problems. Sometimes a task assignment will not be acted upon by the family member, but will catalyze change in an important area that is related to the one focused on by the task. This is more likely to occur if the therapist will empathize with the family member's emotional reactions to carrying out a difficult task.

The personalistic approach to task assignment implies that sometimes the therapist needs to persist in his endeavors to assign a task and sometimes to desist. Furthermore, it implies that sometimes the therapist needs to switch tactics and to use other family members as levers of task assignments. Each family is unique and the type of task, timing of the task and reactions to the task must be carefully tailored to each different family.

FAMILY THERAPIST AS LEADER, ADMINISTRATOR, NEGOTIATOR, DEMONSTRATOR, EXPERIMENTER, COACH AND PARENT

The family therapist often temporarily becomes the leader of the family while they explore new territories in family relationships. He lets parents know that it is alright to talk about most emotional conflicts in the presence of their children. He asks questions that will elicit these conflicts and reassures the parents that the family, including the children, will benefit by openly discussing and resolving family problems. Thus, in one family which was very overcontrolled in their emotional and physical expressions, except for the 11-year-old son's uncontrolled bowel movements, the therapist prodded the parents to talk about their marital and family difficulties in the presence of the children. The parents protested that this would be harmful to the children which included a 17-year-old son, and 4- and 8-year-old girls. They did not want to bring the children to family sessions and even attacked the therapist for firmly stating he would not see them alone.

Since this family had had previous therapy in which the mother, father and oldest son had been seen in their own group or individual sessions, the therapist perceived that the family needed to work on problems as a family. He admitted to the family that it would be difficult for them but that he would lead the way for awhile. By the third session the father began talking about his inability to be sympathetic to his wife and children and his wife started talking about her inability to express direct anger to her husband or her own mother who lived nearby. The oldest son complained that he only got through to his father after constant arguing with him, and the 11-year-old son said that he was scared when he heard his parents fighting because they might hurt each other. The mother, moreover, admitted that she and her husband could never reach agreement on any decision. These open revelations enhanced communication among and between family members.

There are times when the personalistic family therapist must demonstrate to the parents how to express affection, verbally and physically, to their spouse or children, and how to control or enforce limits on aggressive or disruptive behavior when it occurs. In this sense he serves as a model to the parents (Friedman, 1968, 1971, 1972; Liberman, 1970; Patterson, et al. 1970). In one family the father indicated that he had never received praise or physical affection from his father, so he found it almost impossible to give affection and praise to his sons. The therapist would spontaneously put his arm around one of the sons, rub his hair or compliment him. Soon after, the father would tentatively reach over and touch his son. Eventually, the father could put his arm around his son or rub his hair affectionately or compliment him on helping around the house. However, the father needed to receive some affection and praise himself since he had never received any as a child from his father. When the therapist complimented him for being affectionate to his sons, being considerate of his wife's needs, or completing assigned tasks, he was being like a "good parent" to this father. The personalistic family therapist tries to recognize the needs of each family member and is not reluctant to be a "parent" when it is necessary. In the case of this family the therapist also demonstrated how the father could compliment the mother when she stopped criticizing him or the children. Not only did the wife receive praise from the therapist which she had rarely received from her parents, but the husband had a model to observe for giving compliments to his wife. The husband gradually became better able to express affection and praise to his wife.

Although it is difficult to define, it is important for the family therapist to demonstrate ways and means for family members to display empathy, compassion and concern for each other. Praise and affection are usually not enough to maintain a cooperative, emotionally gratifying family system. An ability to know what each family member feels in various situations and an ability to communicate that knowledge is an important ingredient of family relationships. Furthermore, the capacity to enhance positive feelings or to reduce negative feelings is often more important than giving praise and affection. Thus, in the previously mentioned family the therapist modeled compassion and empathy for both the husband and wife. He did this by the questions he asked, the statements he made about their feelings and the tone of voice and facial expression with which he made them. Eventually, the wife learned that when she complained that her kitchen was too small and ranted and raved about it, her husband's feelings were hurt. He considered himself as the family provider, and perceived his wife's criticism of the kitchen as an indication that he had inadequately provided for his wife's needs. When the wife realized that by "letting off steam" she was hurting her husband's feelings, she found other ways of venting her emotions. The husband also learned that his wife felt neglected when he listened to music through earphones and worked late at night. He not only learned to identify his wife's needs but to care about them by spending more time with her.

The personalistic family therapist models empathic concern for each spouse's feelings towards their children and towards each other, and for their feelings towards their own family of origin. The events which disturb or concern each person in relation to his own parents may have occurred in the past or in the present, but one's feelings exist in the *present* and consequently are contemporary experiences. It is this therapist's belief that some degree of compassion or empathy by one spouse for the other spouse's feelings toward his own parents is necessary for a successful marriage. Moreover, the children will perceive the compassion one parent has for the other parent's feelings and learn how to show empathy and compassion themselves.

In one family the mother constantly blamed the family's problems on her husband's "neurotic" family who caused her husband to be so "mixed up." The husband, on the other hand, blamed many of the problems on the wife's family for not having been considerate of his wife or children. Both parents had strong feelings of despair, rage and guilt toward their parents, but rather than receiving empathy for their feelings from their respective spouse they each gave and received condemnation. "Because of your parents, you hate and despise them, which messes up our children and causes me grief," was a fairly typical paraphrase of their statements. The family therapist replaces condemnation with compassion. He demonstrates how each parent can help his spouse to show concern and respect for the other's feelings. The children in turn learn to appreciate and show compassion for their parent's problems not only with each other but also with their family of origin.

Roleplaying scenes can sometimes be used to elicit intense feelings that otherwise stay submerged. When these feelings do emerge, the personalistic family therapist models empathic concern. Naturally, he must himself experience these emotions before he can demonstrate to others how he feels. For example, in the M. family the husband was asked to have a conversation with his natural mother, Carol, who died when he was 6 weeks old. The wife played the role of Carol while two chairs were placed back to back. Mr. M. quickly became very emotional and said that he simply could not do it. The therapist encouraged him to do so, after which Mr. M. said the feelings he had were very painful. The therapist then played the role of Mr. M.'s father. A long conversation ensued in which Mr. M. spoke to his "father" about his natural mother and his stepmother. Again Mr. M. said it was very painful for him to talk about his feelings towards his two mothers. He told his father that he thought life would have been very different for him if his natural mother, Carol, had lived. He wanted to know what she was like as a person and what her desires were. Mr. M. indicated how much resentment he had to his stepmother for putting him down all the time and to his father for supporting his step-mother and not wishing to talk about his natural mother. The therapist empathized with his feelings of hurt, sadness and anger while at the same time trying to convey in the role of "father" how upset he felt when his "wife" died.

In the most emotionally moving sequence of this role enactment, Mr. M. started crying because of his sadness over never having met his natural mother. He had not cried in 30 years. His 11-year-old son, referred for hyperaggressiveness, became restless at this point and looked as though he wanted to participate. The therapist asked him to play the role of Mr. M.'s father. He did so and responded to Mr. M. in an extremely soft, concerned tone of voice. Mr. M. then reached out for his son and pulled him toward him. His son started crying profusely and Mr. M. wrapped his arms around his son and continued to talk to him about how painful and distressing life had been for him for 30 years of his life. At the same time, Mr. M. was very reassuring to his son who indicated he wanted to spend more time with his father. As Mr. M.'s other two sons began to cry, the therapist also felt tears streaming down his face. He had never seen the sons express concern and care for their father in this way.

In another family the therapist demonstrated how to enforce limits on disruptive and aggressive behavior in 4-, 6- and 9-year-old boys. The young mother of these boys, who was divorced, was noticeably affectionate with her children, at least with the two youngest ones, but she was unable to restrict them when they ran around inappropriately, hit each other, talked incessantly or threw temper tantrums. The therapist demonstrated both time-out and incentive procedures for controlling her children's behavior. The children were told specifically during a family session that if they got out of their seats during a five (later ten and fifteen) minute period, or if they hit each other, interrupted the ensuing discussion or threw a temper tantrum, they would be put across the hall in an empty room for five minutes. Whenever these behaviors occurred, the therapist promptly put the disruptive child or children in the "time-out" room for five minutes. If the child stayed quiet for specified lengths of time, he would receive M and M's, praise and later earned time as "keeper of the clock" (kitchen timer). After watching the therapist demonstrate this procedure a few times in the clinic and once in the home, using the bedroom as time-out room, the mother gradually became fairly adept at administering the contingencies herself. In fact she improvised upon them by substituting toys and television time for "good behavior." At first, it was somewhat difficult for this mother to deprive her children even briefly, because of her very deprived background. The therapist empathized with her feelings about her past and by modeling "time-out" procedures reassured her that she would still be a "good" mother if she deprived her children of attention and toys for disruptive behavior as long as she continued being affectionate with her sons when they were not disruptive.

The family therapist serves as a negotiator among family members.

He helps them bargain amongst each other for behavioral changes that are most meaningful to each person and to the family as a whole. His job is to aid family members in evaluating what changes in other family members they desire most, how intensely they feel about these behavioral changes and what changes in their own behavior they are willing to make in exchange for behavioral changes in the other family member or members. The family therapist encourages family members to engage in this "exchange process" on their own but coaches them in the bargaining process when they appear to need guidance or support. In many ways the personalistic family therapist does what Zuk (1966) calls the "go-between" process, while aiding family members to learn what Bach calls bargaining or constructive fighting (Bach and Wyden, 1969).

In one family, for example, a 15-year-old son referred for effeminate behavior and two homosexual episodes wanted his mother to stop babying him by constantly asking him if he had cleaned up his room, brushed his teeth, finished his homework, eaten his vegetables, etc. The mother, in turn, wanted her son to start participating in teenage male activities instead of spending all his time engaged in feminine activities with girls. The therapist supported both mother and son by affirming that these were legitimate requests for behavioral changes and every effort should be made by both parties to exchange one desired behavioral change for another. This twosome needed to be prompted in subsequent weeks to keep their end of the bargain, but eventually they succeeded. In a married couple, the therapist mediated a bargain between husband and wife for more affection expressed verbally and physically by the husband and more uninhibited sexual involvement by the wife. This meant that the wife would engage in more physical movements and vocal sounds during sex and the husband would put his arm around his wife, kiss her, compliment her and smile at her more frequently. For the first few weeks this couple complained bitterly that each spouse was not keeping to the bargain, but by the fifth week the husband was not only showing more affection but he was also taking his wife out to shows and movies more often and the wife in turn was willingly initiating sexual activities in an uninhibited way for the first time in their marriage.

Sometimes a family member may wish to exchange some behavior that the therapist does not consider especially relevant or important. For example, in one family the mother was willing to exchange television time with her sons for cleaning up the living room and bedroom every day. In the process of negotiating an agreement between the mother and her sons, the therapist was aware that the mother was not completely satisfied with this arrangement and was bothered by something else despite her harangues against her sons. Further questioning revealed that she wanted her husband to supervise her sons' cleaning up since she claimed that he almost never helped her out with the children. She was, however, afraid that he would get very angry at her for mentioning this. The therapist then started to mediate a behavior exchange between husband and wife. This led to further complaints by the wife about something which she felt more intensely than the fact that her husband failed to supervise their sons' house-cleaning activities. She wanted her husband to pay more attention to her even when the children were not involved. He wanted more respect from her and fewer attacks on him as a father, a husband and a provider. The bargain that was finally negotiated was for the husband to spend at least two hours twice a week talking to his wife about things that bothered her, and for the wife to stop attacking the husband for not making enough money and for being a poor father. The therapist's task was to elicit the strongest concerns of each person, support each person in bargaining for those concerns, and try to keep the discussion from becoming a vicious battle rather than a negotiated exchange of desired behaviors. In subsequent weeks, the sons in this family asked their father to spend more time with them by going bowling, going to the museum and taking rides in the car. The implicit contract agreed upon between father and sons was for the boys to help their mother more in exchange for more time with their father.

Another area in which the family therapist often has to aid families is in negotiating conflicts between spouses and in-laws. Wives frequently complain that their mothers-in-law are the first to hear about a promotion or an argument on the job, or that their husbands speak to their mothers when they want comfort and not to them. Husbands complain that their wives spend endless hours neglecting them while talking to their mothers on the telephone and taking advice from their mothers and not from them. The therapist mediates these conflicts by trying to establish what bothers each person the most and negotiating with the couple for the desired behavioral changes.

The family therapist serves both as an administrator and negotiator when arrangements are being made with school principals, teachers and counselors to change a child's behavior. Thus, when one school felt extremely harassed by the destructive behavior of an 11-year-old boy, arrangements were made with the principal to restrict the boy's school day to afternoons and to eliminate all free play periods and lunch hours when the hitting, kicking and screaming were most prevalent. This administrative decision was arrived at by the principal in consultation with the therapist and imposed on the family as a precondition of family therapy. The family was told that when the boy's behavior became less disruptive he would gradually be allowed to come to school for a longer part of the school day. At first the boy was delighted to be out of school for half a day, but his mother did not like it very much. Moreover, after a week this boy felt lonesome and left out of school activities since all of his friends were in school. In addition, the boy's father made a contract with his son that helped to eliminate the disruptive behavior. He offered his son five dollars if he did not get any bad conduct marks on his next report card. However, one bad conduct mark, that is an F in conduct, would cost the boy ten dollars. When the boy was abusive in school, the teacher sent a note home to his parents. The father reminded him of the potential ten-dollar penalty. The son reported later that after this occurred he became scared that he would lose two months allowance if he was not careful. The aggressive behavior in the school situation ceased rapidly after the principal's time-out from school contract and the father's reward-penalty contract were put into effect.

The personalistic family therapist is continually trying out new approaches to family therapy in order to increase his effectiveness. Some of these new approaches will eventually be incorporated into his repertoire and others will be discarded. For example, encounter group and psycho-motor techniques appear to offer promising methods of enhancing family therapy. Family members have been instructed to yell at the top of their lungs together, hug each other, arm wrestle with each other, or hit pillows held by each other while indicating how angry they are at the other person. They can also be asked to mimic another person, to physically suppress another person or to caress a family member. These and other non-verbal encounter techniques may eventually expand many of the approaches currently being used. The personalistic family therapist espouses an atheoretical orientation to the methods he employs. He is always experimenting and searching for ways to be more effective with more families. If he is willing to learn and grow, his only limitations are his own abilities and ethical restrictions.

OVERVIEW OF PROBLEMS SEEN, BACKGROUND AND RESULTS

Of the twenty families seen between January 1969 and June 1970 which did not involve a psychotic family member, six were seen exclusively for marital problems. In fifteen of these families one or more family members was markedly depressed or suicidal. In five of these families separation or divorce was seriously contemplated. In six of these families there were sexual problems. Three families were headed by a mother only. In over half the families, at least one family member was withdrawn or noticeably unassertive. In seven families one person was excessively aggressive. There were major psychosomatic or hypochondriacal complaints in two families, underachievement in four, excessive alcoholic drinking in three, theft and lying in two, and overweight in two. As previously mentioned, symptoms were evident in an average of 60% to 80% of family members. Different symptoms existed in different family members, although it was not unusual for depression to exist in more than one family member or for one family member to be depressed while another one was overly aggressive. Based on the occupation of the father, or of the mother if there was no father living, eight families were of middle class background and twelve were of working class background. Eighteen families were white and two were black. Depending on how stringent the criteria for success one employs, between 70% and 80% of the families were successfully treated and between 45 and 50 people in these families benefitted from the treatment. These figures are based on the therapist's estimate of behavioral changes in the family and the family's reports of decreases in symptomatic complaints. Whenever possible, follow-up questionnaires and phone calls were employed. The length of treatment ranged from three hours to sixty hours. Eight families had ten hours or less of family therapy, four had between ten and twenty hours, three had between twenty and thirty hours, and five had between thirty and sixty hours of therapy. Even in the families receiving from thirty to sixty hours of therapy per family, the amount of therapy time was only between eight and twenty therapy hours per person helped. Since the possibility of bias always exists when a therapist evaluates his own cases, additional independent, objective research is needed to adequately determine the effectiveness of the personalistic approach to family and marital therapy. It is expected, however, in keeping with the personalistic emphasis, that as this approach is applied to a wider range of families, particularly the lower socioeconomic, disadvantaged families, some variations of the present approach will have to be made.

SUMMARY

The personalistic approach to family and marital therapy is an outgrowth of a broad-spectrum behavioral approach to therapeutic interventions, a system-oriented three-generational approach to conceptualizing family and marital problems, and a humanistic concern for the uniqueness and worth of each family. The personalistic family therapist respects the values, attitudes and behavior of each family member as well as the interrelationships among the values, attitudes and behaviors of family members. He tries to establish a personal relationship with each family member and empathizes with each individual family member's distress. However, he also engages in the relabeling, cognitive restructuring and reconceptualizing of maladaptive family behavior patterns for the family in order to clarify the sequence of events leading to disturbed or dysfunctional behavior. This is a preliminary intervention which, along with giving behavioral feedback to family members and pointing out the interpersonal consequences of each family member's behavior, sets the stage for the therapist's direct and indirect interventions.

Direct interventions consist of having family members stop engaging in maladaptive behavior patterns and engage in more constructive behaviors in the therapist's presence. The therapist redirects behavioral sequences, instructs family members in new behaviors, elicits suppressed behaviors, and uses modeling and roleplaying techniques. In addition, he uses his own affect to facilitate behavioral changes in the family. Indirect interventions center around the tasks and assignments the therapist gives to a family between therapy sessions. These interventions are designed to increase assertiveness and affection while decreasing destructiveness, reduce sexual inhibitions, fears and guilt, produce emotional release, and generally improve family relationships. The personalistic approach to task assignment recognizes that family members often carry out difficult tasks only after considerable emotional turmoil and delayed compliance with the tasks. Consequently, the therapist deals with the family's reactions to assigned tasks in a variety of ways designed to maximally facilitate change.

The personalistic family therapist tailors his interventions to meet the specific needs of each family. Moreover, he willingly reveals something about himself as a person to the family in order to serve as a model for intimate relating. He tries to demonstrate to the family ways to express affection, anger, disappointment, sadness, and delight. Finally, the personalistic family therapist realizes that to be effective with families he will often have to adopt at different times a variety of roles, such as leader, administrator, negotiator, demonstrator, experimenter, coach and parent.

REFERENCES

ACKERMAN, N. W. *Treating the Troubled Family.* New York: Basic Books, 1966.

BACH, G. & WYDEN, P. *The Intimate Enemy.* New York: Morrow and Co., 1969.

BEELS, C. C. & FERBER, A. Family therapy: a view. *Family Process,* 1969, 8, 280-332.

BERNAL, M. "Behavioral feedback in the modification of brat behaviors" *J. of Nervous Mental Disease.* 1969, 148, 375-385.

BOWEN, M. The use of family theory in clinical practice. *Comprehensive Psychiatry.* 1966, 7, 345-374.

ELLIS, A. *Sex Without Guilt.* New York: Grove Press, 1965.

FRAMO, J. L. Symptoms from the viewpoint of the family therapist. In N. Ackerman (Ed.) *Family Therapy in Transition.* Boston: Little, Brown & Co., 1970.

FRIEDMAN, P. The effects of modeling and roleplaying on assertive behavior. Unpublished doctoral dissertation. Univ. of Wisconsin, Madison, 1968.

FRIEDMAN, P. The effects of modeling and roleplaying on assertive behavior. *Advances in Behavior Therapy,* Vol. II., New York: Academic Press, 1970.

FRIEDMAN, P. The effects of modeling, roleplaying and participation on behavior change. In B. Maher (Ed.) *Progress in Experimental Personality Research.* Vol. VI. New York: Academic Press, 1972.

GINOTT, H. *Between Parents and Child.* New York: Macmillan, 1965.

HALEY, J. Toward a theory of pathological systems. In Zuk, G. and Nagy, I. (Eds.) *Family Therapy and Disturbed Families.* Palo Alto: Science and Behavior Books, 1967.

HALEY, J. Marriage therapy. *Archives of General Psychiatry,* 1963, 8, 213-234.

HAWKINS, R., PETERSON, R., SCHWEID, E., & BIJOU, S. Behavior therapy in the home: amelioration of problem parent-child relationships with the parent in a therapeutic role. *J. of Experimental Child Psychology,* 1967. 4, 99-107.

HOMME, L. *How to Use Contingency Contracting in the Classroom.* Champaign, Illinois: Research Press, 1969.

KNOX, D. & MADSEN, C. Behavior therapy and marriage problems. Unpublished manuscript. East Carolina University and Florida State University respectively.

LAZARUS, A. Behavior therapy and group marriage counseling. *Journal of American Society of Psychosomatic Dentistry and Medicine,* 1968, 15, 49-56.

LAZARUS, A. In support of technical eclecticism. *Psychological Reports,* 1967, 21, 415-416.

LAZARUS, A. *Behavior Therapy and Beyond.* New York: McGraw-Hill, 1971.

LIBERMAN, R. Behavioral approaches to family and couple therapy. *American J. of Orthopsychiatry,* 1970, 40, 106-118.

LINDSLEY, O. R. An experiment with parents handling behavior at home. *Johnstone Bulletin,* 1966, 9, 27-36.

MINUCHIN, S., MONTALVO, B., GUERNING, B., ROSMAN, B., & SCHUMAN, F., *Families of the Slums,* New York: Basic Books, 1967.

NAGY, I. & FRAMO, J. L. *Intensive Family Therapy.* New York: Harper and Row, 1965.

O'LEARY, K. D., O'LEARY, S., & BECKER, W. C. Modification of a deviant sibling interaction pattern in the home. *Behavior Research and Therapy,* 1967, 5, 113-120.

PATTERSON, G. R., COBB, J., & RAY, R. A social engineering technology for retraining aggressive boys. In H. Adams and L. Unikel (Eds.) *Georgia Symposium in Experimental Clinical Psychology,* Vol. II, New York: Pergamon Press, 1970.

PATTERSON, G. R. & GULLION, M. E. *Living With Children: New Methods for Parents and Teachers.* Champaign, Illinois: Research Press, 1968.

PATTERSON, G. R., RAY, R. S. & SHAW, D. A. Direct intervention in families of deviant children. *Oregon Research Institute Research Bulletin,* 1968, Vol. 8, No. 9.

RUBIN, T. *The Angry Book,* Toronto: Macmillan Co., 1969.

SATIR, V. *Conjoint Family Therapy.* Palo Alto: Science and Behavior Books, 1964.

THARP, R. G. & WETZEL, R. *Behavior Modification in the Natural Environment.* New York: Academic Press, 1969.

WAHLER, R. G. Oppositional children: a quest for parental reinforcement control. *J. of Applied Behavior Analysis,* 1969, 2, 159-170.

WAHLER, R. G., WINKEL, G. H., PETERSON, R. F., & MORRISON, D. C. Mothers as behavior therapists for their own children. *Behavior Research and Therapy,* 1965, 3, 113-124.

WATZLAWICK, P., BEAVIN, J., & JACKSON, D. *Pragmatics of Human Communication.* W. W. Norton and Co., 1967.

WERRY, J. & WOLLERSHEIM, J. Behavior therapy with children: a broad overview. *Journal of the American Academy of Child Psychiatry.* 1967, 6, 346-370.

ZUK, G. The go-between process in family therapy. *Family Process,* 1966, 5, 162-178.

ZUK, G. Triadic based family therapy. *International Journal of Psychiatry,* 1969, 2, 538-549.

The author wishes to acknowledge the fact that Dr. Arnold Lazarus first introduced the term personalistic psychotherapy in his book *Behavior Therapy and Beyond,* McGraw-Hill, 1971.

The author is extremely grateful to Dr. Lazarus for the many hours he spent with him discussing the application of the personalistic approach to specific therapy clients. The extension of the personalistic approach to the family therapy field lies primarily with the present author, however.

The author would also like to thank Dr. Lazarus, Dr. Munjack, Dr. Crocco, and Margaret Olsen for their constructive comments and suggestions on the first draft of this paper. In addition, the author would like to thank his colleagues Dr. Ivan Boszormenyi-Nagy, Mrs. G. Spark, Dr. G. Zuk, Dr. L. Robinson and Dr. R. Crocco for the many hours they have spent talking with him about family therapy and for all he has learned from them. He recognizes, however, that the point of view taken in this paper is not necessarily consistent with his colleagues' frame of reference.

8

Training Patients to Communicate

GERALD W. PIAGET, Ph.D.

IT IS UNFORTUNATE that our society spends so much time teaching its members arithmetic and history, and so little time showing them how to share thoughts and feelings with one another. The result is a large group of alienated, lonely, anxious people who do not know how to communicate effectively, are not as creative, productive, or as happy as they could be, and who do not understand why they feel vaguely unfulfilled. Our consulting rooms are full of these people.

Much of the worth of traditional psychotherapeutic interaction probably results from the communication training opportunities inherent in its structure. However, these specific training benefits often become lost within some sort of subjective process orientation, and are never exploited to their fullest extent. Based on the tenets of learning theory, behavior therapy with its more technical approach is uniquely suited to optimizing the development of communication training benefits in the one-to-one setting.

Behavioral anxiety reduction procedures and communication training techniques have much in common and serve complementary needs. Anxiety reduction techniques alone provide nothing to replace the dysfunctional habits they remove. Successful desensitization creates a kind of behavioral void, one which can facilitate the recurrence of maladaptive response patterns. (In some cases, of course, the desensitized patient "fills the void" himself by learning adaptive responses to previously feared stimuli.) Most communication responses are incompatible with anxiety, and may help overcome certain fear reactions. However, communication training often generates new behavior patterns which, initially at least, are not powerful enough to counteract the mountains of anxiety experienced by severely neurotic individuals who are asked to change long-standing social habits. *Combining anxiety reduction therapy and communication training into a single, integrated program serves to minimize the problems inherent in each individual approach, while maximizing the potential benefits to be gained.*

In practice, a good many therapists successfully employ a broad spectrum therapy-training potpourri of one kind or another. This chapter describes one such program.

CHARACTERISTICS OF GOOD AND BAD COMMUNICATION

For training purposes, communication may be defined as *an ordered process of data transfer from one individual (the sender) to another (the receiver).* The sender's job is to transmit a message as clearly as possible; the receiver must accept the message without modifying it in any way, and then let the sender know that his message was received. Then the participants usually switch roles: the new sender originates a message based in part on the information he has just received, transmits it to the new receiver, and the process continues. Spontaneous, two-way communication involves the rapid and continual exchange of roles, with each party alternately functioning as sender and receiver. (This model describes dyadic peer-level communication; however, it is easily expanded to cover group interaction and other types of interpersonal behavior.)

On a behavioral level, interpersonal communication is a very complex process. The "sender Gestalt" is made up of a large number of discrete, but interrelated, movements; the power with which a message is sent is determined by the nature, quality, and pattern of these molecular behaviors. Similarly, a large number of discrete behaviors combine to generate a "receiver Gestalt" that determines the power (sensitivity) with which a message is received. *The concepts of sender power and receiver power are central to this communication training model: essentially, the patient/ trainee is taught to be a powerful sender and receiver of messages.* The powerful sender transmits messages clearly, quickly, and accurately, in a manner the listener finds easy to understand. The powerful receiver facilitates transmission, makes sure he understands what was sent, and then firmly acknowledges receipt of the message.

Several patterns of behavior which seem to characterize powerful communication have been isolated. Some are individual in nature and others involve interpersonal skills. A few require extensive training to master, but most are quite simple and can be learned with little effort. The presence of these qualities in dyadic communication promotes rewarding and successful interaction; in their absence, communication is not effective and eventually breaks down.

Some of the performance characteristics which facilitate powerful communication are described below. The list is not exhaustive, and not every item on it must be reflected in successful communication. Some are specific to particular kinds of communicative behavior and may even be contraindicated in certain situations. As communication skill can be rated in terms of the presence or absence of these characteristics, the following list can be used to advantage as a training guideline in communication courses and therapy/training sessions. It is presented in greater detail by Piaget (1971).

1. *Intention to communicate:* The sender looks and acts as if he wants to be understood, and makes sure that he is understood. The listener looks and acts as if he wants to understand, and makes sure he does understand. Communication vehicles include attention, acknowledgment, reflection, verification, vocal quality, and other nonverbal cues.

2. *Role clarity and division:* The sender sends, the receiver receives. Participants try not to do both at once or send simultaneously. Problems involving role division (how much time each party spends sending relative to how much time he spends receiving) and related expectations are handled.

3. *Verbal skill:* The sender delivers his message clearly and concisely. He speaks in concrete terms when possible. He sends the message he wants to send and not some other. Vehicles include a well-developed, topic-related vocabulary and verbal fluency.

4. *Affective skill:* Participants take responsibility for and advantage

of their ability to communicate on a feeling level. Communication vehicles include verbal and nonverbal cues, emotive expression, and the ability to employ such process skills as empathy and positive regard.

5. *Congruence:* The sender looks and sounds the way he says he feels. His verbal and nonverbal behaviors transmit similar messages. Participants send and receive only when they wish to do so. Attention and interest are never faked. Termination occurs on time.

6. *Facilitation:* The sender makes it easy for the listener to hear his message by tailoring the method and intensity of its transmission to the particular strengths and weaknesses of the receiver. The receiver makes it easy for the sender to send by creating a receptive, nonjudgmental atmosphere. Participants reinforce one another for communicating.

7. *Troubleshooting:* Participants can recognize and modify contracommunicative behavior in themselves and one another. Bad communication may involve unintentional response patterns, destructive intent, manipulative intent, or the absence of such qualities and skills as are described in this section. Successful troubleshooting depends primarily upon perceptivity, feedback, and technical skill.

8. *Personal qualities:* Intelligence, personality, sensitivity, flexibility, anxieties, tension level, self-image, energy level, and many other personal characteristics help determine an individual's ability to communicate effectively. Willingness to be trained also falls into this category.

Communication breakdowns occur when several desirable performance characteristics are absent from the dyadic interaction. These breakdowns reflect the presence of maladaptive habits and/or the absence of necessary skills. Usually, both problems are involved.

1. *The participant may possess certain response patterns which serve to inhibit, rather than facilitate, effective communication.* This category may be further subdivided:

a) When part or all of the sender's behavior is designed to produce internal gratification *directly* (bypassing the receiver), a "short circuit" develops, resulting in considerable energy drain. Short circuit reactions usually occur in the service of anxiety reduction, although other types of motivating behaviors (e.g., anger, sex drive) may be involved, as well. "Nervous" habits (such as giggling, loss of eye contact, and inappropriate anger) exemplify the kind of behavior which leads to inefficient communication. Anxiety reduction is a powerful reinforcer, and such habits are often difficult to eliminate.

b) Certain spurious reactive components may be reflections of residual habits: responses which at one time served a purpose, but are no longer necessary and have become more of a hindrance than a help. These behaviors are maintained through a self-reinforcement mechanism: they have been a part of the sender's response pattern for so long that dropping them would introduce anxiety-producing novelty into his life. It is easier for him to go on as always, carrying the unnecessary weight of antiquated behaviors with him in spite of the long term annoyance they cause.

2. *The sender or receiver may not possess certain interpersonal skills necessary for effective, powerful communication to occur.* It may not be what the patient/trainee is doing wrong that matters as much as what he is not doing right. Consider the enterprising, young shoe salesman who arrives home from work each evening, promptly, at 5:30, heads straight for the television set, and seldom emits more than a grunt until dinner is served at 8:00. He may not *wish* to treat his wife as if she were unimportant to him; part of the problem may be that he does not know how to implement appropriate expressions of empathy and warmth. Through the years, his lack of interpersonal skill may have led to reward patterns which extinguished behaviors involving emotional expression. Similarly, the recently terminated desensitization case who no longer fears the interpersonal setting may, yet, avoid attractive females at parties simply because he does not know how to "break the ice."

SETTING UP THE PROGRAM

The patient who stands the best chance of deriving benefit from a regimen like communication training is the one who believes that the program is in his best interest and, therefore, is well-motivated to participate actively in it. Certain individuals are surprised and somewhat threatened by the training model (communication training does not fit many people's projection of what psychotherapy is like). However, a brief description of the importance and desirability of being a potent communicator is usually sufficient to allay the patient's initial fears and give him a "common sense" understanding of the approach. In addition, if the therapist tailors his discussion as closely as possible to his patient's presenting complaints and other specific needs, he should have little difficulty in presenting the concept of supplementary communication training in an appealing manner.

The amount of session time that should be spent on anxiety reduction and the amount spent on communication training vary with each patient.

Usually, the first few sessions are used to reduce anxiety. As therapy progresses and hierarchies are completed, the balance of time spent often sways toward training. Both approaches can be used in each session as long as anxiety remains a major problem. (It is not always easy to say which procedures are aimed at which goal. Several techniques provide the simultaneous benefits of training and conditioning; this is particularly true of roleplaying technologies.)

As the behavioral anxiety reduction procedures used in the program are well known (systematic desensitization, implosive therapy, and modifications thereof), the present discussion will relate itself primarily to the implementation of communication training. However, in practice the two approaches are employed together.

Data Collection

During the first few sessions the therapist attempts to experience the patient as both a sender and a receiver in order to decide how his communicative behaviors might be improved. A recommended starting point is to ask the patient what communication skills he would like to develop, and whether there are any related behaviors and/or feelings that he would like to change. Roleplaying, in its many and varied forms, is helpful—particularly in conjunction with the use of participant-observers. A behavior checklist can be used to mark target behaviors and facilitate objective comparison between observer reports. The use of standard checklists and objective rating scales yields specific information which is difficult to obtain in other ways. Occasionally, stress interview techniques are helpful. Consulting with the significant others in the patient's life often produces valuable information.

Feedback

One major problem facing the therapist/trainer is how to implement necessary training procedures without seeming critical or judgmental to his patient. The individual who begins by saying, "Well, here is a list of the things you are doing wrong," stands a good chance of limiting his future worth as a reinforcing agent. By allowing the patient to make his own decisions regarding those communicative behaviors which warrant change, it is possible to circumvent unnecessary power struggles and increase the patient's chances for positive movement. The therapist's initial task is simpler when his patient's problems revolve primarily around lack of adaptive response patterns, rather than the presence of dysfunctional habits. It is easier for most patients to entertain the possibility that they do not possess certain communication skills than it is for them to confront the idea that some of their pet mannerisms are contraproductive.

The therapist's opinions, biases, phraseology, topic selection, etc. have a decided effect on the patient, no matter how "nondirective" he tries to be. The important variable is the *skill* and *sensitivity* with which his selected experience is fed back to the patient. This phase of the operation can be initiated by saying something like, "Now, let's take a look at some of the communication techniques you, yourself, use and try to get some information about how they affect other people." Subsequently, any number of procedures may be used.

a) The participant-observer may be asked to return and give the patient feedback. (A checksheet proves valuable in this context.) This method provides the patient with outside opinion, and allows the therapist to remain somewhat neutral.

b) If equipment is available, videotape feedback of patient behavior proves uniquely valuable in that it allows the patient to respond to himself as a "third person." The therapist may facilitate the encounter by asking his patient such questions as, "How does it make you feel, when he (pointing to monitor) moves his arms like that?". Some individuals are powerfully motivated to change certain response patterns simply by seeing themselves on tape. When videotape is unavailable, verbal recordings of roleplaying situations may serve a similar, if less impressive, function.

c) In the absence of videotape equipment, the therapist may employ role reversal procedures to show the patient how he looks and acts.

d) Another valuable roleplaying device calls for a modification of the Gestalt "two-chair" procedure. The therapist has his patient play himself while sitting in one chair, and a specified third party (wife, boss, enemy, stranger, etc.) while in the other chair. While in the "other chair," he is asked to see and react to himself as he might do were he the individual whose role he is filling. He switches chairs at will to facilitate role clarity during this interaction. The patient is instructed to give himself feedback from the "other chair," regarding the quality and effect of his communicative behavior. The therapist may provide the alter-ego in either role to get his own points across. In another variation, the *therapist* roleplays with the patient's "other chair," or with a personality of his own choosing. The patient, as observer, listens passively. In this way, it may be possible for the therapist to "allow his patient to overhear" information which would be threatening to the patient if communicated directly. Variations on these themes are nearly endless.

No doubt, many feedback techniques can be devised. Again, feedback information is meant to help the patient decide which behaviors he wishes to drop from his repertoire and which interpersonal skills he wishes to develop. The therapist should reinforce those decisions with which he agrees. Obviously, he has a good deal of control over the target behavior choices his patient makes, no matter which feedback techniques he employs. The important thing is that the patient feels no one is telling him what is right or wrong, what is good behavior or bad. For optimal training results, the patient must feel that the training emphasis decisions he has made are primarily his own.

Contract

It may be helpful to draw up a written or verbal contract containing the target behavior(s) the patient has chosen to attack and the behavior change goals he has set for himself. The contract goals can be set forth in "graded structure" form for reinforcement value. (In this modification, the patient's training goals are organized into a series of progressive steps, and usually are presented to him in writing. As the training sessions proceed, he is allowed to "graduate" from one step to the next, each graduation being enthusiastically reinforced by the therapist. It is felt that the reinforcement value of this procedure provides the patient with increased motivation to change.) In some cases, a "time-limiting" clause may be added to the contract: certain goals are projected for specific dates. The contract is signed by both patient and therapist, and is kept handy for easy reference at all therapy/training sessions.

Technique Selection

The therapist/trainer is acquainted with a large number of communication training techniques; it is his job to suggest and then to implement those he feels are most suited to his patient's specific needs. As noted above, training techniques differ as to function: some are oriented toward removing maladaptive behavior, and some are intended to sharpen desirable communication skills. Cross-sectionally, they may be subdivided in terms of focus: some techniques develop sender power, some receiver power, and others facilitate both aspects of training. All good communication training techniques, however, have three qualities in common:

a) They provide a vehicle for the *modeling* and/or description of effective behaviors.

b) They provide a vehicle for the *reinforcement* of desirable behaviors.

c) They provide a vehicle for rapid and accurate *feedback control* (letting the trainee know when he is doing something right or wrong).

THERAPY/TRAINING TECHNIQUE APPLICATION

The communicative techniques described below are as diverse in theoretical origin as they are dissimilar in training function. They are fairly representative of the range of techniques which can be used to supplement anxiety reduction procedures in a therapy/training session, although many more than these are available. Most of these procedures are essentially unresearched; the data that do exist to support their effectiveness are largely empirical. In the following section, technique sources have been referenced for the reader who wishes more detailed process information than is presented here.

Elimination of Dysfunctional Behavior

Janet L. was an attractive, intelligent twenty-nine-year-old divorcée and mother of two who came to treatment seeking relief from what she described as "constant tension, nervousness, and worry." Further discussion revealed that Janet had a current boyfriend whom she "loved," but of whose affections and marital intentions she was not sure. She said that she was often the "life of the party" with friends, but wished she could feel more confident among strangers. When asked to describe herself, she mumbled such phrases as "kind of pretty" and "sort of fun to be with" in a tone of voice that screamed, "Boy, I really think I'm blah, and so will you!". These responses were directed, not at me, but at a spot on the floor three feet in front of Janet's chair. It soon became apparent that Janet planned not to look at my eyes at all unless she absolutely had to. When I suggested that she maintain eye contact while we talked, she did manage to focus on me for a short while. However, simultaneously with this new found assertion, her hand shot to a curl on her forehead and from then on she managed to hide at least one eye and half her face behind her forearm at all times.

Several additional "short circuit" behaviors became evident during that first hour. Janet "talked with her hands" excessively, and repeatedly varied the volume and tone of her voice more than was necessary to emphasize her point. She stressed words in a manner which suggested that she was not sure she could say what she wanted to say in the way she wanted, but did not quite know what else to do. Her tone of voice was vaguely apologetic and her occasional assertive verbalizations were invariably accompanied by compromising behaviors, such as: nervous laughter; shrugs; arm, leg, and hand movements; and the inevitable breaking of eye contact. While she talked, her body was turned away from me about sixty degrees. She constantly, crossed and re-crossed her legs. When not weaving in the air, her right arm was clasped tightly across her stomach, held in place by the "death grip" she maintained on her left bicep. Her left forearm, as noted earlier, was usually held in front of her face.

In reaching our therapeutic contract, procedures such as those described in the preceding section were employed with no major problems arising. As a result, Janet and I agreed to work toward the following therapeutic goals, and attempt further progress in other areas once these goals were reached.

1. *Anxiety reduction* through relaxation training and the systematic desensitization of hierarchies developed in three related areas: criticism, rejection, and expression of anger.

2. *Communication training* aimed at a) increasing assertive behavior (basically, Janet needed to learn how to stand up to people like her boyfriend) and b) decreasing the number and frequency of spurious movements and unnecessary sounds accompanying her verbal response patterns. Specific target behaviors cited were: breaking of eye contact, arm or hand in front of face, unnecessary arm and leg movements, inappropriate tonal emphasis, and unnecessary sounds (particularly, nervous laughter, clearing of the throat before speaking, and use of unnecessary antecedent words, such as "well").

Desensitization and assertive training are familiar techniques which need not be described here. However, it may be interesting to consider two of the retraining procedures used to help Janet reduce some of her communication-inhibiting patterns. They are not often applied in this context. The first involves a form of negative practice, a procedure which has been notably successful in reducing the severity of stuttering and multiple tics (e.g. Yates, 1958). It also seems to be effective in helping patients like Janet control undesirable, but semi-voluntary movement patterns.

TECHNIQUE #1: *R. I. D.* Patients who are made to imitate maladaptive habit patterns at some length and in the absence of anxiety-producing cues sometimes learn to control the habit. Proponents of the mnemonic device may introduce this technique to their patients as a means of getting R.I.D. of problem behaviors, explaining that the capital letters represent the words *recognize, imitate,* and *drop.* For negative practice to be successful, the patient must imitate precisely the maladaptive behavior he wishes to eliminate, and then repeat it many times. In this way, he either a) extinguishes the behavior via repetition *sans* reinforcement, and/or b) brings it under more precise, conscious control, thereby acquiring the power simply to *choose* not to perform it (depending on which theoretical system one happens to prefer). Whatever the dynamics, negative practice seems to work relatively well for certain stubborn habits.

The second procedure was developed by L. Ron Hubbard (1961) to help his students practice behavior control in the face of anxiety-producing cues.

TECHNIQUE #2: *Bullbaiting.* The therapist presents his patient with a graded series of increasingly stress-producing, verbal and behavioral cues (gestures, jokes, criticisms, insults, references to embarrassing situations, etc.). The student is not permitted to respond to the therapist at all, but must continue to perform some specific communication-related task (e.g. asking a question). Any visible reaction to the therapist is noted as a mistake, and the process is begun again. Successful trials (specific periods of time during which the therapist is unable to elicit a reaction from his patient) are strongly reinforced (praise and attention are the usual rewards). This procedure bears a resemblance to *in vivo* desensitization, the major differences being that in bullbaiting no hierarchy is written out beforehand, and no counter-conditioning response, such as relaxation, is specified.

In Janet's case, R.I.D. and Bullbaiting proved quite effective in reducing the frequency of target behaviors specified in our therapeutic contract. In all, we spent seven half-sessions using these techniques. Janet was surprised at the initial difficulty she had in deliberately duplicating some of the patterns she had been performing spontaneously and perfectly for years. Incessant verbal feedback from me and visual feedback from a mirror especially positioned for the purpose soon helped her recognize and master the necessary movements. For repetition practice, we implemented a roleplaying process in which Janet held imaginary two-way conversations with a life-sized Joe Palooka punching bag. During her conversations with Joe, Janet initiated her various target behaviors, first in response to a signal from me, and later on her own. Daily homework sessions of a similar nature were assigned. During her fourth session of R.I.D., Janet reported feeling in control of most of her target behaviors and said she was bored with the technique. We initiated Bullbaiting procedures at that time. Janet acted out conversations as before, this time with me, while I applied a graded series of anxiety-producing stimuli to try to force her to react, particularly in the form of target behavior. Although Janet later reported feeling anxious occasionally during the Bullbaiting sessions, she evidenced a marked reduction in incidence of target behavior almost from the beginning, and continued to improve with each session. I soon found myself hard-pressed to come up with a Bullbaiting cue that would elicit so much as a twitch. Janet reported concurrent improvement outside of therapy as well. At that point, we switched our primary training focus from the elimination of maladaptive habits to the development of positive, assertive response patterns.

At termination three months later, Janet and I were both quite pleased at the extent of her progress with regard both to skill acquisition and anxiety reduction. Could Janet have sustained similar gains without help from the learning techniques described above? Only controlled research can provide answers to such questions. Empirically, these techniques seem to facilitate the elimination of dysfunctional habits, and help provide a solid behavioral base upon which to anchor the subsequent development of adaptive communication skills.

Training in Emotional Expression

It is commonly believed that unexpressed emotion can generate considerable physical tension which, in turn, can lead to anxiety. Several therapeutic approaches to this problem are popular today. For instance, the Reichian therapist trains his patients to scream on the assumption that the consequent tension release is intrinsically therapeutic. Alexander Lowen and other proponents of the bio-energetic movement stress the need for congruence between feeling and physical expression. Behavior therapists (e.g. Goldstein, et al., 1970) have used anger responses coupled with violent physical activity to counter-condition anxiety and facilitate subsequent assertive behavior. Encounter-oriented therapists encourage free expression of emotions for a variety of reasons.

From a communication standpoint, emotional expression is an efficient way to send certain kinds of messages: for one thing, little doubt is left in the receiver's mind as to how the sender feels. Unfortunately, many people find it difficult to express intense emotion in a congruent manner. Instead, they bottle up anger and fear until the tension becomes unbearable. The catharsis value in the resulting explosion seldom compensates for the negative social consequences and guilt reactions which usually follow.

TECHNIQUE #3: *Emotive expression.* The patient is given a book from which he is asked to read aloud into a taperecorder for approximately a minute. Then he is requested to read the same passage three additional times, donning a different *emotional role* with each repetition. On the first repetition, he is to sound as happy as possible. On the second run he is to sound very sad. During the final repetition he is to express as much anger as he possibly can. After completing these assignments, he is allowed to listen to the tape. Patients who are chosen for this kind of training usually sound pretty much the same all four times. (One effective feedback technique is to stop the tape at random during rewind and ask the patient if he can tell from the sound of his own voice which emotional role he was attempting to portray.) If the patient is unhappy with his performance and requests training in this area, the therapist may proceed as follows:

a. The therapist role-models various modes of verbal expression which communicate pleasure, and asks the patient to mimic him. When the patient can do so accurately, he is asked to reread the book passage while modeling happiness. The therapist coaches his patient, enthusiastically praising all positive gains until the patient really does sound happy while reading.

b. The procedure is repeated for sadness and anger in that order.

c. When both therapist and patient are satisfied with the latter's improvement, another session is taped. The patient is asked to compare his "before" tape with his "after" tape for additional reinforcement effect. Patients who are concerned with the artificiality of the training situation are assured that a generalization of learning will take place.

d. The patient's homework assignment is simply to try to sound happy, sad, or angry whenever he experiences these emotions. The therapist discusses with him the implications of being able to sound the way he feels.

TECHNIQUE #4: *Shout training.* This is an expressive training technique for the individual who finds it difficult to raise his voice. Basically, the patient is instructed to say a neutral sentence or phrase again and again, each time slightly louder than before, until he is yelling at the top of his lungs. If desired, the patient may be requested to pound a hassock or punching bag while he yells. Later in training, he is asked to shout appropriate material directly at the therapist, another trainee, other third party, or at an inanimate object. Gradually, the complexity, emotional content, and personal relevance of the target phrase may be increased. The training is complete when the patient no longer feels reticent to raise his voice in nonthreatening situations. The response may then be used as a counter-conditioning agent in desensitization, or as a bridge to more socially appropriate anger responses in assertive training.

Roger T. was a smallish, balding, married, thirty-five-year-old drafts-man who had received analytically-oriented therapy off and on for a period of years. Somewhere along the line, his condition had been diagnosed as endogenous depression, although he suffered from a wide range of emotional problems and maladaptive habit patterns. From a communications point of view, one of Roger's most significant characteristics was his chronic flatness of affect. He never raised his voice in anger or joy, but spoke in a constant nasal monotone. Assertive training, which was the major therapy technique used, was only moderately successful. Of the many procedures tried with Roger, emotive training was one of the few that seemed to have any lasting effect.

Roger T.'s reaction to these techniques was rather interesting. This mild, sullen, passive-aggressive individual became an accomplished shouter, and learned to express several different kinds of spontaneous emotions. His wife, for one, was delighted; evidently, Roger was becoming increasingly more bearable to live with. Even Roger seemed to be deriving more pleasure from life. Unfortunately, he moved from the area before completing treatment and no follow-up was attempted.

Training in Receiver Skills

Listening is anything but a passive art. The powerful receiver of communication is adept in at least four vital areas: he can focus much attention on the sender, he knows how to check up on the accuracy of his intake, he is good at rewarding the sender for communicating, and he can understand the feelings behind the message he receives as well as the thoughts contained in it. Learning attentional focus is a pursuit beyond the scope of this discussion. (One major requisite is the elimination of energy-draining extraneous behaviors, which has been treated earlier.) Checking intake and reinforcing communication are skills that are relatively easy to acquire. It is more difficult to train patients to receive feeling messages accurately; in most cases, previous experience accounts for more performance variation in this area than does short-term communication training.

To reinforce communication it is only necessary to 1) pay close attention to the sender and 2) communicate to him that he is receiving attention. This must be done in such a way that his sending behavior is validated without being interrupted. Patients can be trained to acknowledge the receipt of messages through a roleplaying modification.

TECHNIQUE #5: *Acknowledgment training.* Practice takes place in dyads; therapist and patient may roleplay together or a third party may be used. The participants, say Bob and Alice, engage in a discussion. Bob makes a statement. Before Alice can reply, she must acknowledge that she received and understood Bob's message. She may do this by saying, "Thank you," "OK," "I understand," or words to that effect. A nonverbal response, such as a smile or nod, may be used only if it is clearly understood by both parties to be an acknowledgment. If Alice did not understand Bob's message, she must ask for clarification: "Would you repeat that?", or "I don't understand that." Bob will then repeat his statement. If Alice now understands, she acknowledges the communication and continues with a statement of her own, which Bob must then acknowledge, or she waits for Bob to continue the discussion. If Alice is still confused, she must again request clarification; she never originates a statement until she understands the content of Bob's message. In this technique, the participants police one another, immediately calling one another's attention to missed acknowledgments. (If the therapist is roleplaying, he may omit acknowledgments purposely toward the end of the session, and judge training success partly in terms of how quickly the patient calls his attention to the omission.)

> *EXAMPLE:* Wrong: Bob: "Alice, your blouse is dirty."
> Alice: "So is your shirt."
> Right: Bob: "Alice, your blouse is dirty."
> Alice: "OK," (or "Thank you," or "Yes, I see that it is.") Then, (if she still wishes to reply) "So is your shirt."

The patient should be reminded that it is the *act of communication,* and not communication content, which is being acknowledged. For instance:

> Bob: "Alice, I don't like you."
> Alice: "Thank you."

In this example, Alice is not being facetious or sarcastic, although it may seem so at first. She is not thanking Bob for his negative feelings; she is thanking him for *sharing them* with her. Honest feedback is a valuable gift. Alice may not be particularly pleased that Bob dislikes her, but now, at least, she does know how he feels. (The preceding discussion ignores the possibility that Alice may have a need to respond to negative feedback in an emotional or assertive manner. It is not being suggested that simple acknowledgment is the appropriate response in every interpersonal situation, but only that it is one good receiving technique.)

A more involved listening procedure was described by Rogers (1961). Its purpose is to facilitate the settling of disputes as well as to sharpen listening skill in general.

TECHNIQUE #6: *Intake verification.* A dyadic training setup is used, as above. Bob makes a statement. Before Alice is allowed to reply to that statement or make one of her own, she must paraphrase Bob's message and repeat it back to him. If Bob acknowledges her accuracy, she may continue. However, if she has repeated the essence of Bob's statement incorrectly, Bob tells her so, repeats himself, and Alice tries again. Alice must get Bob's message right before she can send one of her own. At that point the roles are reversed. Again, if the therapist is directly involved in the roleplaying situation, he may verify the content of his patient's message incorrectly on purpose to check training quality.

> *EXAMPLE:* Bob: "The house is always filthy when I get home from work—the dinner is never ready on time. I want you to shape up and start doing your job!"
> Alice: "You think it's my job to clean house and cook, and that I'm not doing it very well these days."
> Bob: "Right on!"
> Alice: "Well, I think you're being too hard on me; I'm human, too. The house is usually clean. Besides, why don't you ever offer to help me, like with the dishes?"
> Bob: "You think I expect too much of you and never do anything around the house myself."
> Alice: "No, I didn't say that. You do a lot to keep the house and yard up. But, you never offer to help me with anything."
> Bob: "Oh, you'd like to see more of a team effort on some things, like the dishes.
> Alice: "Yes, I would."
> Bob: "Well, I don't think that I should be expected to . . . (etc.)."

Continuing in such a manner for more than a few minutes at one time would, of course, be maddening. The verification technique is primarily a troubleshooting device, used during conflict or when it is important that complicated information be received accurately. It is perfect for, say, the young married couple who profess undying love, but seemingly would rather fight than listen to one another. In addition, verification provides excellent receiver practice, in that he who uses it quickly gets into the habit of really listening to what the other person has to say. Finally, there is considerable reinforcement value in hearing one's own thoughts repeated back to one by a listener who obviously is trying to understand.

Although the training procedures are somewhat involved, patients can be taught to reinforce and facilitate the communication of feelings as well as of factual content. The basic technique they must learn is called *reflective listening*, which probably has been taught to more students in one form or another than any other single communication device (e.g. Gordon, 1971). Procedurally, *reflection* is much like *verification*, except that the primary focus is on affect feelings and not verbal content.

Three qualities of reflective listening make it a valuable communication tool. First, it catalyzes self-exploration and thus serves as a means of gathering information. The listener can induce the sender to talk about himself without "putting him on the spot" by asking a lot of questions. Second, as noted above, accurate reflective listening promotes feeling expression and reinforces constructive interpersonal behavior, in general. In new relationships, it may serve as a base from which other, more direct, forms of communication grow. Third, the dynamics of its implementation are easy to grasp; almost anyone can become an adept reflector of feelings in a relatively short time if he wishes to do so.

TECHNIQUE #7: *Reflective listening.* Patients are acquainted with the basic strategies of reflection, and then are presented with the following set of guidelines, mimeographed for home use.

a. Listen attentively to the sender's words and try to understand the meaning behind them.

b. Try to understand how the sender is feeling as he speaks, and watch for feeling implications in his words, tone, facial expression, body language, etc.

c. Repeat back to the sender, succinctly and in your on words, the essence of his message as you heard it and felt it. Your *primary* purpose here is communicating to the sender that you understand how he feels, accept his feelings without judging them as good or bad, and want to hear more about them.

d. Your secondary purpose is content verification.

e. Don't choose not to respond rather than risk being wrong. It is not mandatory that all your responses be blindingly accurate, as long as you continually check on and rectify your mistakes.

f. Respond often to the sender, even "with only a nod, to let him know you are still there with him."

Roleplaying procedures, particularly role-reversal, can be used to implement training in the office. In role-reversal, the therapist first plays himself; the patient sends feeling messages, and the therapist models reflective listening. Then they reverse roles: the therapist sends the same messages he received and the patient reflects. When the patient can imitate reflective listening in this manner, the therapist may begin sending him "unrehearsed" feeling messages, and critically evaluate the quality of his reflection. Taped sessions are valuable in that they allow the patient himself to evaluate his performance. Toward the end of training, the use of a third person in the role of interviewee provides the patient with "training under fire" and allows the therapist to check his progress.

> *EXAMPLE:* Bob: "That damn Richardson made it look like I fouled up the project again at staff meeting today."
> Alice: "He sure does annoy you with the tricks he pulls."
> Bob: "The really amazing part is how he gets the staff to buy it so easily. He comes out smelling like a rose and. . . ."
> Alice: "And you get left holding the fertilizer. . . ."
> Bob: "Yeah! I don't know how the little weasel gets away with it, but I can't handle much more of this."
> Alice: "Boy! You're damned mad at him and the whole place. It's so frustrating not to be able to do anything about it."
> Bob: "It's definitely getting me down. . . ."
>
> (and so on)

A trainee's ability to listen reflectively may be considerably improved by teaching him to function at high levels on certain interpersonal process dimensions. Research indicates that psychiatric inpatients, as well as outpatients and "normal" trainees, derive considerable benefit from process training. *Empathy, respect, concreteness,* and *immediacy* are a few of the more common variables which may be taught. Essentially, process training involves learning to 1) discriminate between good and bad communication in terms of specific variables, and 2) communicate at facilitative levels with regard to each variable in question. Training is conducted on the didactic and experiential level simultaneously, with the therapist functioning as role model for his patient/trainee. Elaborate criterion measures have been developed to assist the participants and insure training objectivity (Carkhuff, 1969). Implementation of process training in the therapy setting may, in some cases, be limited by practical considerations such as available training time and the therapist's own facilitative ability.

REFERENCES

CARKHUFF, R. R. *Helping and human relations: Volume I.* New York: Holt, Rinehart, and Winston, Inc., 1969.

GOLDSTEIN, A., SERBER, M., & PIAGET, G. W. Induced anger as a reciprocal inhibitor of fear. *Journal of Behavior Therapy and Experimental Psychiatry*, 1970, 1, 67.

GORDON, T. *Parent effectiveness training.* New York: Peter H. Wyden, Inc., 1971.

HUBBARD, L. R. Mimeographed communication training manual. East Grinstead, Sussex, England, 1961.

PIAGET, G. W. *Toward effective communication.* Unpublished manuscript, Palo Alto, California, 1971.

ROGERS, C. R. *On becoming a person.* Boston: Houghton Mifflin Company, 1961.

YATES, A. J. The application of learning theory to the treatment of tics. *Journal of Abnormal and Social Psychology*, 1958, 56, 175-182.

9

The Multiple Techniques of Broad Spectrum Psychotherapy

BARRY M. BROWN, M.D.

BROAD-SPECTRUM PSYCHOTHERAPY is a technique-oriented system of psychotherapy in which all facets of the therapeutic process are considered to be composed of multiple techniques. The term "technique" will not be limited to such specific, much-discussed methods as clarification, interpretation, counterconditioning or assertive training. It will encompass, as much as possible, every way the therapist and patient interact. From the first phone call to the end of the last session, there are numerous interactions involved. Many of these are taken for granted, yet may be of great significance. For instance, the length of time a therapist spends with a patient, especially the first session, may be of great importance. Forty-five minutes may be anti-therapeutic, one and a half hours greatly therapeutic. The reverse may be true. The therapist's tone of voice, facial expression, his decisions as to when to speak or when to listen are likewise important. Again, how does he word things to the patient? Does his choice of words and their order convey blame or stimulate thinking? What techniques does he use to change the patient's concepts, beliefs and attitudes? What specific behavior therapy techniques does he use and when?

It is the premise of this chapter that every phase of Broad Spectrum Psychotherapy—RAPPORT, MANAGEMENT, BEHAVIOR THERAPY, and COGNITIVE THERAPY—is composed of multiple techniques. To be considered techniques, however, in the true sense of the word, they must be under the conscious control of the therapist and based on his working hypothesis of human behavior. Since little is proven about what is and what is not therapeutic, I am only suggesting that attention be paid to these areas and that they be given a more careful consideration in the study of psychotherapy. Hopefully, the techniques alluded to may someday be backed by experimental proof.

It is my intent to describe the techniques that I use in all phases of psychotherapy and to give my rationale for using them. Clinical material will be used widely, with emphasis on both successes and failures.

RAPPORT TECHNIQUES

Rapport is defined here as an optimal relationship between therapist and patient during the entire course of therapy. An optimal relationship is one where the patient likes the therapist, trusts him and has confidence in him. Rapport is imperative if the therapist wishes:

1. To motivate the patient to attend further therapy sessions.
2. To give the patient the feeling he is understood.
3. To enhance the patient's self-esteem.
4. To stimulate a free flow of attitudes and feelings from the patient.

Rapport techniques may vary during a session and during the course of therapy. If rapport is to exist the therapist must be constantly aware of himself and the use of his characteristics as part of his rapport regime. The following factors are important to the establishment of rapport:

1. The therapist's appearance, mannerisms and charisma.
2. The therapist's facial expressions.
3. The therapist's knowing when to talk, as well as when to listen.
4. The therapist's intensity, phrasing and general tone of voice and his choice of words.
5. The choice of subject matter.
6. The role that a therapist plays.

7. The attitude of empathy, warmth, and positive regard.
8. The therapist's ability to allow fulfillment of the patient's expectations early in therapy.
9. The occurrence of a remark by the therapist that captures the way the patient feels.
10. The use of a specific technique for relief of a troublesome symptom.
11. The educating of the patient as to what will occur in therapy and how it may work for him.

The appearance, age and charisma of the therapist can be only minimally controlled or altered. It is pointed out here because it must be considered a factor in the development of rapport. Very often, the reason for a patient leaving therapy can be explained on the basis of his not feeling any attraction for the therapist. The patient may be repelled because the therapist does not measure up to his own preconceived notions of what a therapist should be.

A therapist can be particularly skillful in the way he senses what constitutes optimal rapport with each individual patient. From the beginning of the first meeting, the therapist should note what he does that produces a favorable reaction. Does the patient seem more at ease, more open, more talkative, more intent on working on his difficulties when the therapist smiles and is friendly or when he is poker-faced and reserved? Does the patient like to do the talking or does he seem to respond better to being questioned? Does the therapist's tone of voice affect him? The therapist can speak in a very authoritarian way or can speak in a matter-of-fact way. To which does the patient seem to respond more readily? In the past, I feel that I have had a tendency to be too serious with patients, especially early in therapy, possibly from my own anxiety and possibly from wanting to "get down to business." However, I find that many patients come to therapy in an anxious state and seem more responsive when I am relaxed, warm, friendly, and spend some time discussing trivial matters.

It is also important to emphasize that a patient's personality may evoke responses in the therapist which may block effective therapy. The therapist should be aware of these responses and deal with them.

For example:

C.N. is a thirty-year-old white female, discussed in the management section. She can best be described as an obsessive-compulsive personality with tendencies toward depression, self-criticism, skepticism and an inability to enjoy life. In the early sessions, I noted how annoyed, critical and bored I felt with her. I realized my facial expression conveyed this feeling. I tried responding with a more pleasant, smiling, approving, and interested facial expression. On occasion, I started joking with her. Over our next four sessions her eye contact increased markedly, skeptical remarks about therapy decreased, and she began discussing highly personal matters more openly.

J.J. was an extremely attractive, mini-skirted twenty-two-year-old white female who talked incessantly about her "horrible" husband. Her talkativeness decreased her attractiveness. This, plus the frustration of not being able to get a word in edgewise, made me feel quite negative about her, and I am quite sure my facial expression conveyed my feelings. I decided to stop trying to interrupt her and spent the sessions looking at her "admiringly." The results were gratifying as she soon ran out of steam and not only listened to what I did have to say, but also adopted and put to use my suggestions.

In regard to actively taking a history versus letting the patient tell his own story, I have converted more to an inactive role in the early sessions and have found that giving the patient more time to talk or some gentle prods reveals much more information and is preferred by the patient. When the patient is having difficulty getting started and has no idea what is expected of him in psychotherapy or what he is to talk about, I will then help him along by asking questions.

As a therapist, as well as in my own interpersonal relations, I have felt my "vocal image" left something to be desired. I have particularly concentrated on improving my phrasing, intensity and tone of voice and my choice of words. A therapist should learn to speak in a more mellow, softer tone, to be less intense, and to watch his phrasing of sentences and choice of words. Instead of saying, "You are looking very hostile today." I might state, "Have things been annoying you?" The latter is less critical and more indirect. Rather than saying, "You are a sensitive person," one may say "You seem very alert to the environment." Words that may bear a psychological "stigma" or negative implications of any kind like "hostility," "depression" and "fear" tend to upset patients more than those with fewer psychological overtones—"sadness," "concern" and "scared." Usage of the latter increases rapport.

Often the therapist gets so engrossed in his thoughts of "What is going on here?," "What are the dynamics?," that he forgets to be the reinforcer and does not give his full attention to what the patient has said. Because of this, he may lose rapport. It must be emphasized that while rapport techniques are important throughout therapy, it is basically the first sessions that are the most crucial because early in therapy patients often need motivation, which good rapport helps establish. Later in therapy I may discuss the rapport techniques, "the way I've had to be," to demonstrate to a patient one of his characteristics. For example, in the nineteenth session with N.A. (cognitive section) I said, "Look, some days I get the feeling I have got to let you do all the talking and other days I feel you are disappointed if I don't say much." My purpose in making this remark at this time was to lay the groundwork for pointing out how his moods change, and later to relate his moods to changing predominant cognitive themes. His answer to the statement was "You're right. Today I was impatient and wanted you to talk and yet other times I am annoyed and tell you to be quiet."

I generally allow patients to discuss whatever subject they desire. Allowing certain important issues to be left unsaid may be a necessity in early sessions in order to keep anxiety low and rapport high. Once the patient has become relaxed and optimal rapport is operating, the therapist may then call attention to the issues. For example, N.A., discussed in the cognitive section, brought up little talk about girls and sex prior to the fifteenth meeting. Early attempts to encourage discussion in this area had met with resistance, so were not pursued further.

Patients tend to differ in the level of confidence they want in their therapist. Some patients prefer humility; others want certainty. The therapist should recognize early in treatment into which category the patient belongs and act accordingly. This is not necessarily constant and the therapist must "tune in" at each meeting to determine how he should act.

J.D. is a twenty-four year old white female whose father and married boyfriend are strong willed and assertive. She did not respond in the first half hour of our first session to my occasional soft-spoken statements. When I spoke louder and with more confidence, she responded more to me, i.e., had better eye contact and showed facial signs of agreement.

Then at a second session where she was overwrought about the boyfriend's loss of interest in her, she only responded after I switched from an assertive, confident role to a soft-spoken, sympathetic one.

Whereas I was originally trained in the traditional model of distance and aloofness, I find that this stance often leads to lowering of the patient's self-esteem and an increase in self-critical feelings. I have become much more prone to using techniques involving empathy, warmth, and unconditional positive regard. This approach also involves the wording of interpretations. Sentences that traditionalists use, such as "You have a need to suffer," or allusions to one's hostilities or traits in a critical light, contribute to the loss of self-esteem and also increase self-blame. An approach that views human behavior in terms of traits which are adaptive or maladaptive has been more effective for me than the traditional approach which, while disclaiming this in theory, in practice tends to see traits in "bad" or "good" terms.

Patients often have preconceived ideas as to what therapy is about and what they are supposed to say. Interrupting the patient as he is telling every detail of his past life or of a seemingly irrelevant situation may prevent him from realizing his expectation. Once the patient has told what he thinks he should tell, the therapist may then direct the session to the significant points.

A statement that is emotionally meaningful to a patient, that is, one which really "hits home," causes the patient to feel understood. This is usually evident by the response of the patient: a brightening of the eyes, nodding of the head or verbal expression of agreement.

C.M. (described in management section) showed anxiety, irritability and inappropriate affect to the point where she was considered borderline psychotic. At a marital session, my female cotherapist said to her, "I have the feeling you're protecting your husband." Her facial expression changed, her voice dropped in pitch, she couldn't speak for a moment and for the remainder of the session she was more relaxed and showed no irritability or inappropriate affect. Furthermore, she rationally discussed the statement made to her. Clearly the statement increased rapport.

Many patients have been thought to leave therapy because of the failure of the therapist to recognize at an early session the need to treat the specific symptom of the patient. I have found this particularly true regarding psychosomatic cases, specifically some headache cases. I have seen three patients referred by their physician for headaches of no known physical cause and explored their life situation, past and present, with particular emphasis on events surrounding their headaches. These patients did not see the value of this approach and therefore did not respond. A better approach for these cases would seem to be an initial treatment of the specific symptom. This may be accomplished by generalized muscle relaxation, particularly the neck and scalp muscles. This hopefully would give a therapeutic result at an early session. I feel that treating the symptom successfully will set the stage for later psychological exploration, should the relaxation treatment be unsuccessful in giving the patient complete relief. If the patient is made aware of the fact that some psychological difficulty may be contributing to his symptom, he may then be more receptive for exploratory psychotherapy. Illustrative of the effects of early symptomatic relief would be the case of a stutterer with whom I initially took a behavior therapy approach. A marked improvement in his stuttering occurred in four sessions with the use of generalized relaxation and selective relaxation of throat muscles. He then began discussing other areas of his life and a cognitive approach was used. (See Behavior Therapy, Section—D.C.)

A final technique used to develop rapport is one used with the patient who is not sure what psychotherapy is all about or what is really expected of him. This type of patient would probably respond much more readily if the first session or two were devoted to educating him in any areas of psychiatry or psychotherapy in which the therapist feels increased knowledge would relieve anxiety. Sometimes a case example may be used.

L.C. is a thirty-year-old white male who presented with a history of five panic attacks. He was most anxious at the meeting and his wife indicated he had not wanted to come at all. He revealed skepticism about therapy for "financial reasons." He had no previous contact with psychiatry and was quite unsophisticated about psychological matters. The story he gave revealed little to explain his attacks. Because of his anxiety, I limited the session to forty minutes and because of possible similarities to another case (W.B.—Cognitive Section), I described the case to him, emphasizing that certain ideas or fears always preceded the patient's anxiety attacks. I also mentioned that the patient had improved in four sessions. The patient acted most interested, and said, "That sounds just like me." He left in a more relaxed, apparently optimistic state than that in which he had entered.

MANAGEMENT TECHNIQUES

The management of patients includes six important areas: the length of therapy sessions, the frequency of sessions, the collection of fees, the use and abuse of phone calls, the involvement of parents and peers, and the role of a married patient's spouse.

Length of Sessions

It is frequently necessary for a new patient to be seen for ninety, rather than fifty minutes. I find the longer time period necessary for the patient to become sufficiently relaxed so that he can openly relate his difficulties in detail, obtain relief from catharsis, and develop a feeling that the therapist understands and can help him. The therapist needs this time to make multiple decisions involving the specific information he wishes to obtain, the meaning of information gained, the techniques to be employed to maximally lessen the patient's suffering in this initial session, and the tentative plans for future therapy.

On the other hand, I often limit the first session to thirty minutes. This is done with patients who come to a psychiatrist reluctantly and appear to be in an anxious state relative to the experience itself. Since it is my goal in these situations to lower the patient's anxiety and to increase his motivation, I concentrate on rapport techniques such as relaxed affect, warmth, and discussion of trivial matters. In addition I attempt to educate the patient about what occurs in psychotherapy and how it may help him. This use of rapport and education acts to "desensitize" the patient and, more often than not, he will return in a less anxious state, more prepared to discuss his life.

With many patients, throughout an entire course of therapy, it may take fifteen to twenty minutes to relax sufficiently to talk freely. For these people, I usually allow sixty to seventy-five minutes at early meetings and later rarely see them for less than one hour.

Frequency of Sessions

Frequency of sessions varies if there is a crisis involved. Crisis patients may be seen daily for up to four days, and may then be tapered off. Regular patients are seen more than once a week only if there is a pressing problem.

Sometimes the verbal, psychological-minded, contemplative patient feels he gains more by coming twice weekly. I never see these patients more than this as I feel no benefit is gained.

Some patients who would profit more from weekly therapy will only come biweekly or monthly because of the financial strain that weekly therapy imposes.

Fees

The handling of patients' fees varies with the type of patient with which one is dealing. Poor risk patients, such as certain character disorders and alcoholics, are told by the clinic bookkeeper, at my suggestion, that they must pay prior to each session. This promotes responsibility in the patient and avoids hostility in the therapist. Conscientious patients, known to pay their bills regularly, are allowed extended time to pay their bills should their finances be tight. Patients are not charged if they miss an appointment. Most responsible patients cancel in advance except when there is an emergency. If the patient has a poor excuse for cancelling or is absent without explanation, the therapist should look into the patient's motivation for continued treatment. Often, these are signals that the patient is dissatisfied. Calling the patient who misses an appointment and does not telephone often verifies dissatisfaction or ambivalence, is an excellent way of learning the patient's reasons for stopping therapy, and gives clues to what errors, if any, the therapist made in technique.

With patients in an explorative cognitive therapy, the implications of delayed fee payment and missed appointments may be examined in terms of life patterns.

Cotherapy, which we feel is an excellent modality for marital problems, is, unfortunately, quite expensive. Because of our interest in this, we have each decreased our fees and have tended to use combined sessions more sparingly due to their long length.

Telephone Calls

Patients conscientiously working in therapy are permitted to call for any crisis, with no fee charged or reprimand made. Patients who have avoided regular therapy and who call the therapist at home are tactfully managed by being billed at a higher rate than that of an office visit. Patients who overly concern themselves about "bothering" a therapist and who may get into difficulty, such as a severe depression in between visits, are often given specific instructions to call on a given day. I also will not hesitate calling any patient about whom I am concerned.

Involvement of Parents and Peers

In the treatment of adolescents I usually involve members of the patient's family and/or peer group in the therapy.

C.K. was a thirteen-year-old white female referred by a neurologist because of an inability to walk without falling for three months. This had been preceded by a viral illness and a facial palsy necessitating complete medical and neurological studies. There were no positive findings and because of the bizarre character of the girl's gait, the neurologist was convinced that her ataxia was functional in nature, a conversion reaction. At the initial interview, the mother revealed that the daughter might have some concern about school, but she denied family difficulties, any particular precipitating events or other potential problem areas such as menarche or boyfriends that might have catalyzed the daughter's walking difficulty. When seen individually, no obvious concerns were evident in the daughter. At this time the mother was advised to "pay less attention" to the walking problem and the daughter was told she would gradually improve in her walking. The daughter was seen individually on two further occasions where all interview techniques known to the author failed to elicit possible anxiety-producing areas for the girl. The patient and her mother were then seen by the social worker and myself so their interaction might be examined. The session was awkward, the girl being quite silent and the mother fruitlessly urging discussion. Since there were allusions to some hostility from the father and sixteen-year-old sister we decided to involve them in our next meeting. When the whole family was seen, some interesting interactions occurred which gave us an idea for a therapeutic approach. The mother was noted to be consistently understanding and protective of the patient, while the father and sister were consistently sarcastic and unsupportive toward her. Seeing these relationships and having gleaned nothing further in the areas we had continued to explore—school, boys and menarche—it was decided to instruct the family on some rules for the management of the patient. These were: only the sister and father could help the patient get to her crutches or wheel chair; the mother was to do nothing for the patient in these areas nor attend to anything she had not done before the patient "got sick." The patient was to use her crutches as her main source of ambulation, to gradually stop using the wheel chair over a one-week period and to practice walking without crutches, increasing daily the number of steps without them. The rationale was that the patient liked using the wheel chair and had complained that the crutches were most uncomfortable. The patient had always been able to take two or three faltering steps without crutches. During the entire course of therapy, suggestion had been used—"This will improve over a matter of time. The neurologist has told us that these conditions always get better. Your condition appears good enough that you should be able to increase your walking by at least one step a day."

Two weeks after this regime was started the patient walked with no abnormality and needed no assistance of any type. Her flawless walking was demonstrated at our next visit. The family was advised that we were glad of the girl's success but felt followup therapy was necessary. They were quite happy with the results and did not see the value of further therapy.

C.G. was an eighteen-year-old white female brought into my office in a catatonic-like state—staring blankly ahead, showing no spontaneous speech, laughing inappropriately and giving brief answers to all questions. The parents stated that the girl had always been a "model child," but in the past six months had been telling lies, taking illegal drugs, and had recently stayed away from home for three weeks. The family had always been most strict and in the last two months increased their strictness in response to the patient's dating a boy of a religion of which they disapproved. There were no other known objections to the boy.

It was decided to hospitalize the girl. When seen in the hospital, she was angry about being hospitalized, but otherwise her clinical picture had not changed. She was able to briefly discuss her current boyfriend and could not understand her parents reaction to him since he was not involved with drugs and was an ambitious college student. Since he had assumed such great importance in her life I thought that I would involve him in her therapy. She perked up when I suggested this. The couple was seen together for two meetings and their relationship, the patient's past problems with her parents and the current conflict were discussed. At the same time, the parents were seen by the social worker and myself. The social worker was a very warm, supportive woman and was able to establish an excellent relationship, even with the extremely rigid father. Once good rapport was established, their reasons for strictness were discussed and the fact that extreme strictness often led to rebellious behavior was pointed out. The religious issue was discussed and the boyfriend's many good traits were emphasized. The parents were able to see that the boy had been a good influence, had gotten their daughter away from drugs and had stimulated her interest in going to college. It was also pointed out that the boyfriend had excellent credentials: he was from a good family, was a conscientious premedical student and was interested in the well-being of their daughter. We brought out to the parents how they had always overreacted to many things the daughter had done and were now overreacting to the dating of a well-intentioned man on the basis of religious difference.

The parents responded well to therapy and softened their limits on the girl, allowing her to continue dating the boy. The girl showed marked clinical improvement and she and her boyfriend cancelled their plans to run away and marry. She was able to return home and the relationship with her parents went well. The truce that developed from the involvement of all family members plus the involvement of the most important person in the girl's life at that time led to a clinical remission of all her presenting symptoms as well as an understanding by the parents of what they had been doing that led to the girl's rebelliousness. At last report the boyfriend was thinking of converting to the girl's religion and the plans for secret marriage were postponed indefinitely.

Involvement of the Patient's Spouse

A married person presenting for therapy poses a challenging management problem: In what way should the mate be handled? Should the mate be ignored, the presenting spouse becoming the "designated patient"? Should the mate be an "adviser" informing the therapist of the spouse's past and present life and giving his views of the spouse's current difficulty? Should the marriage partner be a patient in his own right, needing some form of individual therapy or should he be treated as part of a marital system which then becomes the "designated patient"?

Factors involved in assessing the extent of the mate's involvement include the presenting problem: Does the presenting patient pose difficulties which do not appear related to the marriage or does the complaint involve the marriage, either some form of marital disharmony or an attitude of apathy in one or both partners? Is the patient willing for his spouse to be seen? Will the spouse come in and, if so, what aspects of his personality influence the therapist's decision as to the role he will play in the patient's treatment? These important factors in management can be demonstrated in the following cases:

D.W., discussed in the cognitive therapy section, was a twenty-eight-year-old pregnant white female with agoraphobia. Even though she indicated no marital problems, I decided, with her consent, to interview her husband. This was done to evaluate his personality, to get his views on their marriage, to elicit the meaning to both of them of her pregnancy and to learn how he responded to her phobic condition. When it became clinically evident to me that he was well adjusted, that there were no obvious marital problems, that the pregnancy was wanted by both of them and that his responses to her symptoms did not encourage secondary gain, it was decided to see her in individual cognitive therapy. Treatment on this basis was successful.

C.H., discussed in the cognitive therapy section, was a twenty-nine-year-old white female with an obsessive thought that she was going to kill her six-month-old son. Her history revealed nervousness, obsessions, compulsions and phobias dating to her teen years. She was treated with traditional psychotherapy for one year at age twenty. Even though the long history of difficulty antedated her marriage by four years and she denied marital difficulties, it was decided that the husband be seen once in order to clarify some of this patient's magnifications and distortions. She agreed to his coming and when seen he was found to be appropriate and understanding and put things in a clearer perspective than the patient had. There was no evidence from either him or his wife that there had been any worsening of her marked obsession secondary to the marital situation. He did point out that the child actually was extremely irritable and had occupied much of the wife's day and night. It was decided that her obsession to kill the child was most likely related to feelings of hostility and resentment of which she was unaware. I therefore encouraged further care of the child by the husband, relatives, friends and baby sitters, so that the patient could get some relief from the child and spend some of her time at activities she found relaxing and pleasurable. The husband cooperated fully and the decreased pressure from the care of the child and the gains made in cognitive therapy, as described in that section, led to a resolution of the obsession.

P.P. is a forty-six-year-old white male wealthy accountant. He has been married twenty-five years and has four children. He presented in a state of agitation and depression because the young married woman he had been dating and intending to marry had been wooed back by her husband after she had told him of her romance with the patient. After three weeks of supportive therapy, the patient recovered from this "loss" and began to discuss his marriage. He stated he had never felt romantic with his wife, was disappointed in her sexually, and repeatedly mentioned his resentment for her many interests and activities and the fact that she controlled the household and the children. Early in the marriage he had had one brief affair because he was "not getting enough sex" from his wife and over the years saw a prostitute on three single occasions when out of town on business. However, he states he always felt that he was looking for a "true romance." I thought it was significant that, before developing this intense relationship with the young woman, he had been transferred from a small town where he moved among the social élite and where he was a significant man in his firm's small office to a large city where he was unknown to the élite and less important to the larger office of his firm. This was felt by me to be a blow to his self-esteem and the statements relative to his wife indicated she had always reinforced this poor self-opinion. Statements concerning the girlfriend displayed a theme of how important he felt when with her.

The patient had moved out of his house prior to losing the young woman and, after the grief period, he decided to move back and "try it again." He had told his wife candidly all along of his relationship with the woman and then of her loss. She reacted sympathetically, indicated she cared for him, would take him back and never was vindictive in any way. However, the patient did not like living at home even though he felt his wife had acted favorably in every way he could ask, including her sexual reactivity toward him. He returned to the house, did not feel happy and moved out again on three occasions. With his agreement, I decided to see the wife. She was much as he described her and anxious to cooperate in any way she could. She was concerned about him and hoped he would return. It was decided, however, at that time, that the main contribution to his leaving was intrapsychic rather than interpersonal, so no marital sessions were planned. Also, I advised the wife to not allow the husband back home until I talked with her. At our next meeting, I told the patient that he was not to return home until he honestly desired his wife and until further therapy cleared up some of the issues involved. My reasoning on this matter was that this would give him time to examine possible intrapsychic causes leading to his current situation. Also, by not going home, at my suggestion, his guilt would be relieved and his positive feelings for his wife would possibly intensify. Many cases similar to this, that is a mate apathetic to his spouse and on the look for romance, were formerly handled by seeing the marital couple together with a female cotherapist present and by emphasizing examination of the communication and the ways each was being reinforcing or adversive. However, this did not meet with great success. It is my feeling that putting the couple together to treat their marriage was done too early, when motivation of the apathetic mate was low. This patient is still in individual therapy, having to date a total of fourteen meetings. He has spent most of his time recently talking of his wife; themes of his low self-esteem are quite frequent. The plan now is to continue cognitive therapy and see if the awareness that self-esteem has played a part in his "problem" leads him to return to his wife, without being vulnerable to the intensity of a new romance, particularly in regard to its esteem-building potential.

E.U. is a twenty-eight-year-old white female married ten years and having two children. She stated she has been "bored" with her husband for five years and now wants "out," "freedom." She described her husband's actions over the years as very "controlling." She has always been afraid to do anything without his approval. Her desire for freedom increased markedly when the family moved into a new home. "I felt like having a home was like going to jail for the rest of my life, as if the house had bars." The husband was seen once, did not appear especially domineering and was vaguely aware of the issues the patient had brought up. The wife during the first six sessions of therapy was intensely desirous of freedom and had obtained a job and hired a divorce attorney. Marital therapy was not suggested because of her need to avoid the husband. In individual therapy, other than mentioning marital therapy in the first session and seeing the husband once, I always acted as if I assumed she was going to get the divorce, even though I felt her dependency might prevent her. The main pattern seen and discussed in the eight meetings to date has been her continual giving into people and doing what they wanted. This was noted not only in the marriage, but also in the job she had taken. There, she had allowed herself to become the busiest secretary in the office. At our seventh meeting, one month before the husband was scheduled to move out of the home, the patient mentioned that the husband and she had had two dates, both very enjoyable and ending with satisfying sex. "When I think of myself as free from him, I can enjoy his company and the sex. But the next day when he assumes all is well and says,

'I guess we will stay together,' then I feel just as turned off by him."
Assertive training was started at the seventh session since the theme
of low assertiveness permeates her relationships with her parents and
siblings, work situation and marriage. At the eighth session she stated,
"I'm not so sure now about the divorce. C. has shaped up." It would
seem from this that she is showing more motivation toward her husband.
It is felt, however, that to maintain the good feelings she is now beginning to experience, she must continue to feel some degree of assertiveness
and independence in her marriage. Individual therapy will continue with
an emphasis on attitude exploration and assertive training.

J.T. is a thirty-five-year-old white female married twelve years and having
three children. In the past five years she has suffered recurrent severe
depressions, abused tranquilizing drugs, made at least three serious suicide
attempts and was hospitalized five times. She has been treated with drugs
and electroshock therapy. When seen by me after her last serious suicide
attempt, she was markedly depressed and appeared to be a "hopeless
case." As we talked daily, it became evident that much of her unhappiness
related to the different life styles she and her husband had and the
consequences of living in a small town. She was markedly extrovertish
while he was an introvert. Her husband was in business in a small town
and felt it was important for her to act in a more "straight-laced" way.
He was public opinion oriented, she was not. Her actions of the past few
years did not involve immoral acts of any kind; however, there was some
sexual acting out after a hysterectomy eight years ago. The husband
worked very hard and rarely took her out. Her depressions always began
with decreased attention to the children and the housework. It was my
opinion that there were no reinforcers in her life for which to work. Also,
she suffered repeated reprimanding from him for being seen with women
of the wrong race, religion or social class in the town and for outgoing
behavior at social functions. During her past illnesses the husband was
handled as the stable, "well" member of the marriage and only interviewed
by her doctors "to obtain a history." I decided that her illnesses had as
much to do with him as it did with her. This was explained to her and
drew a marked response of appreciation. She felt what I said was very
true. The husband was seen both alone and with his wife and my cotherapist. Emphasis was put on the wife's needs for attention, and his
fears concerning her friends and actions. Also, they were educated as to
their marital interaction. This was all presented in a non-blameful way,
making it fairly palatable. In the sixteen months since the patient was
first seen, she has come in every four to six weeks and he has been seen
four times. She has not been hospitalized nor has she made any suicide
attempt. She still is occasionally nervous and depressed, the marriage is
not perfect and she requires tranquilizing medication. This is a good
clinical result considering her past history. It is attributed to making the
patient and her husband aware of the causation of her illness and to both
of them recognizing the other's needs more acutely. More frequent therapy

might lead to even further lessening of the patient's symptoms and needs for medication, but financial realities have limited their attendance. The wife is seen alone until she shows signs of increased depression or anxiety, whereupon the husband is brought in and the above conditions are reemphasized.

S.H. is a twenty-six-year-old white male systems analyst married seven years and having two children. He sought help for his "troubled marriage." I saw him individually for three meetings and characterized him as bright, sensitive and persistent, with a tendency to distort and magnify things and to use multisyllabic words and detailed explanations. This made him difficult to understand, but I did not feel he was schizophrenic. His wife was then seen twice and appeared calm, intelligent, honest and motivated to improve the marriage. The focus of their conversation was on the recent arguing that had been occurring. The husband said the marriage was good until the wife had gone out to a nightclub with a divorcée who he did not feel was a good influence on her. He claimed all would be well in the marriage if she did not see this woman or go to the club again. The wife complained of the husband's lack of attention, their lack of social life and her husband's working long hours on nights and weekends. She felt they had never communicated well. I felt she was the healthier member of the marriage.

Since they had daily bitter arguments and were talking of divorce, I decided to see them together with the assistance of a female cotherapist. Our goal was to make some basic agreements to establish a truce so that we could explore with them the factors contributing to their difficulties. In the combined sessions the husband reacted quite intensively to even the most benign remarks from the wife. We attempted to point out his distortions and magnifications when they occurred. At times it appeared that he got the message and would calm down, but the next session usually revealed that he intensively goaded the wife after the session. His demands on her led to her continually going out to the nightclub, having an affair on one occasion and admitting it to him. This led to his moving out of their apartment. We supported this separation because we thought it would be good for them to avoid each other's aversive behavior. The wife was upset by the husband's leaving and at one of our sessions she agreed to stay in at night and not go out again with the divorcée. This did not satisfy the husband. He stayed apart and decided to divorce her. A three-month followup revealed he was going through with the divorce as planned. I regard this case as a failure but would like to discuss some further points not mentioned above.

1. Good rapport was established between the therapists and the patients—even though Mr. H. was exquisitely sensitive to his wife, I found I was able to relate well with him in individual and marital sessions.
2. Mr. H. was seen individually by me between marital sessions to further

point out his cognitive distortions and magnifications. I felt he got some understanding of the points made.

3. The couple was seen very frequently during acute periods to avoid a worsening of the situation.

4. Other points in the history that may be significant include:
   a. Mr. H. had always been a premature ejaculator, but the wife denied this bothered her or that she was looking for sex with other men.
   b. Mrs. H. had felt the husband was interested in affairs with other women from the way he acted at parties and spoke. Mr. H. said he appreciated looking at other women, but had always been faithful. Late in therapy when separated, Mr. H. revealed in the joint therapy meeting that he was seeing another woman. This was said in a boastful, vindictive tone of voice.

5. Our hypothesis about the precipitating event of the overt marital discord was that the wife, who had always been quite active in school, limited her activity and money spending while the husband was in college and the children were being raised. She had also spoiled her husband, waiting on him excessively and keeping the children quiet during this period. When he began his career seven months before consulting us, she was disappointed that despite having more money and less academic pressure, the husband still paid her little attention, took her nowhere, worked long hours and still demanded much from her. She stopped doing housework, and began pushing the message that she wanted more out of life. He had become accustomed to having complete control over her and could not tolerate anything like this. It is hard to explain, however, why he persisted in separating and divorcing once she acceded to his demands. It is possible that he felt inadequate about his premature ejaculation and the threatened loss of his wife may have made him feel more insecure in this respect. His leaving her, before she left him, may well have been an attempt to build his self-esteem.

M.W. is a forty-five-year-old white married female who had multiple somatic complaints, called her family physician almost daily and went through multiple physical exams, laboratory tests and x-rays. Her symptoms had developed over the last five years, but were worse in the last three after her son was killed in a skirmish with the law. She blamed herself for the son's death and the husband never denied this. Whereas she had formerly been active with the husband in camping, fishing and other activities, she became much less active over this period and the husband did not go out without her. She had also lost interest in sex. She had been hospitalized several times for her somatic complaints, marked depression and, when I first saw her, for deeply cutting both wrists. I interviewed the husband and found him to be cooperative, disappointed in the wife's apathy of recent years, and having no abnormal psychiatric signs or symptoms. Because of his apparent stability, he had never been involved in the patient's therapy except as historian. It was decided to see them together and discuss their interaction. This revealed the tendency of the wife to blame herself for the son's lawlessness and death, and the husband's tacit agreement. This assumption was challenged and the shared role in childrearing was emphasized, but put in a non-blameful perspective. That is, the fact that people's personalities may be determined by factors parents cannot control, such as genetic influences, was pointed out.

It was further emphasized that there was nothing wrong with the wife physically and that she tended to magnify aches and pains. She was encouraged to be more active with the husband again. Three combined meetings were held. Followup therapy was done one and two months after this and revealed the patient was asymptomatic physically and mentally. She was not obsessing on her son's death and was going places with her husband every weekend. He was delighted with the change in her and was taking her out to dinner during the week. The patient ceased calling her family doctor and has maintained her improvement with no further therapy. A friend of mine reading this case said it sounded too good to be true, but it is my impression that just by including a mate as part of a patient's problem, taking the onus of sickness off the patient and putting it on the marriage where it is dealt with, is a highly therapeutic maneuver.

C.M. was a forty-four-year-old white female married twenty-four years and having six children. Her husband made an appointment for her because she was irritable, continually starting arguments with him and the children and was not doing housework. She had acted similarly two years before and was treated with electroshock therapy with moderately good results, according to the husband. When I saw her, she was indeed sensitive, irritable, and appeared depressed. At times her thoughts were a bit inappropriate and she complained of feeling nervous. Diagnostically I saw her as having a depressive reaction and as possibly being borderline psychotic. Others may have seen her as an agitated depression or a schizophrenic. Her husband was seen and appeared very rational, helpful, annoyed by her condition and with no signs or symptoms of psychiatric disorder. He related that she had consulted other psychiatrists in the last ten years and if they felt it was just "her problem" and did not blame him, she did not stay with them. My initial plan was to treat her with tranquilizers and antidepressants and see her for individual psychotherapy. I felt she might well need hospitalization if she did not respond to these. In individual therapy her thinking became more logical and she related dissatisfactions in her marital life and an interest in another man. Further sessions made me feel the marital interaction was more the problem than a primary interest in romance with other men. The patient responded amazingly well to statements that captured her feelings, and became relaxed in the therapy. However, her husband would call between sessions and complain that she was "irritable, depressed and getting on everyone's nerves." I then decided that marital therapy was indicated and saw the couple with a female cotherapist. Some of the issues brought up in individual therapy were the different philosophies of raising the children and handling of finances. This woman had allowed her husband much responsibility with the children but then resented the children's dependency on him rather than on her. She also stated that she resented her husband because of his Ph.D. She had many inferior feelings and for some reason these had recently begun to dominate her thinking. She also felt a need for more stimulation than a housewife gets. As with most wives seen, she complained that the husband had an active interesting job and wanted to stay home and do nothing in the evenings. She was bored and wanted to go out. Even though her complaints centered around the marriage, she repeatedly denied wanting marital therapy. Despite this, it was decided by me to involve the husband. In two sessions of marital therapy, the patient was much more inhibited and complained little of the husband's characteristics. My cotherapist referred to Mrs. M's extremely high expectations of herself. It was also mentioned that she seemed to protect the husband in therapy. This remark seemed very meaningful to the patient. It was also pointed out that Mrs. M. got much responsibility without having the authority. As the communications between the couple were discussed, in a non-blameful way, the husband appeared more anxious and depressed. Significantly, they cancelled their next appointment one day before it was scheduled. They did not reschedule. When I called one and two weeks later I did not get either parent, left a message with an older child and the call was never returned.

One month later I learned by chance that the couple had sought out a hospital-oriented psychiatrist, told him that drugs and therapy had not helped and almost demanded electroshock treatment. This was done and the psychiatrist felt the patient showed moderate improvement.

I called Mrs. M. one month later to get some followup information for this chapter. She was very cold, did not volunteer any information about the shock therapy and simply said she was "fine."

We felt these patients left therapy because the guilt-prone wife could not tolerate seeing the husband being "blamed."

C.N. and J.N.: C.N. is a thirty-year-old white female married for seven years. She was referred by a physician because of depression. When J.N., her husband, heard this he made an appointment with me, stating to her and to me that he was her problem and that he needed treatment. When interviewed he was depressed and complained that he was not involved in his marriage, work or any activities. I agreed to see him for individual therapy. When I reported this to the referring physician, he insisted that I still see the wife as he felt she, too, needed help. The wife was seen and found to be depressed, pessimistic, perfectionistic, self-critical and tense. Individual therapy was suggested to her and she agreed. Both are now being seen in individual therapy. J.N. is discussed in the cognitive section.

He has stated, after each of them had about six sessions, that his wife is better than ever, worrying less about the housework and the kids and treating him with more respect. The emphasis in his therapy is on his fears of talking spontaneously and of involving himself in activities. Her therapy has centered around her extremes in thinking. I am treating both of them, feel they both trust me and that with this couple there is no harm in the procedure. There is no serious marital problem, though of course they are sensitive to each other's moods and acts. Marital therapy is felt not indicated at this time.

Mr. and Mrs. W.E. are in their late twenties, have been married for seven years and have two children. Mrs. E. brought her husband in because "he drinks too much and is always wanting sex." I saw the couple alone at the first meeting. The next three sessions involved my seeing the wife first, while my female social worker saw the husband. The four of us would then meet for a combined session.

In brief, the marriage had been "good" for four years but then for some reason the wife became less interested in sex and cut down its frequency. The husband, always a beer drinker, increased the number of beers he drank. At the time neither complained about the changed conditions. The wife's alcoholic father died one year ago and it was then that she got increasingly critical of her husband, mainly of his drinking (which consisted of four cans of beer in the evening), of his smoking, of his not hanging his clothes up, and of his not knowing how to manage money. In individual therapy it became evident that she was sensitized by her father's death, stating he would have lived another ten years if not for alcohol. She also revealed a premarital sex adventure with another man which she enjoyed very much, but which led to pregnancy, illegal abortion and to near death for her. She never liked sex much after that, even though she took careful birth control precautions. Whereas at first this girl presented as a hostile demanding, complaining spoiled brat, she was very responsive to both individual and marital therapy. My cotherapist saw the husband as a capable, but meek man who did well at his job, was liked by his bosses, made decisions carefully, handled his children well, both in giving attention and disciplining them, and gave his wife whatever she wanted. His chief weakness was his inability to stand up to her. His drinking was not felt to be excessive. In the combined meetings we pointed out some of the patterns we saw operating. One statement made to her was, "Despite this fighting, I get the feeling you love your husband very much. Because of this you get very scared of losing him through death at a young age. This is why it would seem it is upsetting you when he drinks and smokes." At another session, we had them list each other's good traits. Both came up with many. We then discussed the impossibility of perfection in marriage and stated that there seemed to be many things they really did like about each other. The husband's lack of assertiveness was pointed out in individual therapy and then he was urged to practice acting assertively during a combined session. We had him repeat the behavior several times until it sounded convincing. The wife, when asked about this "new way" of his acting, said she preferred him this way.

This couple was only seen four times but showed marked improvement in several respects.

1. The wife seemed to understand both the probable etiology of her sexual disinterest and the reason for her complaints about her husband, relative to her own fears of his dying, like her father, and to the fact that he never stood up to her, thus reinforcing her complaining.
2. The wife became more agreeable to sex.
3. The husband gained less insight but, according to the wife, was acting more assertively.

Unfortunately they moved from the area and no further therapy was done. Also no followup is available. We feel these people could have explored, in more detail, their personal fears—hers about sex and his about asserting himself in the marriage and other areas.

BEHAVIOR THERAPY TECHNIQUES

Muscle Relaxation

I have taught muscle relaxation much the same way Wolpe does but have emphasized specific wording and imagery to implement it. As the patient focuses attention on the various parts of his body, he is told to attend to that part only, not to let his mind wander elsewhere. He is then told the feeling he should be experiencing is a "letting go," a letting out of all tension from this part of the body. He is told he does not need to use this part for the next half hour and, therefore, can let all muscle tension out of it. Sometimes the word "paralyze" is added. "You don't need to use your arm; it feels as if it is paralyzed." If I detect a fear of loss of control, I assure the patients that this is not hypnosis. They will be fully aware of what is going on and remain in control of themselves. If a noise occurs in the room, I tell them what caused it. I then have them take frequent deep breaths and suggest that they feel more relaxed with each exhalation. I suggest all along that the relaxed feeling is a pleasurable one; all tension is going from their body and they are feeling very good. Sometimes I add pleasant imagery such as, "You are lying in a grassy field on a warm, sunny day with gentle breezes and feel very good, without a care in the world."

I have used relaxation as a modality in itself, along with other procedures such as cognitive techniques, and of course as part of counterconditioning methods. I have obtained an excellent response. Patients often spontaneously report how much better they feel just by using relaxation on a daily basis or in tense situations.

C.S. was a twenty-eight-year-old white male treated for fears of separation from his geographical home. He worked for a company that wanted to send him to a six-week training course in a distant state. On two previous occasions he had anxiety attacks when going to this course and the approaching training course would be his "last chance." The case was explored fully, revealing anxiety in many similar situations. The patient was treated mainly with a cognitive approach in which the therapist continually pointed out the patient's magnifications and challenged his ominous predictions. "Even if you were to get sick, there are doctors all over the country." He was taught muscle relaxation, but counterconditioning could not be used as he found it most difficult to imagine vividly the scenes described.

Unfortunately, it is impossible to answer whether the treatment, of twenty sessions, was a success or failure. He and his family drove to the distant state but left there after a brief stay. The patient claimed, and his wife later verified, that the living accommodations were extremely bad, and since they were unable to find better ones, they returned home. An extensive review of the happenings of the trip convinced me that anxiety factors were not prominent in their decision to come back.

The only relevant fact about this case was that the patient used simple muscle relaxation to relieve anxiety before, during and after the trip and stated that this helped him on many occasions. He gives some lip service to the cognitive aspects discussed, but there was no evidence that he magnifies conditions less or that his thinking has changed in any other way.

I have used relaxation techniques at times in relation to sexual problems. One young man whom I was treating for multiple anxieties and occasional depression told me that he also had premature ejaculation, having orgasm some thirty seconds to two minutes after penetration, always too quickly to build up his own sexual tensions and never capable of satisfying his wife. Discussion revealed an awareness of tension relative to sexual performance. A brief discussion and demonstration of muscle relaxation was given. A few weeks later the patient related how he handled this problem. Fifteen to thirty minutes before sexual relations, he tried to relax his entire body, and since shortly before sexual penetration he noted increased tension in the lower part of his body and legs, he focused on these areas and relaxed them. He stated that this had consistently and considerably increased his performance time.

Counterconditioning

Two cases with whom I have used counterconditioning techniques are as follows:

B.D. was a thirty-five-year-old sergeant in the military who was seen by me for fears concerning a fast pulse. This patient had a four-month history of taking his pulse repeatedly and if he felt it was too fast, he would rush to the emergency room, state that he thought that he was having a heart attack, and demand an EKG. When his symptoms had first begun, he had been treated with a traditional approach for two months with no improvement. A second therapist then attempted paradoxical intention—having him do ten to twenty push-ups whenever he noticed a fast pulse. This made his anxiety worse. When I began asking questions about his present and past life, as the traditionalist had done, he became somewhat annoyed and bluntly denied problems in all areas mentioned. I therefore decided to use what information I did have without pushing him for more history. First, since it was evident to me that he was overly aware of bodily processes and magnified the significance of any pain or slight increase in pulse, I pointed out to him that his pulse increase could be due to a number of things, such as exercise, heat, an exciting or upsetting thought or other phenomenon of which he might not be aware. I also told him that he seemed to get aches and pains just like other people, but he seemed to notice them more and to magnify their importance. At the same time that these cognitive processes were being discussed, I began training the patient in muscle relaxation. Imagery was added to this: "You are lying in a grassy field on a warm sunny day with gentle breezes and not a care in the world." When he was imagining this scene and in a deep state of relaxation, I had him take his pulse in the imagery. At first I had him imagine that his pulse was seventy-six. As he became more relaxed, through muscle relaxation and imagery, the pulse was raised to eighty, but I always gave him a reason for the increase. For instance, "Your pulse is now eighty since you have been lying in the sun for half an hour." "You feel like running from one area to another fifty feet away, but now you have been in the sun a half hour and even though you run slowly, you take your pulse again and it is up to eighty-four." Again, another scene was introduced such as, "You have been in the sun for an hour. You run and when you lie down again, you begin thinking of an exciting football game. You take your pulse, and it is eighty-eight." Through the use of imagery and relaxation, the patient was able to imagine his pulse at one hundred without feeling any anxiety. During the early relaxation training he had one visit to the emergency room. After he had reached a pulse of eighty-four in imagery, he did not return there again. When his pulse reached one hundred in imagery, he stopped therapy, stating that he was feeling "great." This patient has been in complete remission for over two years. The reason I emphasize the relaxation with imagery as being the more effective technique, even though cognitive techniques were used, is that the patient felt this is what helped him. He also started using relaxation techniques for other tensions that he had. He gave no credit nor mention to his tendency to magnify things. This, of course, does not rule out that the cognitive techniques contributed to his improvement.

G.L. was a twenty-eight-year-old white male first lieutenant in the military service. This man had a history of being in three tornadoes at ages sixteen, twenty-one and twenty-eight, the last one occurring one month before coming to the Psychiatry Service. He had been hurt slightly in all three of these. In the last one he was in his trailer with his wife who was pregnant and both of them were thrown around but not injured seriously. Two weeks later his wife delivered a normal baby without difficulty. However, since this last tornado the patient would become extremely nervous when going outside and seeing even a single cloud in the sky. A complete life history revealed excellent functioning in all spheres and no additional phobias or other psychiatric symptoms. Interestingly, however, he mentioned that while in college he studied tornadoes as a special project and had become somewhat of an expert on the conditions leading up to them. This knowledge did not alleviate his fears, however, and he would become anxious on hearing a weather forecast that presented conditions that could even remotely lead to a tornado.

It was felt that this was a case of pure associative learning and, therefore, would be very amenable to counterconditioning procedures. Hierarchies were constructed in three areas, the first being the actual weather conditions—one cloud, then two, then many, darker clouds, rain of increasing intensity and wind of increasing speed. A second hierarchy involved information heard on the weather report—with increasingly ominous data, and a third hierarchy involved seeing the weather map on television with increasingly threatening conditions. After the patient learned deep muscle relaxation, he was started on the hierarchy of actual weather conditions. This was the main hierarchy employed and each session was begun with it. When the patient could not advance past a particular scene, he was switched to one of the other hierarchies. This man was treated for sixteen sessions. There was no improvement. Even though he seemed capable of attaining a good degree of muscle relaxation and stated he was imagining the various scenes quite vividly, he denied any improvement in his condition.

Assertive Training

Lack of appropriate assertive behavior appears to be present in a large percentage of psychiatric patients. This would include depressives, phobics, homosexuals and passive dependent personalities—about seventy-five-percent of my practice.

The techniques that I have used to promote assertiveness include advice, education, exploration of the inhibiting factors, modeling and behavior rehearsal.

Advice merely involves telling the patient they need to be more assertive in particular situations. It is notable that few people seen in psychotherapy can respond to direct advice without being somewhat resistant. An example of a woman who did respond to direct advice and became more assertive, thus benefiting greatly, is E.W.

E.W. is a forty-eight-year-old white female seen one week following discharge from a hospital after taking an overdose of drugs. In the past six years she had experienced frequent depressions, with three drug overdoses requiring hospitalization, and had seen three psychiatrists. One treated her for a year in weekly psychotherapy. Her last doctor had placed her on multiple drugs, including major tranquilizers and antidepressants.

She described her family life as chaotic, with an alcoholic, abusive father. She was the oldest of five children and was the peace mediator between the parents. She always had been the only one to assert herself with the father. As a child she felt society looked down upon her because of her father's alcoholism. She had divorced her second husband six years before, after eighteen years of a marriage in which "he let me do anything I wanted, but I was bored." She appeared nervous, moderately depressed and not very intelligent. There was no evidence of a psychosis. The diagnosis was a depressive reaction with anxiety features. As she talked, she calmed down, but I did not feel she would turn out to be a good candidate for cognitive therapy. My plan was to continue her medicine and see her for supportive therapy. During the second session, however, she began openly discussing her five-year relationship with a married man. I was much surprised that she was able to relate upsetting events to her moods. At this session I was able to markedly reduce her drugs to a low dose of anti-depressant, a mild tranquilizer and a sleeping pill. During the third session, the boyfriend was discussed in more detail and the bind the patient was in became evident. Her lover had been promising a marriage, borrowing money from her and allowing her to date no one. He continually promised her that he was going to divorce his wife. She believed him, but during the entire period she had almost constant nervousness and depression, made three suicide attempts, was hospitalized three times, and saw three psychiatrists. My therapeutic comments were along the lines of, "It seems you've put a lot of emphasis on R. and that the chances of his marrying you would appear slim. Why not develop an interest in other men?" When she came in for the fourth session, she stated that the entire week had gone better. She stated she had not heard from R., but she was not upset. She had one episode of nervousness, decided to go out dancing, and then felt better. During this session, while she discussed the money that this lover had borrowed from her and how angry she was at him, it was pointed out that during her relationship with him, she did not seem to assert herself much with him. Therapist: "Do you think there is a reason why you don't ask for the money back from R.?" Patient: "Yes, it might drive him further away." The patient was reticent about involving herself with other men and stated that she would still see R. if he called. At the next session, she stated that she had asserted herself with R., and he agreed to give back some of the money he had borrowed from her. She felt very good about this and had no guilt feelings. During this session, after a discussion of men, I pointed out that she only seemed interested in men who played hard to get. This seemed to make sense to her. This woman was very responsive all along to observations I made. She was also able to take direct advice. At this session she was advised to continue seeing other men and not to depend on any one of them for her entire social life. At the next session she reported that she was dating a new man whom she liked and who wanted to date her exclusively. She stated she would date him, but not limit her dating to him. She seemed to be feeling good. Therapy was then put on an every other week basis. At the next session she reported that she had taken steps to legally get her money back from R. She also reported an increased intensity in her new relationship. Advice was again given in this session regarding R. and the new boyfriend. At the next session, the patient revealed that she had had an anxiety attack when the boyfriend she had been going with most actively seemed to be losing interest. It was pointed out that she seemed to be searching for an intense relationship, perhaps marriage, and when she appeared to be losing a prospect she went into great panic. Her tendency to catastrophize was pointed out. At the same time, it was mentioned that considering she was forty-eight years old, she seemed quite adept at meeting men and gaining their interest. I told her that since many men were available to her, she should "keep many irons in the fire." The next session showed her to be in an excellent mood. She stated that she had been doing wonderfully the last two weeks. She had been going out and meeting new men and stated, "I've done what you told me and not gotten serious with anyone. I plan to date ten men." At this session she enthusiastically claimed that she was "doing great," had had no depressions and was feeling better than she had in the last five years. She stated that during those five years she was depressed almost continuously. She had now gone completely off all medication. "I have a new outlook. I feel free for the first time in five years." When seen five weeks later, the patient was in excellent spirits, stating that she had no depression and had not needed any medication. She stated she felt independent from men and felt that she was assertive in more areas. She stated that her friends had told her, "You're not the same person." She said to me, "No other doctor could get me over the depression or off the depression pills."

Five weeks later the patient had a slight setback. She had begun dating another man, but let herself increase her expectations of him. He was very attractive to her, and fairly wealthy. However, like the first man, he was still married and told her that while he cared very much for her, he still had to go through a divorce. Two things seemed to upset her from the weekend she had had with him. One was that the man could only be seen occasionally because business kept him moving around the country. He had asked her not to date other men and she had agreed to it, thus again putting control on her and dampening all social life. Also, for the first time in their relationship, he had gotten angry at her over a minor issue. Again, several things were pointed out to her: that she was put in an impossible situation where there would be no reinforcement from other men for possibly two or three months, that the probability of marriage to this man might not be high because of his as yet unfiled divorce, and that she had expected the man to be perfect (have no angry moods), and when he wasn't, her image of him was shattered. She improved during this session and when seen one week later was in a much better mood. She had decided that she would not be tied down by this man because of his inability to give her a guarantee of marriage and she had again begun to see other men. One week later she was back in good spirits. When she spoke with her potential fiancé, she had been more assertive with him, and while she did not tell him that she was dating other men, she did tell him that she thought he should write her more if he was as interested in her as he had said. She continued dating other men, and again she was completely asymptomatic. One month later she again experienced a rejection from a man she had been dating four weeks. However, within the session, where the old patterns were pointed out to her, that is, the high expectations and tendency to read rejection into situations, she recovered almost completely and one week later again was completely recovered. Two weeks later she was continuing at an asymptomatic level. When asked by me, "What things that we have talked about have helped you?" she replied, "Your statement, 'Don't underrate yourself.'"

Essentially then, this is a woman who was seen fifteen times in eight months and treated largely with assertive training. She is regarded as a successful case from seven points of view:

1. From the history she gave, and all other indications, she had been much more anxious, depressed and suicidal during the five years preceding therapy than in the period since.
2. Her daughter and friends told her she had been looking much better than she had in the previous five years.
3. "I told my daughter what has helped me in therapy with you. I told her you let me talk, but you will also talk back to me; you tell me things to think about and I think about these things when I leave. When I am nervous you give me medicine. I take as little as possible. I will never go back to a hospital."
4. She was acting assertively in her interpersonal relations and with me.
5. She had incorporated much of what we discussed into her thinking.
6. When she did get upset, it was quite easy to snap her out of it.

7. The therapist has a feeling of the specific events she is vulnerable to and what to emphasize in therapy.

Education about assertiveness and its importance in human interaction can serve as an indirect way to get some patients to begin developing an awareness of its role in their lives. I will educate a patient by making a general statement somewhat applicable to the patient and then amplify this by discussing another case.

"Look, in general, while being a nice guy certainly has its virtues and usually leads to one's being well liked, it also has its drawbacks in that people, unknowingly, tend to expect and demand more from agreeable people. For instance I have an extremely conscientious patient who is an excellent worker. However, his boss is never satisfied and the patient is constantly pushing himself harder to please this essentially unpleasable boss. The patient has asked for a pay raise twice in the past year and has been turned down. He is invaluable to his boss's operation, yet he does not use his power to help himself, either by pushing himself less or demanding more money. When he decided to use his power, that is by turning in his resignation, his boss gave him everything he wanted, more assistance at work and a pay raise. Timidly asking for changes had been totally unsuccessful because it was no threat to the boss, whereas threatened loss of his prize worker brought the boss to terms. Of course, if the patient had not been a conscientious, hard worker, he would have had no power base from which he could bargain."

The technique I use most often to stimulate assertive behavior is the exploration of the inhibiting thoughts that prevent a patient from expressing himself more effectively. The inhibiting thoughts are usually some fear of loss or harm that the patient is predicting.

For example:

"If I ask the boss for a raise, he'll fire me."
"If I dispute the mark with the teacher, I'll get a poor grade next time."
"If I say the wrong thing, people will think I'm stupid."
"If I express my views, people will not like me."

There is a most important secondary implication to the harm that will be endured and that is that it will be *catastrophic* in nature.

"If I lose my job, I'll *never get another one* and *I'll starve.*"
"If she doesn't love me, *my life is ruined.*"

This second belief is usually less accessible to awareness than is the primary one. It is important, however, to stress its presence since once the intensity of the "catastrophe" is lessened, the inhibiting power of the primary fear is lessened. A patient, after gaining awareness into and learning to challenge the catastrophic remark, may say the following to himself:

"It is important that I feel less pressure and make more money at this job. I'll probably have to get fairly assertive and may have to resign to show them that I mean what I say. This may accomplish what I want, but there is a chance my resignation will be accepted. But I am a good worker and can get another job. I may miss working here and it will be disappointing to leave, but it is not the end of the world."

J.N., who is described in the cognitive section, is markedly inhibited about talking. At this point in his therapy, he is beginning to focus on the numerous times he doesn't say or do things "because people will think I'm stupid." Every time he focuses on one of these fear predictions, I add "and wouldn't that be awful." Hopefully he will begin to see that, he, too, has been adding this statement and thereby keeping himself blocked and uninvolved.

Modeling procedures are carried out on only a small scale by my speaking assertively to a nurse or secretary on the phone in the presence of a patient who would benefit from seeing or hearing this.

"Look, that report has to go out today. If you are overburdened, ask the other girl to help you." This is said in a firm but non-hostile tone.

Behavior rehearsal has sometimes been effective with dependent personalities such as W.E., discussed in the management section. W.E. was urged to repeat the same assertive statement to his wife several times. After about eight attempts he sounded convincingly assertive to his wife and the two cotherapists, and was praised for this. His wife later reported that he was maintaining this assertiveness at home and that she liked him much better this way.

An area where appropriate assertive behavior is of particular importance, but difficult to develop, is with depressive syndromes. Many depressives vacillate between sulking depressions and annoying hostility, neither of which helps them attain their goal. These people need a multifaceted approach to help them develop appropriate assertiveness. This includes education and other cognitive procedures to make them aware of the extremes of their behavior, behavior rehearsal, and modeling.

Advice rarely works with them. My results even with this multifaceted approach have had limited success in the treatment of depressives.

Imagery

I have used imagery but only to a limited degree to date. As mentioned before, I use pleasant imagery to aid muscle relaxation. I first try to find what scenes a person would find to be especially relaxing.

Imagery in the form of caricatures or animal forms, as I described in a previous article, has been used minimally by me with few worthwhile results. I have discovered that patients find it is hard to put their feelings in the form of a caricature or animal form. When they can do it, I find that it does give me clues to their fears and distortions.

With married couples, we have tried to get them to conjure up images of their early dating or early marriage scenes that were very romantic. We then have them fully describe the scene and try to put themselves back in that scene as if it were now occurring. The hope is that if we can do this, we might be able to have these emotionally divorced couples feel a bit more *"turned on"* by each other. We have even suggested that they practice these scenes several times daily. This, of course, is used in combination with other techniques we are using with marital couples which involve communication and increasing their awareness of how they reinforce and are aversive to each other. At this writing, we have attempted the imagery techniques on only two couples. However, there has been little enthusiasm on their part. During a marital session, they are unable to come up with any good description of a scene and there has been little, if any, practice. It is our feeling that their negative feelings about each other probably have to be sufficiently low to get them motivated to apply this technique.

The use of imagery as an aversive technique sounds interesting. I found that twenty-four hours after I read an article on the use of aversive imagery for the treatment of alcoholism, I went to take a drink and as I approached the liquor cabinet, I got a slightly nauseated feeling. I remembered the article but still did not take the drink. This technique appears to have much to offer.

Symptom Removal

An interesting case that involves symptom removal is as follows:

D.C. is a twenty-six-year-old married, white male who presented with a chief complaint of stuttering. Significant in the patient's history is that his father was a well-known personality in the government. The patient was conscientious and had worked hard and accomplished much in his vocation. He was motivated to rid himself of the stuttering so that he could make a better verbal presentation of his work. He had been working for someone and had planned to go into business on his own. Notable in the mental status examination was the fact that this patient was extremely polite, friendly and anxious to please. He did not talk unless spoken to and I had to watch my tendency to overtalk.

The patient was able to identify those situations where he did get nervous and stutter. The first phase of therapy was concerned with pointing out that his stuttering did not seem to be a catastrophe and that he had so many attributes that the stuttering, even if it did continue, would not ruin him. The patient accepted this but not with any great enthusiasm. Relaxation training was given, with emphasis on the muscles of his tongue, jaws, and neck. The next week he came in and said he was able to do the relaxation as taught and that he was able to relax his throat muscles. He said that when he found himself starting to stutter, he would stop talking, relax himself completely and then focus on relaxing the throat muscles. When he started talking again, he was able to proceed with great success. This patient's stuttering disappeared so quickly (in four sessions), that it had the therapist a little concerned. I was not sure if he was better or just trying to please me, or if he was not really that serious a stutterer at all. After his stuttering had improved (it had been evident only about five to ten times during any one session and at those times it was mild in nature), he started discussing other anxieties he had. His dynamics in these areas seemed to me to be related to the fact that he was a nice guy and that people pushed him to do things and that he did them without complaint. He was encouraged to be more assertive. However, in the ensuing meetings it became evident that this man was willing to accept a certain degree of subservience to please people. He assured me that he really wasn't walked on by people and knew where to draw the line. One motivation that brought him to therapy was that his brother was willing to use his father's name and rely on his father to advance him in his career. The patient said he was never like that and did not like it in his brother. He stated that he wanted to be excellent in everything so that people would not think that he had achieved on the basis of his father's connections. As a result of this, he worked very hard at not only educating himself in his career field, but in other areas as well. He picked subjects that he felt would be interesting to people and would study them in great detail. Since many of his friends were hunters and he, too, hunted, he became an expert on marksmanship and ballistics. It occurred to me during the seventh session that his coming to therapy was motivated not by a sense of an extreme disabling stuttering disorder but by some very strong need to improve himself in every area possible. Even a slight amount of stuttering, therefore, to him was an impairment and anything to improve this was necessary.

COGNITIVE THERAPY TECHNIQUES

The role of the cognitive therapist is to familiarize himself with his patient's thought content, thought processes, feelings and behavior; to note the relationships between thoughts, feelings and behavior; to organize the data from each of these areas into what appears to be recurring patterns; and to use any one of numerous techniques to add to, subtract from, or in some way change or reorganize the patient's thought content and processes. Changes in these areas, in my opinion, are basic to and precede emotional change.

Thought content is defined as the themes, concepts, attitudes and beliefs which dominate the patient's thinking. The patient may be aware of only a portion of these. Examples of thought content in different patients are as follows: The themes dominating the thinking of a depressive would be those of hopelessness, loss of interest, self-criticism and concerns about health; those of a paranoid would concern injustices done to him and dangers that await him.

Thought processes may be defined as activities postulated to occur in the mind. These would include: *magnification*—the tendency to view things as being much more important, fearful or catastrophic than they objectively are; *selective abstraction*—the tendency to take certain features out of context and emphasize them to the exclusion of others; *overgeneralization*—the tendency to make far reaching conclusions on the basis of little data; and *thinking in extremes*—the tendency to see things as absolutes, either white or black, good or bad, right or wrong. This is often exemplified by remarks such as, "I must do my job perfectly," or "The world should be fair."

The information sought varies with the therapist, and is a reflection of the model of personality he uses. For example, the traditionalist usually seeks an extensive history of early family relationships. My own tendency is to take only a brief past history initially and devote most of my efforts toward ascertaining the patient's present-day thought content, processes, feelings and behavior. I listen for what motivates or reinforces him and what discourages him or is aversive for him, as well as evaluating his ability to assert himself in different settings. If the patient is unable to give the therapist enough information to work with, either spontaneously, nonverbally or with facilitating procedures such as direct and indirect questions, comments, paraphrasing correctly (or purposely incorrectly), or repeating the last words of a sentence, the patient may be helped to talk by using several techniques. The therapist can: educate him as to the reasons that talking is necessary in psychotherapy, inform him that his remarks are confidential, and assure him that there are no right or wrong answers; use rapport techniques to decrease anxiety; or specifically focus on his inability to talk freely by exploring what fears might be involved in the therapy situation. Pinpointing and discussing these fears usually lead to the patient's talking more and may, in addition, help him with inhibitions he is having outside of therapy.

If these procedures fail to give me enough information to organize the patient's difficulties in a meaningful way, I turn to other methods to get the necessary information. These are more indirect techniques than the aforementioned and include areas more removed from the patient's here-and-now concepts. They are in a sense projective techniques.

For example:

I may ask for a more detailed history. As mentioned, with most patients I do not gather an extensive past history since I rarely find this of value; however, when I need clues to a patient's unrevealed conceptual systems, I will probe for more details of the past. "What was your parents' marriage like?" "What do you remember about your sex education?"

I rarely encourage patients to discuss dreams because if it is to be done correctly, this is a time-consuming procedure involving a complete description of the dream and the patient's associations to each detail. However, in patients where information is sparse, I urge dream description to give me additional information on the patient's governing attitudes. N.A., cognitive section, described a dream without my urging him to and without extensive associations to each detail. The dream in itself and the remarks he made about it verified some of the ideas I had about his feelings toward women. It also served to have him discuss these feelings more at this session.

I have used imagery techniques, to some extent, to increase my knowledge of the patient.

"Try and put your feelings on this matter into a picture. It can involve people or animals or caricatures."

With a man felt to have serious sexual inhibitions: "Try to imagine that your father is watching you having sex with your wife. What would his facial expression be? Would he say anything?"

Other statements used to indirectly gain information may include:

"What TV personality are you most like? Why?"
"Do other people feel the same way as you do?"
"How would your friends react if you told them you did this?"

These four ancillary information gathering techniques—detailed history, dreams, imagery and projective statements—are usually used when information gathering methods mentioned earlier are at a stalemate. The data thus far gathered from these auxiliary procedures have been minimal at best.

Just as the type of information sought reflects the therapist's concepts of human behavior, so does the organization of that information in the therapist's mind. This is demonstrated in the case of N.A. (mentioned in more detail later in this section). His traditional therapist was apparently seeing his problems as "oedipal"—his inability to work hard and become a success being caused by unresolved anxieties about the father's harming him or being angry with him should he succeed. My current working concept of the case sees his inhibitions as due to his tendency to overthink, to carefully weigh the pros and cons of everything he does so that he does it right. Only if there is certainty that he is doing the right thing (his strongest reinforcer) can he embark on any venture. Without this certainty he cannot proceed with it at all.

Once the therapist has gathered sufficient information for his own understanding and organized this into some conceptual scheme (that further information should verify), the problem is: what techniques does he use to help the patient? It is the author's opinion that one helps the patient by influencing his thinking: adding to it, subtracting from it, and reorganizing it on the basis of what the therapist has decided is maladaptive about it.

One can add to a patient's thinking by direct education. Many patients are prone to fears and misconceptions in areas in which they are least knowledgeable. When educated in these matters, misconceptions are lessened and concomitant fears are alleviated. This is well demonstrated in the cases of W.B., who was aided by education on body processes, health data and doctors' examining procedures; and J.N., who was taught about sexual norms in the United States today.

One can also add to a patient's thinking by making him more aware of his thought content, thought processes, feelings and behavior. Techniques used to do this include those already mentioned for information gathering, such as direct and indirect questions and paraphrasing, and asking him what he thinks when experiencing certain feelings (what is he telling himself, what is going through his mind). One substantially increases a patient's awareness by repeatedly pointing out recurring themes: "You always blame yourself when something goes wrong," and recurring processes: "You have a tendency to magnify things. Every time you get a pain in your chest you are certain it is a heart attack." It is felt that increasing awareness in these areas gives patients a mastery over them.

A second means of relieving patient suffering is by decreasing thoughts which are maladaptive, those which underlie unpleasant emotions. After the patient becomes aware of his current thinking, his thoughts can be challenged. I repeatedly focus on and challenge maladaptive thoughts during a therapy session and promote the patient's doing the same during the intersession period, thereby causing thoughts to lose their effect on the patient's feelings.

For example, with J.N., who was afraid to talk in many situations because he told himself he might "sound stupid," I focused repeatedly on this thought, thus bringing it more clearly into his awareness, and challenged his statements by saying, "Why would it be so awful, even if they thought what you said was stupid, which they probably won't, would that ruin your career, end your life?" Repetition usually leads to the challenging remark being incorporated into the patient's thinking. Every time the maladaptive thought occurs, the challenging remark is triggered and hopefully "defeats" the maladaptive thought. The patient is no longer anxious that a catastrophe will occur if he speaks. The maladaptive thought has become absent from, or inactive in, his thought repertoire.

While all of the techniques thus far mentioned do tend to reorganize thinking by adding to or subtracting from one's thought repertoire, other procedures may likewise reorganize the patient's thinking. The most commonly used of these would be the therapist's reduction of a large amount of data into a sentence or two. I refer to this as "making order out of chaos." This reduction to a simpler form enables the patient to understand more clearly a basic concept and to have a certain mastery over it. An example of this would be a statement of N.A. such as, "You seem to have a need for certainty." His awareness of one dominant thought motif may simplify the often confusing thought data which are processed by the human mind.

A second means of promoting the reorganization of thinking is asking the patient if there are alternative ways of looking at a situation just described. I try to get a patient to list five to ten alternatives. So when a man states that he feels uncomfortable with a girl who is quiet and gives as his interpretation of her action, "She doesn't like me," I have him list other possibilities such as, "She might be shy," "She might not have felt well," "She might have problems on her mind," or "She might feel this is the way a man wants her to act." Continually getting patients to list alternatives to the one stereotyped maladaptive thought they get in specific situations gradually increases the repertoire of explanations they have to choose from. Choosing a more adaptive thought constitutes a reorganization of thinking in the specific area involved.

During the course of cognitive therapy, I am most interested in learning if cognitive changes are occurring, and if so, is there a concomitant improvement in the patient's feeling and behavior. Many times patients in psychotherapy show complete symptom removal without the cognitive change that would be anticipated. This is demonstrated in some of the cases that follow where statements made to the patient never seemed to be incorporated into his thinking and other statements never even discussed are mentioned and sometimes credited with the patient's improvement. This is seen in the cases of W.B., D.W., and E.E. In other cases the patient begins using remarks made by the therapist earlier in therapy and attributes changes to these remarks, as did E.W. (Behavior Therapy Section). N.A., on the other hand, shows cognitive changes along the lines the therapist planned, but without the therapist ever having had the opportunity to make the remarks. In other words, the therapist and patient are in conceptual agreement without having traded specific information.

The following cases are presented to give the reader some idea of the way I employ cognitive therapy.

J.N. is a thirty-year-old white male auditor who voluntarily came to therapy after his wife was referred to me by a neurologist for depression. The patient felt he was the cause of her depression. His main concern was that he had put no effort into any area of his life for several years. There was no evidence of psychosis and he essentially presented a depressed picture, talking slowly and with no spontaneity.

Because of his lack of spontaneous information and the fact that he revealed a long-term problem, a rather complete history was taken. Briefly stated, he was the third of five children, none of whom were ever close to the others. He had a poor relationship with his father who frequently hit him on the face. "I resented him. I was never able to do what he seemed to want. My mother backed me up, even when she shouldn't have." He later said of his mother, "I used to work endlessly on my model boats, until fatigued, and hope my mother would praise me. She always did. I would push her until she said something good." As a child he described himself as a loner, having no confidence. He remembers that he could never talk in front of people even in second grade. The picture changed somewhat in high school and college where he described himself as a good student, active in clubs and holding down a job. He liked dating beautiful girls so that other people would "eat their hearts out." Since graduating from college he had been with the same company for ten years, did not like the job in general, but liked his current assignment and planned no change. The company wanted to send him for further education so he could advance, but "I had no goals in mind, so it would be worthless to go to school." He has been married for seven years and has two children. He talked little of the marriage other than, "It's O.K.," said unenthusiastically. There has been fidelity on both sides, but with his having some fantasy life about other women and his mentioning of his wife's lack of orgasm. Also significant but not mentioned specifically in relation to the marriage was that even after his active high school and college life, he maintained enthusiasm in many areas, such as model plane building and sailing. The loss of interest in activities seemed to date from one year prior to his marriage. "Over the last eight years, I have stopped many activities. I don't even sail anymore. I occasionally get overly interested in something like building cabinets. When I first moved here, I was interested in landscaping. My wife felt I was going overboard, I guess I was."

Besides his apathy about work and outside activities, he brought up two other areas for discussion. At the third meeting he stated he had better "confess" some things to me about himself, whereupon he revealed a list of thoughts and activities in the sexual area since age ten. This included masturbation, attempts to see his older sister nude and the admission that he found his mother sexually "stimulating"—"When she vacuumed the stairs, I would look up her dress." He also admitted that he now gets sexual fantasies about his wife, other women, and his wife having sex with another man. These fantasies excite him and lead to masturbation. In reality he felt his sex relations with his wife were very satisfying, except for her usual lack of orgasm. Also his wife gets upset if he looks at other girls because she feels he's not just appreciating their aesthetic qualities but looks like he wants to be in bed with them. He stated, "I guess if our relationship were better, I wouldn't look at girls in the same way."

A third area of concern came up during the fifth meeting. He revealed marked fears about what people think of him. This involved activities such as sailing and skiing, speaking in a classroom, asking a waiter to return a bad steak, and most importantly, talking in any situation where he might risk saying the wrong thing.

From a treatment standpoint this man has been quite interesting. His initial quietness was handled by active history taking. I also decided at the second session to allude to his nonspontaneity, whereupon he said, "I guess it's because you're young. Also you mentioned marital therapy and I'm not interested in that." This is when he revealed his sexual curiosities and acts over the years with much guilt. Nothing that he said sounded terribly abnormal to me and I used simple educational techniques, informing him that most of what he described was done by a large majority of boys and men and that his guilt seemed out of proportion to his thoughts and actions. He was surprised to hear what I said. My impression about this lack in his knowledge and in other areas is that it has been due to little close contact with other people where such information is usually learned. My initial thoughts about his loss of interest in things since just before his marriage were that the wife has had some role in discouraging him. This hasn't been alluded to yet, other than my saying, "It seems you've lost your spontaneity in the last seven years." In the last four sessions (fourth through seventh), each of which had shown the same pattern of no spontaneous talk, I have begun focusing on this. It has seemed to me that this is a carry over of his lack of spontaneity and lack of involvement in the outside world. It has also frustrated me. Working with this phenomenon, which is occurring in the actual therapy situation, I feel is most promising in helping the patient with his outside life and has also relieved my frustration.

Patient: Silent three minutes.
Therapist: Small talk ten minutes.
Patient: Silent three minutes.
Therapist: "Is there anything you'd like to bring up today?"
Patient: "No, we've discussed everything."
Therapist: "Are you uncomfortable coming here?"
Patient: "Yes."
Therapist: "Is it similar to talking in other situations?"
Patient: "Yes, I'm afraid that what I'd have to say isn't important."
Therapist: (I felt at this point, that the patient was sensitive to the asking of questions, the technique I was using on him. It seemed to me that when asked questions he felt he had to give a "right answer." If wrong he feared punishment, so I made the following statements.)
   "Listen, I ask you questions to get you to think about things, but I get the feeling that you feel you must give a *right* answer. However, the answers aren't necessarily right or wrong. They are just designed to learn what occurs in your thinking."
Patient: "I'm glad to hear you say that. I really feel that maybe you understand me. I feel good when you say something that relates to the way I feel."

Discussions since then have tended to center around his classroom fears of answering, fear of looking bad while skiing or sailing and current interpersonal relations. Other comments made to this patient include, "You seem to predict what's on other people's minds." He agreed and revealed he predicted they would be critical. He was later challenged on this, "How do you learn what they are thinking?" When he talked of getting an "F" in class, clarification revealed many people got "F's," and no one got above "C." When he brought up fear of answering in class "because everyone knew the right answer and I might be wrong," I challenged, "How do you know they all have the answer?" Another statement to him concerning his fear of looking stupid by making mistakes was, "You seem to have lost the ability to judge how serious or maladaptive a mistake is. Getting lost looking for a street isn't the catastrophe that driving your car into a pole is."

Remarks indicating cognitive change and general improvement are as follows:

At the fourth session—

"Recently I've felt more enthusiasm for fixing the house up."
"I felt good when you said the things I've done aren't sick."

At the sixth session—

"Things are great—the best things have been in years. My wife and I are talking more. Things don't get her down like they used to. She isn't as upset if the house isn't clean; she's not as upset with our son. She has more respect for me. We are getting along well, talking about things."

The patient's improvement so far is attributed to education and to some extent the challenging of his distortions, particularly in regard to his multiple guilts and to his fears about what others think. It is hard to assess the role his therapy plays in the improvement of the marriage because his wife, too, has responded well to individual therapy.

D.W. was a twenty-eight-year-old attractive, eight months pregnant white female who was seen in consultation in the hospital because of symptoms of depression, panic episodes and a fear of going outside. The patient had been hospitalized two years before, when not pregnant, for similar symptoms. She claims that the psychiatrist she saw two years ago did not help her. However, apparently she had improved and had functioned fairly well until two weeks prior to her admission to the hospital. On examination she was slightly nervous, agitated, emotionally labile, and showed a significant increase in anxiety when discussions of going out of the house or hospital were held. There was no evidence of schizophrenic disorder. She was diagnosed as a phobic reaction. In her early history, it was revealed that her mother died when she was seven and her father, she claims, sexually molested her at age five. This patient was treated for eight sessions in a two-week period by cognitive approach. Discussion was largely on the here and now, a description of what her current life situation was, her relationship with her husband, her feelings about her having another child and the events surrounding her panic attacks. Initially the patient was felt to be somewhat hysterical, overreacting to many things in her environment. She claimed annoyance in many situations. As details of her life were expanded and clarified, it became evident that her fear of being outside was more a fear specifically of seeing people she knew and being delayed by them. She said that everyone in their family, including herself, was always in a hurry. She experienced "sickness" when people would stop her in a store, or when waiting in line, causing her to not want to go out at all. She was afraid that if she did go out she would get sick. She discussed the fact that as a child she felt she used sickness to avoid doing things. When neighbors visited, she was quite annoyed and to get them to leave she would say she wasn't feeling well. She allowed people to be quite dependent on her and was unable to assert herself. She could never tell them that she was tired or had things to do. She could only feign illness to get rid of them. It was pointed out that she seemed to equate, from habit, annoyance with sickness and that now when she felt annoyed, she felt sick. She also catastrophized in many situations, and these were pointed out. While this woman never gave evidence that she incorporated what was being pointed out to her in the eight sessions that she was seen, there was a marked improvement. That is she stopped complaining, she catastrophized less, gained confidence, was not easily upset by disappointments or unexpected events, and began to go on her own to see her obstetrician without fear or attacks of panic. She was able to be discharged from the hospital prior to the birth of her baby and was at home and able to function, going out in public and feeling well in general. There was no problem when the baby was delivered, and a follow-up phone call one month after the patient had had her baby revealed that things were going fine and that there were no problems of any kind. The precipitating event of this severely disabling phobia was never established. Interestingly, after her treatment had been completed, her case was discussed with the therapist who had treated her two years before. The dynamics that he gave, for the first phobic reaction two years ago, concerned what he felt to be an attraction to a man at work and he stated that the phobia was an avoidance of a potentially sexual situation. When her current situation was mentioned to him, he stated dogmatically that the pregnancy was obviously the precipitating event, causing concern over her body image. While this man is a traditionally-oriented therapist and conceptualized her situation in a way that led to successful treatment two years ago, his present conceptualization was far different from the one I had formulated and used for basing my remarks to her. It would seem that his past approach and my present one had both succeeded.

W.B. is a thirty-two-year-old white male who came in with a chief complaint of feeling that he had had a heart attack, "weird feelings," and an upset stomach. The patient had been given multiple medications for his stomach and nerves in the past two months by his family physician, but none had relieved his symptoms. When put on thorazine three weeks before I saw him, his pulse got faster and his fears about heart trouble increased. The day before his first visit he had chest pains and felt that he was having a heart attack.

Present history revealed that the patient's wife had given birth to a baby six months ago and that there had been bleeding necessitating a blood transfusion. The patient had to donate a pint of blood. Even though the wife was never dangerously ill, the patient found the whole experience quite traumatic. Also at that time, the babysitter informed the patient that she knew of a girl who died from the "same thing his wife had." Later, about two months after the birth of the baby, the patient developed a severe case of the flu. One month later, about three months prior to my seeing him, he began developing some sensitivity to body processes, noticed feelings of weakness and loss of equilibrium, and became conscious of his heartbeat. The condition worsened in the past month and one day prior to being seen, he had become acutely anxious relative to the pain in the chest.

Mental status examination revealed him to be a thin, nervous, slightly suspicious man of average intelligence. There was no evidence of psychosis. I diagnosed him as an Anxiety Reaction and took him off all drugs except a minor tranquilizer and a sleeping pill.

At the first meeting, I pointed out that he seemed to magnify things greatly. The suggestion was made that he would be better in four to five visits. The therapist's attitude was firm, but friendly. The patient was seen the next day, and it was evident that any stimulus relative to health led to a panic reaction. Stimuli included TV doctor programs, reading of an auto accident in the newspaper, or hearing anything about air pollution. I decided at that session to briefly explore his past to determine the possible origin of his health concerns. He stated that he was the oldest of five boys, all of whom have always been in good health. His father has mild claustrophobia; his mother is in good health. He was raised in a strict manner. He denies that there was any emphasis on health or bodily processes in his upbringing. He had been in the military for three years and had functioned well. He had been married for ten years. There used to be fights in his marriage, but there have not been any recently. He states that he felt better when they did fight. At present there are no obvious problems in his marriage or job. At this session I told him that it appeared to me that he had always led a healthy life and seemed to have developed a feeling of invulnerability to illness. It was pointed out that perhaps the illness of his wife and the events surrounding it (his donating blood, and the babysitter's remark) and then his own serious case of the flu made him feel more vulnerable. It was also mentioned that since then he seemed to have the tendency to magnify things. The third session revealed marked improvement in his attitude and feelings. He stated that he attributed his whole improvement to the fact that his wife will "take over the bills"; also, that he was able to borrow money to pay for her hospitalization. These issues had not been discussed in the prior sessions at all. Also, he stated, "I decided to put my mind on happier thoughts like camping and doing things together and playing with the baby." He was sleeping and eating better. His medications had been tapered off by himself. On the fourth visit, two weeks after his initial visit, he stated he had an occasional "weird" feeling. This was defined as "like I can't move, like I'm moving when I shouldn't be, a pressing feeling all over my body." He also stated that when someone opened the door and warm air hit the side of his face, he would get a weird feeling and get scared. He stated that, "If the sun goes behind a cloud and the room gets dark, I think it is me blacking out." Again, the treatment was to point out his tendency to magnify and to be overly aware of bodily processes. Because of some continued nervousness and my feeling that he had a need for "magic," I decided to teach him relaxation techniques. Also, since the patient brought up financial concerns, I agreed to see him less frequently and for shorter time periods, so that he might save money. When seen one week later, he stated he was feeling the best he had in many years. There was no anxiety whatsoever. Again, when he began to magnify things, this was pointed out; the relaxation training was repeated. Two weeks later, he was off all medication, very relaxed, and he said that he had been catching up on his bills. One-month follow up revealed no exacerbation of symptoms.

E.E. was a forty-year-old married white female with no previous psychiatric history. Her chief complaint was nervousness, tension, decreased appetite, insomnia, and obsessive thoughts about her neighbors for a period of one month.

The patient dates the onset of her feelings to a mild altercation with a neighbor. This neighbor had never been friendly with any other families on the street and had recently complained to the patient about her son being a wise guy. Mrs. E. seemed fairly depressed and self-critical but, in general, from the history gleaned and the mental status examination, it was felt she was a fairly well-adjusted person. Diagnosis was depressive reaction with anxiety features.

This patient spontaneously talked of her childhood. She reported that she was the sixth of ten children, and described her father as a very critical man, especially hard on the older children, whom he physically beat up. She also remarked that he "wrecked" the oldest girl. She stated that he liked her (the patient, that is). "If he was critical of me, I kidded him back, and he laughed. He was lenient with me. I didn't give him reason to be mad at me."

When she was next seen one week later, she stated she had improved, was less tense and was sleeping better. She again began talking about her father during this session without prompting from me. She stated that between ages 5 and 12 she felt that he would beat her. Then she began talking about her neighbor, stating that he was just like her father. She said her father had tortured and shot a dog that "ate our chickens." "The neighbor beat his dog with a chain. I hate him. . . . We're Irish, and no German is any good. (That was the neighbor.) We're Democrat, and no

Republican could be any good. . . . Mainly my problem is my father. I was affected by him. I wouldn't date boys who might yell at me, even if it meant not getting married. If anyone wasn't nice to me once, that ended it." She again talked of her neighbor. I asked her what her father had predicted about Germans and Republicans. "He said that Germans were war-like and made lampshades out of humans. . . . Republicans hurt the farmers." (Her father was a farmer.) It appeared to me that she had not only compared the neighbor with her father in their strong, hostile, critical ways, but she had learned the father's attitudes, and many of these influenced her feelings toward the neighbor. At this session, I mentioned to the patient that there seemed to be a similarity between the neighbor and the father. This remark drew no response from her. Neither did a later one, "You seem to have the same concerns your father had about Germans and Republicans."

At the next session, I stated to her, "Hostile men seem to scare you." I also pointed out another characteristic she had displayed: "You seem to have a lack of assertiveness in your interpersonal relations and this makes you feel helpless and fearful." She stated, "I won't stand up for my rights. I occasionally told on my brothers to my mother."

At this next session, she talked more about her brothers, both of whom, she claimed, sexually attacked her. Her sixteen-year-old brother gave her sticks of gum when she was eight years old to allow him to try sexual relations with her; she states she didn't think he succeeded because she was too small. Her thirteen-year-old brother, she states, wasn't so bad. "He just felt me all over." This woman kept talking about her family, even though I did not promote this. It was my feeling that she had a preconceived idea that psychiatrists like one to talk about one's past and any possible sexual adventures. It was not clear as to whether these events had occurred or not. She said the referring physician had thought she was having some marital problems. She was encouraged to talk more of her marriage. She claimed her marriage was excellent. She stated she didn't enjoy sex until the fifth year of her marriage and that, since being on the birth control pill for the last four years, she has enjoyed it to a much higher degree. She stated at this visit, her third, that she was "a little less afraid of the neighbors this week."

In the fourth visit, she stated she was feeling much better. "I don't know if it is because school is starting or my sister is coming. . . . I have gone out of the house every day the last four to six days. I am not pre-occupied with the neighbors. Before, I couldn't work or fix a meal. . . . I am back to where I was eight or more months ago. . . . It's a clean break. Up until a few weeks ago there was a partial relationship between me and the neighbors. I was uncomfortable about the relationship, so I was trying to appease them. But now, I don't bother with them at all."

She was then seen one more time three weeks later and was doing excellently. She no longer had the symptoms of nervousness, tension, insomnia, poor appetite, or thoughts about the neighbors. Therapy was discontinued.

A follow-up phone call one year after the patient was seen revealed the following, "I was helped by the fact that I talked my heart out. When you said the neighbor sounds psychotic, I stopped blaming myself." Also of note is the fact that the patient's father died nine months ago and her mother six months ago. The patient states she took this very well. "I had no regrets. They had a good life, they died close to each other, they couldn't live without each other."

This is an interesting case in that this patient had a complete remission of an illness with only five sessions of psychotherapy, her improvement starting even during the first session. She gave little credit to the interpretations that I had made, other than the one concerning the neighbor's psychosis. Actually, I do not recall ever having made that statement. Catharsis about her father and brothers and possibly some awareness of the similarity of the neighbor to the father would seem to me to be the thing that helped her. It is difficult to evaluate whether her improvement came in any relation to the verbal statements that I made.

C.H. was a twenty-nine-year-old white married female, discussed in the management section. The chief complaint was an obsession that she might kill her six-month-old son. Examination revealed that she was an intelligent, nervous, talkative woman who seemed very concerned about her obsession. Her thought content was permeated with morbid and violent thoughts about which she commented with less concern than her obsession. She was appropriately friendly, cooperative and occasionally smiled. I did not feel she was schizophrenic.

The patient's description of her childhood and parents was as follows: "We were a close family. . . . Mother was perfect and always did things for my sister and me. . . . I was always mean to my Mother. I always felt she would die before I could repay her. . . . Grandmother was like me— a hypochondriac. She died of cancer. . . . Mother told me to watch out for men when I was little. A few men followed me home. . . . I was always afraid someone might stab me. I feared leaving the door open. I always felt guilty for not being a good daughter. . . . Mother was calm but did spank us. Father was sensitive and couldn't take criticism. He would get mad, then brood. He once said he understood why people killed themselves. Years ago he took a gun and was going to kill himself. I bit his hand, grabbed the gun and ran outside with it."

The patient had three years of college and has been writing mystery stories for children since that time. She admitted to sexual activity with her husband and others before marriage. She stated that she has always enjoyed sex and never felt guilty about it. She had one year of psychotherapy after her third year of college for reasons never discussed. She dated her history of nervousness, phobias, obsessions and compulsions to her teen years. Her sister, who is five years younger, has been hospitalized more than once and received electroshock treatment. The exact nature of her illness was not made clear.

The patient's main preoccupation was with violence, sickness and death. At our first meeting she brought up the Texas Tower slaying, the murder of eight nurses in Chicago and the movie "Psycho." Throughout therapy she revealed multiple fears: cancer, permanent nervousness, the birth of an abnormal baby, that her husband would get killed, that her son will get germs from old people or a dirty kitchen floor, that if she went outside a bee might sting her, leading to her falling and hurting her baby, and that she'd be bitten by a deadly spider. Three years ago, after her husband had one episode of impotence when she was trying to get pregnant, a fear was aroused in her that "he may become schizophrenic and kill me."

Some interesting relationships were noted in her thinking:

1. She was bombarded by multiple thoughts on every issue that came to mind. These consisted of the pros and cons of that particular issue.
2. Every time she got a pleasant or optimistic thought, an unpleasant or pessimistic one seemed to get triggered off.
   a. "I can't believe I have a normal baby. I keep thinking something is going to happen to him."
   b. "If people say I'm better, I ask a lot of questions, to show them I'm still bothered."
   c. "If I take my son outside, he'll get sick."
   She said of these phenomena, "I get afraid when I get a happy thought. If I think bad things, it will be a big surprise when something good happens."
3. She tried to plan her present according to how she might feel in the future. "Maybe we should have another baby, so I won't feel so bad in the future if we lose my son." This planning ahead seemed to have a protective function for her.
4. While most of her thoughts involved violence, death or some harm to herself or others, and her obsession involved killing her son, she denied angry feelings or even annoyance toward anyone. Even the thought of asserting herself with people, such as asking a relative to care for a child, made her feel bad or guilty.
5. She thought in extremes. This especially involved the baby: "I'm his mother I *should* love him. No one else *should* have to care for him. I *shouldn't* get thoughts like that about my son or husband."
6. She seemed markedly dependent on her parents. "I'm afraid to be away from my parents. I've never gone away without them. I'm afraid of what would happen if I got sick while away from them."

Treatment, other than the initial advice to the patient and her husband to have the baby taken care of by others, involved reducing the patient's data into terms of the recurring thought processes just described and repeatedly pointing these out to her.

a. "You have an active mind, you get many thoughts, both pro and con, and carefully think into things. This has its benefits because you get many ideas for your books, but it always makes you miserable by putting you in a state of indecisiveness." This remark was made to point out her characteristic type of thinking. Eventually she could be trained to say, "There I go again trying to think of every single possibility." Realizing the latter helps control overthinking.

b. "You seem to be superstitious. Every time you get a pleasant thought or good feeling, you get worried that something bad is bound to happen. To prevent the bad event from happening, you bring up bad thoughts. There is no reason that good things always precede bad ones and there is no reason to expect you can prevent misfortunes from occurring just by thinking they will." Repeatedly pointing out to patients their irrational thinking results in their becoming aware of it. This awareness gives them control over it.

c. "It might be more helpful to think of things in terms of probabilities. The poisonous spider has struck only five people in the State and none were in this geographical area. It would seem that the probabilities or odds of your getting bitten are low." This was an attempt to counteract her tendency to overgeneralize. (If one person is bitten, all will be.)

d. "You seem to have a need for certainty. There is no absolute, right or wrong, good or bad answer as to whether you should have another child or not. In two years when, you say, you might want one, why don't you come in and we'll discuss the pros and cons of your having additional children." The first remarks were to point out and challenge her thinking in extremes. The latter was to stop her from obsessing now on an issue that is two to four years away.

e. "From what you and your husband tell me, your son is quite sensitive and hard to manage. He keeps you so busy you can't do any of the things you enjoy. It would seem to me that most people would feel some annoyance in this situation." This remark was intended to make her realize certain children would annoy most people. When one has this type of child, one should limit his exposure to him.

f. "I get the feeling that you feel very guilty even if you experience a small amount of annoyance." This was said to make her realize annoyance is normal and not something one should feel guilty about.

g. "What relationship does a single episode of impotence have to schizophrenia? Even if your husband were schizophrenic, what percentage of schizophrenics are homicidal?" These two remarks were designed to point out her making predictions without any factual material to back them. The purpose was to get her to challenge some of her automatic predictions.

h. The patient revealed two techniques she tried on herself that she found helpful.

"I just thought of the worst things that could happen, then the less worse and I climbed out of things."

"I thought of an iron man to whom I could direct my hostility since he's invulnerable. I used to imagine my son's head over a toilet, then my husband's. Now I imagine the iron man's."

The patient was seen fourteen times over a six-month period. After the first visit, the couple placed the child with the patient's mother for a two-week period and the patient visited the baby two hours daily. After the two-weeks, the patient kept the baby with her for a few hours each day, gradually increasing the time so that after six months the baby was living at home full-time. After four visits (or one month of therapy), the patient stated she no longer had the obsession to kill the son. By the sixth meeting the patient reported she was sleeping better and enjoying sex more with her husband. She had also resumed her working. Her husband called me and stated she was vastly improved. The patient also planned to make a trip with her husband to a resort four hundred miles away— something she had never done without her parents. "I've been feeling less fearful about going out of town lately." She gave examples of some change in her thinking. She acknowledged the presence of every thought process discussed. A few statements she made are as follows:

"I think you're right when you said I *shouldn't* expect myself to be with my son all the time."

"How can I get out of this reflexive thinking?"

"How can I stop thinking so deeply into everything?"

This woman's presenting symptom was relieved by cognitive therapy. She also felt better in general and returned to old activities and tried out some new ones. She became aware of her thinking processes. Despite her improvement I do not think she was exposed to therapy long enough to get the mastery over her automatic thought processes necessary to avoid residual distortions or to prevent recurrence of some of her previous symptoms. She has not been seen for five months, but I would expect some recurrence to bring her in for future visits. Continued cognitive therapy had been suggested to her but the deterring factors were her realistic financial status and her mother's remark, "Psychiatrists will keep you coming forever. They'll tie you to their apron strings."

N.A. is a twenty-nine-year-old research physicist who presented with a chief complaint of: "I can't work; I can't concentrate." This case is significant from three points of view:

1. The patient is an intelligent, verbal, psychological-minded, young man who would be regarded as the perfect psychoanalytic patient.
2. He has a previous history of having had traditional psychotherapy for a one-year period two years ago while in graduate school. He went twice a week for four months and then, once a week for eight months.

When questioned about the therapy, he stated that he had done most of the talking, and that there was much discussion about his relationship with his father. He was told by the therapist after a year of therapy, "I have been looking for indications that you fear you might surpass your father, but I have been unable to find any." The patient, who had been seen for the same symptoms for which he is now seeing me, said that the therapy gave him moderate tension relief and helped him over some bad times, but "that's all it did for me."

3. After one year with his traditionally oriented therapist, he was sent to a very well-known behavior therapist. He was treated once a week for three months. This treatment was described as follows: "He imposed discipline by regimenting. . . . I guess his method would be good for children. . . . I had to keep a record of the time I got up and note whether I quickly got to work. I then discussed this with the therapist each week. He then told me to go right to work after waking and not to diddle my time away. . . . Also, he told me to do all my serious work in one place, to create a special environment. I was not to read a magazine there."

Neither therapy gave the patient symptom relief. He had hoped that moving to a new environment and being in an academic position would help him, but shortly after starting his research work, the same symptoms began plaguing him.

The patient presented as a thin, neat, intelligent, soft spoken white male with slightly depressed affect. The diagnosis was obsessive-compulsive personality. He was quite spontaneous and needed no prompting to talk. The first notable occurrence in therapy was his preoccupation with his childhood. He discussed in detail the lives of his two older brothers, both of whom had problems similar to his. He seemed to believe that there was one single reason buried in his childhood, perhaps in relation to his father, that was responsible for the patient and his two brothers turning out the same way. My impression was that this preoccupation was due to his long exposure to traditional therapy.

My initial therapeutic goals were to challenge his thinking in extremes, urge him to discuss his present-day attitudes and feelings, and elucidate what his reinforcers were.

His thinking in extremes was demonstrated by such remarks as: "I *ought* to be enjoying my work. . . . To be a good physicist one *must* know everything in his field." I decided to confront him on these in the hope that combatting them successfully would help take some of the pressure off him. (An initial thought on my part relative to this man's extreme attitudes was that his expectations of himself were so high that doing his work only held reward if it were done in great detail involving a marked amount of time. The reward was so far off that it could not act as a motivating factor.) The patient was not receptive to my challenging his "oughts" and "shoulds" and after frequent attempts with this method, over a three-session period (third to sixth session), it was discontinued. At this point, after twenty sessions, the patient only occasionally shows evidence that he is using extremes less. He has only minimally incorporated my challenging remarks into his thinking.

I tried to get him to discuss his present attitudes and feelings. On one occasion, when I was actually feeling exasperated with him, calling his attention to his dwelling in the past led, much to my surprise, to what appeared to be an "insight" response.

Therapist: "You continue to discuss your childhood, and I keep trying to get you back in the present."

Patient: "I always go back to the beginning, even in my work, instead of working at the problem at hand. My brother and I always got stuck on the first paragraph rather than going ahead."

The insight response was noted as a widening of his eyes, a "Say, that's right" appearance on his face and a nodding of his head. After twenty sessions he still goes to the past on occasion, but has increased his discussion of the present markedly. I do not know if "the insight," the "demand characteristics of the situation" or other factors led to this.

I felt it important to learn what was reinforcing to him, what he enjoyed doing. The rationale behind this was that many conscientious people function poorly when denying themselves enjoyment. He listed activities he liked, played down their having any real significance and essentially spoke little on this topic.

My impression after six sessions was that, although the patient was discussing the present more, he was not receptive to the "interruptions" I had made with comments, questions, challenges or any form of "activity." I felt that he had come to talk and that he wanted me to listen. Doing anything but listening at this point, I felt, would lead to his leaving therapy. In essence, this patient "trained me" to use, in part, a psychoanalytic approach—that of being silent. However I did not combine this with the other usual ingredients such as aloofness and distance.

In the ensuing sessions the patient has revealed interesting information that leads one to make numerous conceptualizations of what his attitudes, beliefs and themes might be. Several excerpts from our meetings are as follows:

1. "I have a desire to be a great physicist, not just ordinary, having complete freedom with no one telling me what to do."
2. "Marriage interferes with becoming great."
3. "When I read the biographies of Einstein and Bertrand Russell, I wonder what motivated them to become great."
   "To understand what motivated Franklin at age eighty-four to discover bifocals."
4. "To achieve greatness one has to go deeply into every subject and know it completely before one can develop new ideas in it. However, going into things deeply might turn out to be a waste of time. Even if one went deeply into a subject and knew everything about it, he

might not be able to plan the research and therefore all his time would go to waste . . . therefore, why bother."

5. "Father was not an authoritarian. He didn't tell me to study. However, I do remember him saying, 'Did you do your homework?' That got me mad. I don't feel free to enjoy things. This problem has been in the back of my mind at least ten years. I guess my father taught me this. He said it's a man's duty to work. I was raised strictly, under the protestant ethic."

6. "I'm concerned with my performance rather than the sheer joy of doing it. I would like to do something out of the ordinary, to not conform. In a sense, I would like to conform—to work, publish, get a good job, satisfy my employer and my professor. But if I fall into this trap, then I'm going through the mill like everyone else. I haven't stood out, just in a rut, like the middle class. I want to insist that I run my own life, not let external circumstances run it. The great physicists were not afraid to do something out of the ordinary. I'm restless at night if I have a good workday. I am afraid to be successful. It will mean that I have made my commitment. There will be demands on me, and I won't be able to brood as much. In the past, I worked evenings till 3:00 a.m. I'm afraid that if I get a good idea, I may get anxious for staying successful. I'll end up working every evening. This would make it hard to live with my wife and kids. (Patient is unmarried.) If I work well in the morning, I might formulate a different opinion of what I'll end up as in the future— possibly, being an eight-to-five worker and coming up with good ideas during the day and enjoying my family in the evening."

7. "The image of marriage in America is one of tenderness and care, as if love is at its height when one partner is sick or one partner is not doing well, so the other can comfort him."

8. "If I made a great discovery, it would make me feel uncomfortable. I'd get attention from others, but I couldn't command the subject to explain it to them."

9. "There is a mixed expression of independence on my part, yet a reluctance to jump into it. Is it just not wanting to get dependent?"

10. "I'd like to reach an age, seventy, fifty or even thirty-five, and look back and feel pleased with what I've done."

11. In discussing the only girl he has been seeing for one and one-half years he said: "This is not the type of girl . . . if I was sure of my own life. She has no initiative, not an intellectual, only wants a family, kids and happy married life. Dating her is like reverting to home and childhood. It's a drifting—the easy way out—requires no effort on my part. When I feel good this girl is too slow for me. I'd want to be more active and do things. I'd feel more comfortable with a girl who wants to take the initiative."

12. "If married it would intrude on my rights to introspect and be alone, and the girl would see a part of me she hadn't seen when dating."

13. At about the eighth session, the patient reported a dream—"I was climbing a wall—trying to get to the top. I finally got to the top after a hard climb. When I'm on top of the wall, I see a woman there and feel terrified." He awakened screaming. The meaning of the dream to him was "a woman is a threat to my progress."

14. Some of the remarks the patient made about the author were:

 a. "Coming in here makes me bring out my inadequacies. You have to talk about your failures and that you are being dependent."

 b. "I don't like when you say, 'It's a good session.' Or 'You're doing well. That makes me feel like a little boy.' "

 c. "I felt more equal to you today—not as the patient coming in to show his failure."

 d. "I would like you to say that I'm perceptive and intelligent."

 e. "One of the advantages of coming to you is that you're not much older than I—yourself just out of graduate school, so you may appreciate what I'm feeling."

 f. "I wish you were more experienced—an experienced therapist would have a deeper and quicker understanding of the situation. Your questions are in a faltering tone, as if they are not strongly formulated."

 g. "I feel good after leaving here. I work better for three hours. I always learn something here that sets my mind at ease. This has happened several times. It makes me feel free to do what I want and that what I've been doing is alright."

Some signs of improvement may be noted by reports and attitudes discussed in the past five sessions (fifteenth to twentieth): He has had an increased frequency of good work days and more enjoyable weekend activities. He has sent out sixty-three job applications for next year—an activity which he stated early in therapy he should do, but was unable to. Also he had decided, on his own, to come once weekly rather than twice.

Some of his attitudes which appear changed are:

a. "When reading an article, I'm not as bothered as I used to be that the author is smarter than me."

b. "I was able to read a review on a subject without it bothering me."

c. "I guess no one understands everything. This is the proper attitude."

d. "I've been getting some new research ideas lately."

e. "A year ago I felt that not working *should* bother me. Now I don't feel I *should* be bothered."

f. "I was out with my girlfriend this weekend and wasn't thinking of physics."

g. "Why am I such a perfectionist? Most people don't look for a girl that has the perfect reaction to them."

h. "I think these paradoxes are very real—I can exhibit opposite moods."

The plan of therapy is to allow the patient to do the talking, only interrupting him when he's felt to be "receptive."

Concepts that will be pointed out to him involve:

a. His tendency to think of all the pros and cons of the issues that face him.
b. The presence of any negatives deters him from proceeding with enthusiasm in any area.
c. Positive thoughts tend to trigger negative ones.

For example:

He'd like to read an interesting physics topic but he then thinks—'It might be a waste of time; if I come across something I don't know, I'll feel inadequate; if it's an article written by someone my age, it will make me realize how I've wasted my life; if I get interested in the topic, I will want to read everything in that field, and that might waste time (or I might be bored); reading an interesting article takes me away from work I *should* be doing.'

In relation to girls and marriage some of his thoughts might be: 'I'd like to get married and have a family; if one has a family, one *should* devote evenings and week-ends to being with them; if I were to get involved in a physics problem, I might want to work on it into the night; if I worked on my physics at night or on the weekend, I would not be a *proper* husband or father.'

In both cases the chain of thoughts leads to an imperfect situation. Since he cannot tolerate imperfect situations, he refrains from beginning any potentially rewarding activity.

Therapy must be aimed at familiarizing him with his thoughts and helping him to challenge them. This is the only way I feel he can achieve symptom relief, and function effectively. A more appropriate thought pattern might be:

'I'll read this article since it might be interesting. I won't be wasting time because this could add to my knowledge or, if not, may just be enjoyable. If there is some area I'm not familiar with, I can look it up or try to get as much out of the article as possible without knowing that information. Some men my age have done better than I have, but I don't *have* to be the best. I'm doing a good job and am satisfied with my work.'

CONCLUSION

In this chapter I have tried to describe the thinking that goes into the planning of the therapies I use, the techniques themselves and the results obtained.

I see myself at this time as being between two categories of therapist. On the one hand are those traditionalists with their strong belief in stereotyped "dynamics" and rigid rules of therapy (one to one, noninvolvement of relatives, and the fifty-minute hour). On the other hand are those few extraordinary and talented people who have not only familiarized themselves with multiple techniques from many different schools (cognitive therapy, behavior therapy, rational emotive therapy, implosive therapy, eidetic imagery, psychodrama, morita therapy, etc.), but who realize the importance of techniques designed to *influence* people toward favorable change.

I would like to progress still further from my original traditional background to this latter one. I would also hope that the training programs of future therapists will take this same direction.

Index